BREAKING BAD

The Cultural History of Television

Series Editors: Bob Batchelor, M. Keith Booker, Kathleen M. Turner

Mad Men*: A Cultural History*, by M. Keith Booker and Bob Batchelor
Frasier*: A Cultural History*, by Joseph J. Darowski and Kate Darowski
Breaking Bad*: A Cultural History*, by Lara C. Stache

BREAKING BAD

A Cultural History

Lara C. Stache

ROWMAN & LITTLEFIELD
Lanham • Boulder • New York • London

Published by Rowman & Littlefield
A wholly owned subsidiary of The Rowman & Littlefield Publishing Group, Inc.
4501 Forbes Boulevard, Suite 200, Lanham, Maryland 20706
www.rowman.com

Unit A, Whitacre Mews, 26-34 Stannary Street, London SE11 4AB

British Library Cataloguing in Publication Information Available

Library of Congress Cataloging-in-Publication Data

Names: Stache, Lara C. 1981– author.
Title: Breaking bad : a cultural history / Lara C. Stache.
Description: Lanham : Rowman & Littlefield, [2017] | Series: The cultural history of television | Includes bibliographical references and index.
Identifiers: LCCN 2017005726 (print) | LCCN 2017022847 (ebook) | ISBN 9781442278271 (electronic) | ISBN 9781442278264 (hardback : alk. paper)
Subjects: LCSH: Breaking bad (Television program : 2008-2013)
Classification: LCC PN1992.77.B74 (ebook) | LCC PN1992.77.B74 S73 2017 (print) | DDC 791.45/72—dc23
LC record available at https://lccn.loc.gov/2017005726

Printed in the United States of America

To R. M. and O. M.
My stars, my perfect silence.

CONTENTS

ACKNOWLEDGMENTS

Thank you to my friends and family who always give nothing but support and positive encouragement.

Writing can be a quiet solitude, or sometimes feel like solitary confinement. Thank you to those who offered feedback during this process: Jimmie Manning, Kathleen Turner, Jennifer Dunn, Chris Olson, and CarrieLynn Reinhard. You are the best popular culture and gender writing group a gal could ask for.

An extra special thank-you to Mary and Rob Chase, Sheena and Jason Ozbolt, and Rachel Davidson for talking out ideas and giving excellent feedback. I would be as lonely as Jesse in a house full of junkies without your friendships in my life.

Thank you to the series editors, Keith Booker, Bob Batchelor, and Kathleen Turner, for taking on the monumental task of a series that explores the cultural history and impact of television. Thanks especially to Stephen Ryan, senior editor at Rowman & Littlefield, for patiently answering questions and providing feedback.

And, last but not least, thank you to my family. To my parents, Mike and Jan Stache, to my sister and brother-in-law Lindsay and John Altwine, and to my Mangun/Mangun-Porter family—your support is felt a thousand times over.

To my incredible husband, my favorite viewing partner, and the best writer I know, Rob Mangun. I love you more than Heisenberg loves money, yo. And to Ogden—I cannot wait to watch this series with you and see how much the world has changed by then. I love you.

INTRODUCTION

Why Being *Bad* Is So Good

"**L**ive from New York, it's Saturday night!" yells Bryan Cranston, introducing the December 10, 2016, episode of *Saturday Night Live*. The episode aired during a highly contentious time in politics, as president-elect Donald Trump's cabinet decisions were being announced daily, and this night, *Breaking Bad*'s Walter White made an appearance. A talented and popular actor, Cranston opening the show was not surprising; however, seeing the black hat of Walt's alter ego Heisenberg perched on his head was delightfully unexpected. *Vanity Fair* writer Hillary Busis explains, "The sketch show has an educated guess for who Trump may tap to head the Drug Enforcement Administration when he's president: Walter White, the meth kingpin at the center of A.M.C.'s dearly departed drama *Breaking Bad*."[1] Bryan Cranston, in the costume of his most famous character, announced to viewers that he, Walter White, is back on the grid. The short clip references plot points and famous lines that fans of the show can appreciate. More significantly, the use of Walter White to make a statement about contemporary politics, more than three years after the finale episode aired, highlights the cultural resonance of this enigmatic figure and creative series.

Breaking Bad (2008–2013) is a television series that chronicles the life of high school chemistry teacher Walter White (Bryan Cranston) who finds out he has terminal cancer and realizes he needs money to provide for his family in anticipation of his inevitable demise. Created and written by Vince Gilligan, *Breaking Bad* ran for five seasons on the AMC network and ignited a passion for the characters, the story, and the artistry of the series from fans and critics alike. Throughout each creatively written season, the audience follows Walt, a brilliant and complicated man, obsessed with providing for his family, and eventually, with building an empire. Walt secures the help of former student Jesse Pinkman (Aaron Paul), a hoodlum who knows the world of meth as a drug dealer and user. The two make fascinating business partners, creating a complex power dynamic within the relationship of former teacher/student that evolves to, at times, father/son, and other times angry coworkers and enemies.

Walter's wife, Skyler (Anna Gunn), is pregnant in the first season with their second child, and their first child, Walt Jr. (RJ Mitte), has cerebral palsy—all key factors that build layers of complexity into the protagonist's situation. Vince Gilligan discusses the attractiveness of this charac-

The cast of *Breaking Bad* from Season 2: Walter White Jr. (RJ Mitte), Walter White (Bryan Cranston), Skyler White (Anna Gunn), Marie Schrader (Betsy Brandt), Hank Schrader (Dean Norris), and Jesse Pinkman (Aaron Paul). *AMC/ Photofest © AMC*

ter, a "good, law-abiding man who suddenly decides to become a criminal," suggesting that the value of the series lies at the heart of placing an interesting character in an unusual predicament. The first few episodes of the series paint a picture of Walt as simultaneously pathetic, ingenious, devoted, heartbreaking, and enigmatic. His image is crafted as he negotiates relationships with coworkers, friends, and family, including his sometimes overbearing alpha-male brother-in-law, Hank Schrader (Dean Norris), a DEA officer who takes Walter on his first ride-along and produces the fateful reunion with Jesse that leads to their illicit business partnership.

To say that this show is an important landmark in contemporary television is an understatement. On October 5, 2014, my husband and I sat down to watch the final episode of *Breaking Bad*. We had recorded it to avoid commercials, and we set the lighting just right to enjoy the show. As we both settled ourselves on the couch, we looked at each other with anticipation and high-fived. While a similar scene most likely has played out in many living rooms in America (or perhaps not, in homes less cool than mine), what is significant about this moment was that the show's final episode had first aired on September 29, 2013. Throughout September and October 2014, we rewatched a marathon of the series on AMC that previewed writer Vince Gilligan's next spin-off series, *Better Call Saul*. We were high-five excited about seeing the final episode of the series again, even though we already knew what would happen. We miss the show and have not found another series that fills the creative gap for us in quite the same way. What this moment demonstrates is the excitement that is created from experiencing such a complex, moving, sometimes horrifying, and beautifully written series. Extrapolating from the microcosm of our home, this moment also illustrates the cultural significance of *Breaking Bad*.

Within my social network, I have met die-hard fans of the show who have debated with me at length about plot twists, characters, the quality of writing, and why it was so successful. I also have acquaintances who "gave it a shot" and could not get past the gore in the first few episodes. And then, there are those who have it in their Netflix queue but "just haven't gotten around to it yet." I try not to judge them too harshly (I am sure they have other endearing qualities . . . deep down), but I simply cannot on any level relate to the reactions of the second and third group.

This book is for the first group—the fans who love to analyze the show. Maybe not every episode spoke to them the same way, or perhaps they thought some characters were more interesting to watch than others, but they got something out of the show that went beyond the mere one hour of mindless entertainment experienced by casual viewers. But what is it about this show that is so appealing?

VINCE GILLIGAN CREATES SOMETHING SPECIAL

The beauty of *Breaking Bad* is that the writers did not try to force fit anything in the story, and they did not commit to knowing the end of Walt's journey at the beginning (unlike another popular show, which shall remain nameless). The writers of *Breaking Bad* (OK, I'll give you a hint, it is not "Found") did not even know if they would get a fifth season at the end of the fourth, so Gilligan wrote the fourth (I'm referring to *Lost*) season as if it could be the final one. (The writers of *Lost* claimed early on that the group was not in purgatory or a type of purgatory and they straight up lied, infuriating previously loyal fans. It was baloney.) After negotiations with AMC and Sony, Gilligan got his final season and the writers got to work. They gave themselves every option for how Walt's story would conclude. *Breaking Bad* writers Tom Schnauz and Peter Gould revealed a little bit about the process to *Fresh Air*'s Terry Gross at the conclusion of the series. In the interview, Tom Schnauz explains how the writers worked together to set up the beats of the episode:

> We go over every single beat, and we write them on index cards and pin them to a big corkboard and get it in extreme detail and try to get every writer in agreement for every single beat. And once the board is full, the writer will take that board and go off and actually write the script and write the dialogue and the scenes and fashion the script for the actors and the crew to use.[2]

Gilligan and the six main writers for the series would play out all the possibilities, debating the goals of the episode and the character motivations, to come to a conclusion on the best possible ending. In the same interview, Peter Gould enthuses, "It's a great way to work because what happens is . . . you get to do a little bit of jazz while you're writing it and really try to bring something of yourself to it and bring the emotion to it." This writing process produced an organic, logical storyline and created a finale that is the most satisfying conclusion to a series I have ever seen.

I will admit to some bias, however, as *Breaking Bad* had me at "hello" (although *Lost* had me at "hello," and then proceeded to cheat on me with my best friend *and* sister . . . and then drain my bank account, before kicking my dog on the way out). Only great writing, producing, and powerful acting can accomplish the balance of humor and darkness, all of which works perfectly with graphic imagery and clever plot points. The Jesse and Walt combination is like watching a clever slapstick comedy at times, especially in the first few seasons. Juxtaposed with the grisly situations, the dark comedy of *Breaking Bad* is highly entertaining. Whether the two main characters are physically fighting each other or attempting to steal a barrel of methylamine wearing brightly colored pom-pom topped ski masks, the chemistry between Paul and Cranston is delightful to behold (pardon the pun, there is no getting around it). Take, for example, the fourth episode of the second season (Episode 2.4, "Down"), wherein Jesse falls through the roof of a Porta Potty during a bungled break-in. The visual joke of this scene, which ends with Jesse leaving a slimy trail of blue latrine water in his wake, cracks me up every time. It then immediately becomes the saddest scene in the episode as Jesse hits rock bottom and cries himself to sleep wearing a gas mask. The next morning, when Walt finds Jesse parked outside his home, he demands to know why he is there and then, looking at his hands asks, "Why are you blue?" Walt berates Jesse for his terrible decision making; the two men argue and then erupt into a heated physical scuffle. The intense scene ends with Walt inviting Jesse in for the breakfast his own family has refused. Even as the series continues, getting darker and harder to find humor in the destruction of these people's lives, there are funny moments that bring the viewer back to those first few seasons.

Writing for *Forbes*, Allen St. John contends that Vince Gilligan accomplished on television what is typically found in the Great American novel, when "Walter White embarked on an epic journey, tracing an arc reserved for iconic characters of literature and cinema like Jay Gatsby and Michael Corleone."[3] Walt's story is complete; his beginning is clear, his purpose of being, his motivation, and his evolution are fascinating to watch, as is the eventual conclusion to his story. His story arc feels complete, whereas, as St. John argues, not all beloved characters' stories have such a satisfying conclusion. He cites his enjoyment of *The Sopranos* and *The Wire* but indicates something unusual about *Breaking Bad*:

> *Breaking Bad* differs from those shows—and surpasses them—in one important way. This is a story that's moving toward an ending. The ending of *The Sopranos*, whether you loved it or hated it, was largely a non-ending. It was designed to make us think about the show and the act of watching it, as much as it made us think about Tony Soprano. The last season of *The Wire*, despite a number of resonant, even heartbreaking moments featuring Michael, Omar, and Bubbles, was simply not up to the standards of the four seasons that came before. . . . For all their cardinal virtues, those other contenders for the Best Show Ever left us feeling somewhat unsatisfied. *Breaking Bad*, on the other hand, is sticking the landing.

And St. John is not the only critic making these comparisons between *Breaking Bad* and other highly acclaimed television shows. From *Rolling Stone* to *Entertainment Weekly*, debates about a creative revolution that has occurred with a new era of television all include mentions of Gilligan's *Breaking Bad*.

MEDIA MATTER

If you picked up this book in the first place, and if you have made it this far, then you are probably not a reader who needs to be told that media matter, but it is important to understand why media should be analyzed, dissected, and critiqued. Many viewers get more from television and film than simply filling the hours of the day with entertainment. Media give us complex and persuasive messages about the world in which we live and allow us to make sense of the world around us. Media—television, film, advertisements, literature, and so forth—reflect society by creating a specific vision, or story. *Breaking Bad* aired in 2008, during the housing bubble burst, and methamphetamine production was increasing year over year. Media scholars argue that media construct narratives that both mirror and create society. Television and film narratives negotiate the same issues that are occurring in contemporary society, albeit sometimes on an absurd or grander scale.

The choices that are available to the characters, the dialogue, and who says what, are all important indicators of the fictional world in which the characters exist (create), but also indicative of broader cultural conversations about the world in which the viewers and writers live (mirror). *Time* writer James Poniewozik argues, "Great crime dramas aren't the ones that pass the most perfect [judgments] but those that best help viewers understand an imperfect world."[4] For example, discussing the finale of the series, Vince Gilligan commented that if his show had been written in the 1970s, it would have ended with the police clamping handcuffs on Walt as a triumph for the legal system and the heroic efforts of law enforcement. In a similar vein, analyzing the finale of the series in light of the year 2013 reveals something about the social values, political culture, and expectations of viewers, and the choices that were available to the writers in trying to create a satisfying conclusion to Walt's journey. Popular culture scholar Ann Larabee reminds us, "The new television narratives speak of fragmentation, desperation and violence of tragic, atomized figures whose only meaning lies in narcissistic projects."[5] What does that tragic main character say about our world? A critical, deep analysis of media can sometimes reveal new ways of fully appreciating stories that we already love.

To understand the cultural impact of a series, it is important to think about the show from a variety of perspectives. A good television show challenges us to think about the choices made in the narrative, analyze what worked and what did not, and try to figure out where the story might be headed; it gives us a puzzle to solve, whether that is plot related or in trying to understand a character's motivations. In his book *Everything Bad Is Good for You*, cultural critic Steven Johnson argues that the complexity of many contemporary television shows is not just more entertaining, but it actually makes the viewers sift through nuanced ideas and intellectually challenging material in a way that enhances intelligence rather than dulls it.[6] He separates the level of engagement needed for shows like *Frasier* (1993–2004) and *Lost* (2004–2010) to make this point and suggests that viewers are encouraged to puzzle out clues within shows like the latter, as a result of a lack of obvious cues, like those found in the former (e.g., a soundtrack to tell the audience that they just heard a joke).

Although some texts might be more interesting to analyze than others, media are made for us to interrogate and dissect. According to Greg

Smith, who explains why "It's [not] Just a Movie," film and television narratives teach audience members how to be critical viewers often without realizing they are learning anything.[7] Viewers are taught to recognize certain cues within fictional narratives. For example, in horror movies, when tense music plays and suddenly screeches to a halt, we know the killer is going to appear. Audience members are taught how to read a scene, and narratives in the hands of smart, creative writers offer beautifully rich interpretations of the world in which we live.

Breaking Bad's narratives are thick with references to popular films. Vince Gilligan and his writers were not afraid to praise the great stories that inspired many of the scenes in *Breaking Bad*, but they did so in a way that showed us something new and different than what came before. Andrew Leonard, writer for *Rolling Stone*, comments:

> There are elements of *The Godfather* and *The Sopranos* in *Breaking Bad* ("If you're going to steal, steal from the best," says Gilligan), but we've never seen anything quite like this mixture of the mundane and monstrous before. And that's on purpose. Gilligan says he's watched more TV than "any human has a right to," and he is determined to not waste viewers' time by repeating what's already been done. Gilligan insists on pushing his viewers into unexplored territory, to show them "things they've never seen before." He takes the familiar and twists it into nightmare.[8]

As homage to the seed that started the series, a clip from *Scarface* finally makes an appearance in Season 5, while Walt watches TV with Holly and Walt Jr. (Episode 5.3, "Hazard Pay"). It is the scene with the most famous line from *Scarface*, "Say hello to my little friend," and a fitting choice since Season 5 is the turning point where most fans see Walt as the villain. The bloody scene horrifies Skyler, who makes the connection between Walt and the main character immediately, as fiction has become reality in her world.

In addition, Quentin Tarantino's work also has a huge influence on the style and writing throughout the series. *Time* writer Megan McCluskey states, "*Breaking Bad* creator Vince Gilligan did everything but say Tarantino's name to acknowledge his admiration for the prolific director during the show's five-season run."[9] Even the nicknames of the main characters, Mr. White and Pinkman, loosely reference Tarantino's *Reservoir Dogs*. In her article, McCluskey highlights a video compilation from

Jorge Luengo Ruiz that compares a variety of scenes throughout the five seasons to clips from *Pulp Fiction*.

Westerns were also influential to some of the plotting decisions. About the conclusion (Episode 5.16, "Felina"), Vince Gilligan notes, "A lot of astute viewers who know their film history are going to say, 'It's the ending to *The Searchers*.' And indeed it is . . . it's always a matter of stealing from the best."[10] Gilligan and his writers put their own stamp on that ending, though, as the love story of *Breaking Bad* is far more complicated than that in John Wayne and Natalie Wood's world (although their love story is not exactly simple, either).

In addition to popular references, the show also works in complex themes and symbols. One prominent theme in the series is the idea of fate versus control. It could be argued that Walt's greatest downfall is his need to control what goes on around him. His compulsive desire for control explains Walt's rampant lying, the ego that requires he leave a legacy of money coming from no other source but himself, and the desire to craft an image that he wants his family to remember fondly. However, Walt's desperate need to control his world is challenged by the recurring theme of fate. In the second episode of the series (Episode 1.2, "Cat's in the Bag . . ."), Walt and Jesse flip a coin to determine who will kill Krazy-8. Walt loses. This fateful coin toss is what starts Walt down a terrible path; would Jesse have suffered the same outcome if the coin had come up heads? Similarly, in Episode 2.12 ("Phoenix"), had Walt not let Jesse's girlfriend Jane die that night, the plane crash never would have happened, and Walt might not have started the transformation to Heisenberg. If we focus on fate as a theme, then Walt's choices are not the problem; however, we know that the competing theme of choice comes up frequently within the narrative, particularly as the consequences of Walt's decisions build up. There are a multitude of interesting themes and symbols throughout the series, including mirror images (chirality), science versus faith, and masculinity, that will be explored more in the subsequent chapters. The point is that analyzing these themes can tell us something about the world in which we live outside of the fictional narrative.

It is important to be active and engaged critical viewers because Greg Smith reminds us "an examined life is better, richer, and fuller than an unexamined life."[11] While we need to remain open to the fact that there are sometimes multiple interpretations to the media narratives we view, that does not mean that we have to buy in to everything we are told. We should question it; we should ask what examples are available for that interpretation in the text; and, if we don't see it, then we can say it is not a good evaluation, but if we do see it, then we need to acknowledge it is interesting, even if it is not our reading of the narrative. For example, many fans loved Skyler White, but some fans absolutely despise the character. In chapter 7 of this book, I try to offer some interpretations of the narrative that may have prompted the kind of vitriol that led to Facebook pages devoted to fans' hatred of her.

Viewers and fans of popular media should examine the underlying message(s) in a series, interrogate why a specific twist or turn worked in the narrative, and be able to articulate why they were so drawn into a story or character's arc (or not). The themes of *Breaking Bad* are about real life; we make choices and we pay the consequences, or reap the benefits. For the discerning viewer, supremely well-written shows like *Breaking Bad* can be especially rewarding to dissect.

BREAKING DOWN THE BOOK

The goals of this book are to examine the entire series of *Breaking Bad* and detail the cultural significance of the show respective to the time in which it was produced. To do so, this book has been laid out in three parts: Part 1 of the book investigates the main character, "Walter White: The Good, the *Bad*, or the In-Between?," via three themes present in the show. In the first chapter, "Antihero or Villain: How Walter White Resists the Labels," I build a case that explains where Walter White fits in cultural discussions of the antihero. He has been called the villain, the antihero, and even a psychopath. I discuss how characters like Walt are a new breed of protagonist, and one that cultural critics cannot easily catalog as an antihero or villain. In chapter 2, I analyze "The Evolution of Heisenberg," or "How Mr. Chips becomes Scarface," to use Gilligan's famous logline to pitch his series to the network. I detail how the writers had to slowly turn Walt into a bad guy in order for the viewers to want to continue on his journey. Chapter 3 is an exploration of a question that follows the main character throughout the series: "Does Walt Want to Die?" The intervention scene (Episode 1.5, "Gray Matter") and many of his actions throughout the series keep the viewer guessing but also raise questions about what it means to have a life, and to live.

Part 2 of this book delves deeper into the cultural conversations that *Breaking Bad* both mirrors and creates throughout the five seasons of the series. In chapter 4, I explore the theme of morality and legality, and how the characters discuss these distinctions. Chapter 5, titled "Just Say No? Drug Use and Abuse in *Breaking Bad*," is a discussion of the drug narrative told primarily via Jesse's struggles with addiction. The series does not offer the typical cautionary tale about drugs, but instead provides a much more realistic representation of addiction and abuse. The marketing of *Breaking Bad* is the focus for chapter 6, where I explore the connection between the show and the outside world. The series did a wonderful job of planting Easter eggs throughout the seasons and built a robust world for the series online that only made the connection to the characters more real. I also address the importance of Netflix to the success of *Breaking Bad*, particularly for the significant increase in number of viewers between Seasons 4 and 5.

In the final section of this book, part 3 attempts to give the supporting cast their due credit. Chapter 7 is devoted to Skyler White and how she fits within the Boys Only Club of the *Breaking Bad* world. I attempt to offer an explanation for why many fans dislike the character, and explain how her function in the plot is perhaps the most important for the viewers in order to question their own motives and desires. In a show centered on caring about a man destined to become a monster, I explore how Walt's adversaries and partners function in the bigger picture. In chapter 8, "*Breaking* Down the *Bad* Guys," I analyze what it means to be a villain in a show about a bad guy. As a bookend to the first chapter, chapter 9 suggests that perhaps Jesse and Hank are the antiheroes of the narrative, and I explain what that means for television narratives moving forward.

Breaking Bad has been off the air since 2013, and yet, the cultural relevance and fan fervor have only increased thanks to new fans finally catching up on Netflix. Critically acclaimed, and the winner of more than one hundred awards, including an almost full sweep of the 2014 Emmys acting awards with Outstanding Lead Actor (Bryan Cranston), Outstanding Supporting Actor (Aaron Paul), and Outstanding Supporting Actress (Anna Gunn), *Breaking Bad* is a television series that exemplifies what writers M. Keith Booker and Bob Batchelor call the "quality television revolution" of cable television.[12] This book gives the show its due reverence, but also suggests a new way of understanding and critiquing the series as a part of the larger culture in which it exists.

Part I

Walter White: The Good, the *Bad*, or the In-Between?

Walt and Saul Goodman (Bob Odenkirk). *AMC/Photofest © AMC*

I

ANTIHERO OR VILLAIN

How Walter White Resists the Labels

In medieval morality plays, the protagonist begins in innocence, succumbs to temptation and falls into sin, but in the end finds a way back to God and redemption. We have come to know Walter White, however, as a man who was never truly innocent, as a man who may have been tempted not away from virtue, but toward his truer self.—Kevin Clarke[1]

The more believable humanity of Walter White—the discovery that he's not a good man but an everyman—is due to Bryan.—Vince Gilligan[2]

One of the foremost critical debates surrounding *Breaking Bad* is whether Walter White represents the antihero or the villain. Columnist Jaime Weinman writes, "Because Walt bounces between hilarious and horrifying, the show has a feel that's very different from shows like *Dexter*, which play their anti-heroes more straight."[3] At the start of Season 5, *Entertainment Weekly*'s Dan Snierson writes, "With only 16 episodes left, AMC's magnificent meth drama *Breaking Bad* returns with its hero now a villain whose passion for the thug life is downright scary."[4] The article quotes Gilligan, stating, "In the early going, we kept running up against brick walls in the sense of 'How do we make a guy scarier than the scariest guy we may have ever seen?' . . . we suddenly realized: 'We already have the bad guy scarier than Gus Fring—Walter White.'" Many critics and writers similarly highlight the end of the fourth season, when Walt blows up Gus, as his turn from antihero to villain:

> The show has shed its original skin, that of the antihero drama, in which we root for a bad boy in spite of ourselves. Instead, it's more like the late seasons of *The Sopranos*, the first show that dared to punish its audience for loving a monster. This makes *Breaking Bad* a radical type of television, and also a very strange kind of must-watch: a show that you dread and crave at the same time.[5]

I like writer Emily Nussbaum's use of the phrase "punish its audience," because Walt can only be described as scary in the beginning of Season 5. It is difficult for many fans to remember how he could have been endearing at any point in the series. Vince Gilligan himself pitched the show as a tale of how Mr. Chips becomes Scarface, and that tagline has repeatedly been used to describe the evolution of Walter White into a monster, or how a good man becomes a villain.

Critic Kevin Clarke argues in the quote that opened this chapter that Walter White may never have been a good guy, but instead "tempted . . . toward his truer self."[6] Thus, he is the sociopath living among us who finally becomes the one in charge. A friend once made a comment to me about a man with a huge ego hiding deep insecurity. He said this man should never be put in charge of anyone, because it only magnifies the cruelty of his ego. Every time I watch the beginning of Season 5, I think of his comment. As I experience Walt's viciousness with those around him as they become more terrified—like when he intimidates Saul with "We're done when I say we're done" (Episode 5.1, "Live Free or Die"), or how he gently kisses a horrified Skyler up and down her body (Episode 5.2, "Madrigal")—I wonder whether this imperious nature was buried all along within him waiting to surface, or did the seed get planted with the first taste of power?

Though many fans turned on Walt in Season 5, he still had his loyalists. Exploring the popularity of characters that sell drugs, like Walt and the dealers on *The Wire*, cultural writer Chuck Klosterman states, "We feel for them when they kill, and we understand why it had to happen. We actively want them to get away with murder, because we are on their side."[7] Indeed, many fans seem to sympathize with Walt's plight, and instead of turning away from him, as the writers intended, "something unexpected happened. Fans have been reluctant to let go, sticking by their hero's side even if it means being dragged into hell."[8] In order to be true to his character's motivations, Bryan Cranston never saw Walt as the villain. Instead he contends that Walter White "was doing this for his family. And, that to me was a reasonable thing to hold on to for this man, to justify his actions."[9] So, is he an antihero, a villain, or a hero? At the crux of the definitional issue is the fact that some fans see Walt differently from the writers' intentions (of creating the villain), but perhaps more in line with Cranston's goals to understand how Walt "was a man who was given a set of circumstances that created the type of person he became."[10] He is the antihero to some, the villain to others, and the hero to yet another group.

During Season 2, after arguing with Cranston about Walt's motivations, Gilligan stopped himself and realized he might be damaging the quality of the show by forcing the actor to see his character as a bad man. Gilligan quips, "You don't have to be Freud to know that Hitler thought of himself as a wonderful guy."[11] However, the Hitler comparison is not quite analogous to the complex character of Walter White in *Breaking Bad*. Nobody would argue that Hitler is "just complicated"; he is clearly categorized as a villain, and history's most notorious monster. Walt is not nearly as easy to catalog, and this ambiguity of definition suggests we may be looking at a novel category of protagonists. Cranston argues, "The bad guys of poorly written material were just bad."[12] He continues, "A more interesting complex character is someone who I'm not sure if he is good or bad." Writer James Poniewozik acknowledges this doppelganger persona and describes Walt, referencing the aforementioned quote by Vince Gilligan, "He is Mr. Chips, *and* he is Scarface."[13] When the goal of a show is to understand the transformation of an everyman into a murderer, the lines between good and bad get murky. I argue this murkiness suggests that Walter White represents a shift from villains and heroes to a much more complex and terrifyingly relatable character in contemporary television.

CULTURAL CONVERSATIONS: THE ANTIHERO

Before analyzing Walter White's role in the series, including his decisions, actions, and choices, it is important to first explore cultural conversations about the antihero. Writers utilize the term "antihero" to define

Walter White and Jesse Pinkman. *AMC/Photofest © AMC*

flawed, but beloved, (primarily) male leads in contemporary television. Writers and scholars alike identify the antihero by pointing to popular culture characters: Dexter is an antihero; Tony Soprano, Don Draper, Francis Underwood, Jax Teller, and Nucky all wear the label; and, so does Walter White. In the past, villains in television narratives have frequently been easy to identify. They wear the black hats and the good guys wear the white ones. Contemporary television leads make use of both hats depending on the situation (*Scandal* is particularly adept at weaving this metaphor into the dialogue). The antihero of today wears a gray hat, and this reveals something of the world we live in. Jean MacKenzie of Public Radio International argues, "It's exactly in that gray space between good and bad that Americans seem to feel most comfortable these days. Questionable wars, economic misery and a gradual erosion of the American Dream have taken their toll," and in contemporary American popular culture the antihero has become a celebrated figure.[14] In a 2015 article in the *Guardian*, writer Thomas Batten argues that the popular culture antihero has prepared us for a president like Donald Trump. He states that Americans love "scoundrels who move through the world with an inordinate amount of swagger," and *Breaking Bad* may have readied us for a shift in politics:

> Walter White won hearts by going into the meth trade after the American dream let him down. He decided to go against the law because the law didn't seem to have his best interests at heart, and however horrible his crimes became, fans never forgot, or stopped identifying with, the frustration that set everything in motion. So maybe that's why Trump has some segment of the population so excited. He's running his campaign like he's getting away with something. [15]

As we know, hindsight is twenty-twenty, and Batten's connection between the love of the antihero and our contemporary political landscape may explain Trump's eventual win, but rooting for a rogue is hardly a new practice.

To understand our fascination with the contemporary rogue, writer and scholar Ashley M. Donnelly offers us a throwback to the past when she explores how antiheroes of today "all possess aspects of the archetypal cowboy." [16] She continues, stating, "Now on TV the hats are gray and the same day as they ride into town to rid it of an evil sheriff, our cowboys may in fact do some cattle rustling." An antihero is frequently defined as a flawed protagonist, a main character who struggles with living a decent life, and typically comes out from his experiences scarred but alive and better for the fight. In an interview with NPR's Audie Cornish, Chuck Klosterman explains his theory that viewers evolve with the protagonist/antagonist in popular culture narratives. [17] Using *Star Wars* as an example, he argues that as a child, you identify with Luke Skywalker, and then as you enter your teenage years, you side with Han Solo, "but when you really become an adult, you're no longer looking at characters—fictional or nonfictional—as aspirational. You kind of are the person you are. And now when you look at characters, you kind of want to see things in them that help you understand yourself." [18] It is at this point, Klosterman argues, that you "care the most" about Darth Vader. Klosterman acknowledges in his book that his editor disagreed with his theory, arguing that many people continue to identify with Han Solo rather than the dark side. However, my interpretation of Klosterman's argument is that as life throws its curveballs, it becomes easier to understand how somebody might turn bad. And that character, the one who reflects these flaws, tends to capture our interest as adults.

I was in high school when the film *American Beauty* (1999) came out and the teenage boys I knew (my husband included) were enamored with Lester Burnham, the film's antagonist played by Kevin Spacey. He flouted social convention, refusing to participate in the rules of society. He hated his job, so he quit. He hated his body, so he bought a home gym. He hated his life, so he changed it: he smoked pot, drank booze in his pajamas in the middle of day, told his family what he really thought, and got a part-time job at a fast-food restaurant. The main message about Lester Burnham was that he was not going to conform. There was something about having the ability to say no, to take control and thumb his nose at the sheep of society, that appealed to the teenage boy psyche in particular. For young men facing the next phase of life, about to head out into the adult world of responsibility, Lester Burnham was a revolutionary figure that revealed a deep inner desire to fight back against the social pressure and the net of expectations quickly closing in around them. And then, those teenagers grew up, and the television landscape changed as they entered their thirties.

TV began to feature film-quality small screen narratives like *The Sopranos*, *The Wire*, *Mad Men*, and *Breaking Bad*. AMC paved the way for many of these narratives to reach a wider audience. The inclusion on nonpremium channels and the increasing popularity of Netflix broadened that audience even further. We have entered the "third golden age of television," and it offers a clear lead character[19] and a specific kind of story: a plot-driven narrative and a character study mingled together into a beautiful concoction. The *Star Tribune* notes, "Pitching a dark version of 'Leave It to Beaver' would have been unthinkable a decade ago. But in the contemporary world of cable . . . viewers are encouraged to root for serial killers, coldhearted admen, bloodthirsty bikers or meth-dealing teachers."[20] What does the debate about being on Team Walt say about viewers today? Veteran TV director Nelson McCormack comments, "I think we like to see somebody portray the worst in us that we've either felt or wanted to express. It's kind of liberating."[21]

As stated in many of the preceding comments, cultural critics often consider Walter White an antihero. As he enters the fifth season of *Breaking Bad*, this label requires an asterisk. I contend that Walt's evolution defies his categorization as antihero and he instead resides in a new category of character in American television. Popular characters like

Don, Tony and Tyrion [Lannister] are made sympathetic because they're ultimately tragic, at war with their worst impulses and mystified by their inability to settle down and be nice . . . it's the sympathetic men whose endings have created the most debate and unrest among fans. On the other hand, almost everyone seemed satisfied, and perhaps even relieved, to see White exposed as a monstrous fraud, rejected by society, undone by the same qualities his fans once adored and finally worked into a corner he couldn't bully his way out of.[22]

Walt's cruelty and hubris that start Season 5 are ultimately what make it hard to define him as an antihero; however, because of Seasons 1 through 4 and the final episode of the series in Season 5, it is equally difficult to define him as a villain. Walt did not start out bad, and thanks to Cranston's brilliant acting, we spent four seasons sympathizing with his crazy plight. A.V. Club's Donna Bowman suggests, "As with Tony [Soprano], we join Vic [Mackey] *in medias res*, already deep into the contradictions and temptations of life in the shadows," but Walter White is different, because we did not meet him as a bad guy.[23] Instead, Walt represents something similar to Lester Burnham. He appeals to the adult psyche, the one where Klosterman tells us we try to understand ourselves. Walter is no longer a relatable figure; we know he is tunneling down a rabbit hole so deep we would never want to go with him, but we enjoy that he is taking this plunge. This is because we understand that life is full of choices, excuses, and opportunities, both taken and lost. While most of us would never take Walt's path, we can sympathize with his journey and even secretly root for his success, as we simultaneously recoil at the staggering depth of his depravity and applaud his necessary demise. It is an exhilarating ride.

The complex dilemma of categorizing Walter White is best illustrated in the series finale. In this final episode (Episode 5.16, "Felina"), he finally acknowledges his own selfishness to Skyler ("I did it for me") and liberates Jesse from servitude, while also forcing Elliott and Gretchen, of Gray Matter fame, to give what's left of his ill-gotten fortune to his family. He also ironically catches a bullet from a machine of his own making (metaphors galore!) and receives his fatalistic punishment for his hubris, but not before entering a meth lab one last time and reminiscing about his glory days as Heisenberg. In other words, Walt manages to achieve redemption, receive his comeuppance, and also accomplish his own villainous objective of providing for his family (no matter what), all within a single episode. Walt has his cake and eats it, too. Does this ultimately make him an antihero or villain; or, does Walter White fit into some new and exciting character archetype that has evolved in contemporary American television?

WALTER WHITE AS THE TRAGIC FIGURE

One of Vince Gilligan's themes for the series, that life is about "growth, then decay, then transformation" (Episode 1.1, "Pilot"), explains the difficulty in trying to define Walter White. He is not a hero, or a villain, or an antihero, but instead a human who makes terrible decisions. According to A.V. Club's Todd VanDerWerff, Walt's story can be read as a Greek tragedy and a cautionary tale about the flaws of man.[24] Walt can be understood as a representation of the tragic figure of ancient Greek mythology. At the conclusion of the series, Rich Bellis, a writer for the *Atlantic*, attempts to determine "Which Great Literary Work Explains *Breaking Bad* Best," and he analyzes the finale in terms of a Greek tragedy. He notes:

> Time and again, Walter's intentions serve as weak justifications for his crimes, rather than as their ethical motives. That delusion of righteousness was both a source of fascination and the hallmark of his malevolence. . . . If *Breaking Bad* shares anything with [*Oedipus Rex*], it's the illusion of control. "I was alive," Walt finally tells Skyler, when he isn't any longer. Only in death or abjection is there room for free will.[25]

In the Greek tragedy, the main character's flaws bring about a (typically ill) fate. Walter White makes misstep after misstep because of deep character flaws of vanity, insecurity, narcissism, and a justification of immoral actions. He is human and deeply imperfect. When he gives in to his desires and tries to control his world, he enters the fate machine so commonly used in Greek myths.

What convinces me the most that Walt is a tragic figure, is that, although he ties up loose ends and does some good in the final episode (Episode 5.16, "Felina"), there is no sense of redemption. In an interview with Tom Schnauz and Peter Gould, NPR's Terry Gross comments, "He had a much more honorable and redemptive end than I was expecting."

To which Gould responds, "You know, it's interesting, I don't really see him redeemed . . . just the fact that he sort of accepts what he's done and who he is, that's not redemption to me . . . the actions he's taken are beyond redemption." Gross acknowledges this point and responds, "Redemptive was definitely the wrong word, but still like he makes some things right."[26] In a Greek tragedy, the self-awareness of the tragic figure, at least enough to acknowledge that his own flaws were his downfall, is important in the end. Walter White has some major flaws to acknowledge.

A Carefully Crafted Image

Walter White's ego is the nucleus for his tragic undoing throughout the five seasons of the series. A central drive in Walt's character is to control the way others perceive him, and to be viewed at all times in a positive light. Above all else, he desires to be seen as strong, virtuous, and masculine. This drive becomes his eventual downfall. When Walt finds out he has cancer, he does not consider treatment, and instead immediately makes a plan to ensure his family has enough money to live on after his death. Skyler and the rest of the family confront Walt about his refusal for treatment (Episode 1.5, "Gray Matter") and he explains:

> What good is it to survive, if I am too sick to work, to enjoy a meal, to make love? For what time I have left, I want to live in my own house. I want to sleep in my own bed. I don't want to choke down 30 or 40 pills every day, and lose my hair, and lie around too tired to get up—and, so nauseated, that I can't even move my head. And, you, cleaning up after me. Me . . . some dead man—some artificially alive . . . just marking time. No, no. That is how you would remember me. That's the worst part.

Walt is a convincing liar, but it is hard not to believe him in this moment. As an audience member, I take his explanation during the intervention as another reason why he chooses to break bad—a regional phrase popular in Gilligan's home state of Virginia meaning to break the law—instead of choosing to fight the cancer. If Walt borrows money, he will have to undergo the treatment, which only prolongs the inevitable and will perhaps make him too weak to work. If he undergoes the treatment without borrowing the money from his former friends Gretchen and

Elliott, he will eat into his profits, which is what ends up happening through a series of unfortunate mishaps with Jesse. He also knows that even with treatment he is only buying himself a few years; thus, treatment entirely thwarts his (seemingly) altruistic goal to leave a nest egg for his family to live on once he dies. But why doesn't Walt borrow the money for treatment and cook until he is too weak, thus achieving both goals? His ego will not allow it.

What makes Walt likable in the first few seasons is that although he is arrogant and controlling, he also has to suck it up sometimes and eat a generous serving of humble pie. In the third episode of the second season (Episode 2.3, "Bit by a Dead Bee"), after Tuco is dead, Walt has to invent a cover story to explain his long absence. He pretends he had a fugue state and shows up stark naked at a Hi-Lo grocery store, which lands him in the hospital. Not only does he suffer the humiliation of being perceived as weak and vulnerable by his family, somebody who has to be watched and cared for, but he also now has to pay for "the world's most expensive alibi" (Episode 2.5, "Breakage"). When Walt realizes the doctors are worried about letting him go home, he invokes doctor-patient privilege and confesses to the hospital-appointed psychiatrist why he did it: "I am an extremely overqualified chemistry teacher. . . . I've watched all my friends and colleagues surpass me in every way" (Episode 2.3, "Bit by a Dead Bee"). Although he is lying to his family, and choosing to make meth instead of taking a job with Gray Matter, he is someone who is coming to the end of his life and wishes he had made different choices. His desire for a different image, a different life altogether, is understandable.

Even in Season 4, after he has done some unthinkable things, there are moments that simultaneously demonstrate his flaws while also humanizing him. We find out later in Episode 4.10 ("Salud") that part of his desire to avoid the final image of sickness stems from the childhood trauma of witnessing his own father lying sick in a hospital bed dying slowly of Huntington's disease. In a state of drunken despair after sending Jesse off to his death in Mexico, Walter tells Walt Jr. that he does not want to die a similarly undignified death as that of his own father. Walter's desire is relatable; nobody wants to leave his or her family with an image of sickness and sadness. However, Walt Jr. tells him he prefers his tearful honesty from last night to what it has been like during the last year, because at least he was "real." Unfortunately, Walt does not allow this information to sink in, and he takes the cultivation of his image to a new extreme.

Walt's obsession with image eventually includes the desire to be seen not just as a capable provider, but as a powerful man, which makes him arrogant and cruel. In Episode 4.6 ("Cornered"), Skyler confronts him for telling Hank that Gale was not Heisenberg, and suggests he did it because he wants to get caught. She says he is in danger and scared every time someone knocks on the door. Walt lashes out at her and delivers one of the show's most famous lines: "Who is it you think you see? Do you know how much I make a year? I am not in danger, Skyler. I am the danger. *I am the one who knocks.*" Cranston analyzes this moment in the script, when Walt explains to Skyler that he is the danger in their world, stating, "There was some satisfaction to him to being the one in charge, to being the dangerous one." He continues, "[Walt]'s been able to do all these things in total anonymity, which is at first what he thought he wanted. But as he's going along, he realizes this invisible infamy is not enough."27 Power without the accompanying fame and reputation does not satisfy Walt's growing ego, and instead, he must make those around him—like Skyler, Saul, Jesse, and Mike—aware of his power. Ironically, Walt is actually afraid at this point in his career when he tells Skyler that he is the one who knocks, as he knows that Gus hates him and will choose to be rid of him the first chance he gets.

A Disdain for Charity

Part of the image Walt wishes to construct includes a type of rugged individualism where he succeeds on his own, and to that end he develops a deep disdain for anything deemed as charity. Walt values money as the sign of what makes a man powerful. He hints at this in the "I am the one who knocks" speech to Skyler, when he asks her, "Do you know how much I make a year?" We learn early in the series that Walt essentially cashed out on Google, when he sold his shares in a then fledgling Gray Matter and became an Albuquerque chemistry teacher. At Elliott Schwartz's birthday party (Episode 1.5, "Gray Matter"), Skyler and Walt look out of place and awkward mixed with Elliott and Gretchen's fashionable and wealthy friends. Skyler, wearing what looks like a 1980s maternity prom dress, reassures Walt that his sentimental but cheap birthday gift for Elliott will be a hit. Walt and Elliott do share a moment of nostalgia, and Walt almost accepts a job with Gray Matter—that is, until he realizes Skyler told Elliott about his cancer. The job becomes charity in Walt's mind, and he refuses to accept money from the wealthy Schwartzes.

An even more disturbing scene occurs in Season 2 after Gretchen finds out that Walt lied to his family about her involvement with paying for his treatment (Episode 2.6, "Peekaboo"). The heated conversation ends with Walt looking Gretchen dead in the eyes and saying, "Fuck you," to which she recoils and then tearfully leaves the restaurant. Bryan Cranston discusses Walt's reaction in this scene by stating, "Gretchen was kind of placating, and maybe he took it as condescension, 'Oh, we're happy to come to your rescue.' And he doesn't want her to be smug with him. 'I'm fine, so fuck you.'"[28] The backstory is far more telling. By the sixth episode in season 2, viewers know Gretchen and Walt dated at one point. We know that Elliott and Gretchen are extremely wealthy, and Walt is not. We also know there seems to be some residual anger, or frustration, and even some contempt on Walt's part, based on his resistance to their help and his behavior at the birthday party. Vince Gilligan comments, "Most viewers of *Breaking Bad* assume Gretchen and Elliott are the bad guys, and they assume that Walt got ripped off by them, got ill used by them, and I never actually saw it that way."[29] Shortly after "Peekaboo" aired, Jessica Hecht, who plays Gretchen Schwartz in the series, revealed in an AMC interview:

> Vince Gilligan told us exactly what went down between the characters off screen: We were very much in love and we were to get married. And he came home and met my family, and I come from this really successful, wealthy family, and that knocks him on his side. He couldn't deal with this inferiority he felt—this lack of connection to privilege. It made him terrified, and he literally just left me, and I was devastated.[30]

It is Walt's own ego that kept him from the success of Gray Matter all along, but this information is kept out of the script. These little moments are good examples of why fans of the show have such polarizing reactions to Walt. We are only given enough information to let us decide whether we want to be on Walt's side or not. As we all know, Walt is a wonderful liar, especially to himself.

At one point, Walter White has made a sizable nest egg for his family and is frustrated that he cannot tell anybody about it. He has just convinced Gus Fring to work with him, and he has almost $1 million between his and Jesse's cut (minus Saul's fee), hidden in the walls of his garage (Episode 2.12, "Phoenix"). Walt just made a fortune, and nobody knows how capable he is at providing for his family. One night, when Holly wakes up crying, he walks her out to the garage, shows her the money, and says, "That's right. Daddy did that." He tries to take some satisfaction in being able to show someone, even a few-days-old infant, what he has accomplished. Later, in the same episode, Walt Jr. shows his father the website he created, SaveWalterWhite.com. Walt refuses to allow Jr. to put a donation button on the website, arguing with Skyler, "It's charity." To which Skyler replies, "Why do you say that like it's some kind of dirty word?" Although these conversations do highlight his pride about taking money, it is more than not wanting charity. It is about Walt wanting people to know that he earned the money. He goes to Saul for help, arguing, "It cannot be blind luck, or some imaginary relative who saves us. No. I earned that money. Me!" Saul astutely points to this mindset as a character flaw for Walt with the sarcastic quip, "There are no deep-seated issues there." What strikes me most about this situation is that Walt claims he makes sacrifices for his family, but he refuses to let Walt Jr. feel good about himself by making the money for the family instead. Walt's resistance to charity, even as a lie so that he can make sure his family keeps the money, highlights pride as perhaps his most tragic flaw.

HE'S NO HERO . . .

Defining Walter White, and more broadly, what it means to be a villain in the creative revolution of television today, is complicated. Walter White is hardly the clear-cut black-hatted villain gleefully twirling the corners of his mustache. He is not tying women to railroad tracks[31] or killing random people for sport or pleasure. Instead, Walt's evil is far more nuanced and ultimately more terrifying than the strictly evil villain. You never know what he will decide to do next. It is this messiness that makes *Breaking Bad* so good. Walt makes some good choices and some bad choices, and he attempts to control his future, but the fate machine took its toll. He is so singularly greedy (for ego and money) that we have to know that his end will be tragic.

To me, Walter White dies not as an antihero or a villain, but as a tragic and complex human figure, at once an everyman and a villain: Walt *and* Heisenberg. There are moments within the series, like when he lets Jane die (Episode 2.12, "Phoenix"), or when he turns Jesse over to the white supremacist gang (Episode 5.14, "Ozymandias"), where we just cannot on any level relate to the heinous choices he makes. These decisions make him Heisenberg, the villain. And then Walt surprises us, when he refuses to die alone in a cabin in New Hampshire, and sets into motion a plan that attempts to make the lives of the people he loves a little better. The image he carefully cultivates and protects no longer matters at the end, and that makes him more than a villain. Gretchen and Elliott will never see Walter White again; they only see the Heisenberg that will continue to torment them from the grave, when he threatens their lives if they do not fulfill his dying wish (Episode 5.16, "Felina"). He does not care, as long as his son gets the money. Walt Jr. will never forgive the man who ruined his family. The final words he speaks to his father are "Why don't you just die already? Just die," and he will always think that Walt killed his favorite uncle (Episode 5.15, "Granite State"). Walt accepts that he cannot make Walt Jr. see him as a hero. Skyler gets a glimpse of the endearing Walt we all loved, when he finally admits he did everything for himself. He tells her the truth from a place of self-aware- ness for the first time in two years, and her relief is palpable. Throughout the series, Walter White wavers between the two personae of Walt and Heisenberg, but saves Jesse in the end. This final moment makes us question whether he is fully a monster, or a cautionary tale of greed and ego that is ultimately human and oddly relatable. A tragically flawed man, Walter is no hero, but he is also not a villain.

2

THE EVOLUTION OF HEISENBERG

To the rest of us, it felt like, by the middle of the series, Walt had crossed over, had made too many bad choices. But Bryan never let go of Walt—he felt so strongly that there were pure motives there.— Coproducer Melissa Bernstein [1]

*The only thing I saw was the pilot script. And as an actor, you know if it starts to seep into your soul and you start daydreaming about the character and having nighttime dreams about the character, then it's becoming you—or you're becoming it, one way or the other.—*Bryan Cranston [2]

I think it is important to acknowledge, at the very beginning of this chapter, the deep-rooted bias I have for Bryan Cranston's acting abilities and thoughtfulness about his character's motivations. Cranston's analysis of Walter White and the acting decisions he made and his interpretation of the character are fascinating. For this reason, I include many of his comments in interviews about the character throughout this chapter and book. It is the combination of talented writing, excellent direction, and principally, Cranston's devotion to his craft that makes Walter White one of the most compelling characters on television to date. I am clearly not alone in my appreciation: Cranston received four Emmy wins and six nominations for Best Actor in a Drama Series for his portrayal of Walter White during the five seasons of *Breaking Bad.*

AMC executives originally balked at Vince Gilligan's recommendation of Cranston for the role of Walter, arguing that the father from

Malcolm in the Middle didn't have the range required for Walt's disturbing transformation.[3] In other words, the execs felt Cranston lacked the acting chops necessary to "break bad." They suggested John Cusack or Matthew Broderick instead, and luckily both actors passed on the offer. Really, Matthew freakin' Broderick? Babyface Bueller Broderick? After showing AMC an episode of the *X-Files* written by Gilligan ("Drive") wherein Cranston somehow pulls off playing an endearing anti-Semite, he got his way. Speaking about the *X-Files* role, Gilligan notes, "We needed somebody who could be dramatic and scary yet have an underlying humanity so when he dies, you felt sorry for him."[4] This difficult combination is exactly what *Breaking Bad* needed as well; the audience had to care about somebody who was destined to become a monster. Cranston's supreme talent convinced the AMC executives to offer him the role, and he started the journey to forever become synonymous with Heisenberg, blue meth, and pizza tossing.

This chapter admittedly serves as an homage to the hard work of Gilligan, Cranston, and the various writers and directors of the series, as I dig into the representations and motivations of the character. I explore the evolution of Mr. Chips to Scarface, as Walt becomes Heisenberg. The tale of a character suffering a midlife, or end-of-life, crisis is hardly new, but with Walter White we get a fresh take on this plot device and opportunities to interpret it in new ways. In other words, this chapter ultimately attempts to analyze why Walter White became so captivating a character.

THE SPARK

About his decision to take the role, Cranston states, "I never wanted to be in a position where I should make a creative decision based on financial need. I didn't want a 'job.' I didn't need to work ever again."[5] This statement is particularly ironic, considering Cranston's first creative choice after the success of *Malcolm in the Middle* was to play a man whose fateful decision is based on financial need (and ego)—a character so in love with money, and the power it represents, that he allows his whole world to crumble around him in his tunnel vision.

When we meet Walter White in the beginning of the series, he could not be less of an impressive figure. He has a quiet, submissive demeanor and his posture is slightly slumped, as if the gravity of life's disappoint-

Heisenberg. AMC/Photofest © AMC

ments is slowly crushing him. Bryan Cranston said he wanted early Walt "to have the body type of my dad, who's now eighty-nine, like Walt was a much older man."[6] Cranston chose to emphasize not just complacency in Walt's life, but also sadness about his unrealized potential. He said in an interview:

> I had visions of how this guy (should look). I thought he should be a little chunky. This guy went to seed a bit emotionally, and it should manifest itself physically. He should be pale. And I thought that his invisibility to himself, because of his lost opportunities and depression, should kind of form a mask.[7]

The mask Walt wears is calm and accommodating, but meek. Skyler makes him eat veggie bacon, even though he wants the standard kind; his son is a smart-ass but lovable teenager with cerebral palsy; and at work he attempts to convey his love of science to an apathetic class of high schoolers, some of whom even question his authority. When Walt asks douchebag Chad to move back to his seat instead of playing kissy-face with his girlfriend in the back row, the boy flouts Walt's authority by noisily scraping his chair across the linoleum floor. Later at his second job, Walt has to help on the line at the car wash and ends up cleaning the tires of Chad's red Corvette. Realizing the horror of the situation for Walt, Chad rubs it in, telling Walt to "make those tires shine," and takes a picture. Chad's girlfriend is on the phone, presumably with friends from school, and she immediately begins to gossip about Mr. White cleaning Chad's car. The menial task is bad enough in itself for somebody who contributed research to a Nobel Prize (a fact revealed earlier in the episode via a plaque on the wall of his home), but to then be harassed by the same students who challenge his authority in the classroom makes this scene all the more painful to watch. The audience cannot help but feel for Walter White, and wonder, what led him down this path?

In the next scene, Walt's sullen, introverted personality becomes a foil to the boisterous man's man Hank, who oozes machismo and firmly guards his place at the top of the pecking order by picking on the other men around him. Skyler throws Walt a surprise birthday party, and Hank, a DEA agent, shows off his gun to a group of guys. He hands it to Walt, who comments that the gun is heavy, and Hank says, "That's why they hire men." Hank then gives a toast to Walt, where he ribs him for being too smart and not really fitting in with the group, takes Walt's beer, and then asks that they turn on channel 3 to watch Hank's interview about a meth lab seizure in the area. Hank commands the room, the attention from Walter Jr., and even the television in Walt's own home. Hank is the aggressive and confident yin to Walt's milquetoast yang. He offers to take Walt on a ride-along to a drug bust, telling him to "get a little excitement in your life." Walt initially declines but, after his cancer diagnosis, takes Hank up on his offer. When Walt rides along with Hank and his partner, Gomez, he is emasculated in a variety of ways, sitting in the backseat of the car with an oversized, bright bulletproof vest. Every time he asks questions, Hank rolls his eyes at Walt's lack of knowledge. And he has to wait in the car until Hank tells him he can come into the home to check out the lab.

However, Walt's diagnosis almost immediately tugs at the corners of his pale mask of resignation. Somehow, he finds confidence in the desperation of his situation. He yells, "Fuck you" at Bogdan, his boss from the car wash, when he again demands that Walt wipe down cars (a duty that is outside of the scope of the job he was hired to do), and then grabs his crotch, telling Bogdan to "wipe down this." The gesture, so macho and aggressive, is a major shift from the tepid, acquiescing response that Bogdan expects from his employee. When Walt realizes Jesse Pinkman is the Captain Cook Hank is looking for, he threatens to turn him in if Jesse refuses to partner with him on a cook. Jesse calls Walt "Mr. White," establishing the alpha-beta dynamic of teacher and student, a theme that gets played with throughout the rest of the series. At times, Jesse pushes back slightly, as in the first episode, for example, when Walt asks if he learned anything in his class and Jesse says, "No, you flunked me. Remember? Peerrriiick." It's Walt, however, who establishes the rules for their cook. Flasks will be used for their intended purposes only, no chili powder will be added (Captain Cook's signature ingredient), and Jesse will not use the product. In this premiere episode of the series, when a baffled Jesse asks him why he is breaking bad, Walt tells him, "I'm awake."

Walt's awakened confidence frequently translates into hypermasculinity, and suggests why the foil with Hank early in the series is important. Once he is "awake," Walt fights the kid who is making fun of Walt Jr. in the clothing store, and does not back down. He finds he is able to control Jesse; what he says goes during the cook, especially after he shows Jesse how pure they can make a product when they follow the rules of science ("Yeah science!"). Prior to entering this world, sex with his wife consists of a preoccupied hand job on his birthday, but after he experiences the terror that this world can bring, Walt is not only virile but sexually dominant. We see all these changes happen in the first episode, and the contrast between the man we meet at the beginning and who we see by the end is stark; this early postdiagnosis characterization reveals tiny glimpses of what is to come.

TURNING POINTS TO HEISENBERG

In the pilot episode of the series, Walter explains chemistry to his class. He says life is "a constant, a cycle. It's solution. Dissolution. Over and over and over. It is growth, then decay, then transformation!" This lecture is the blueprint for the show, as Walter White transforms into Heisenberg.

At the beginning of his evolution into Heisenberg, Walter is how most of us watching would be if we were new to the drug-dealing scene. He does not know what he's doing. In the first episode (Episode 1.1, "Pilot"), he takes off his clothes to cook in his slightly sagging tighty-whities and it is clear that Jesse is embarrassed by Walt's choice. Walt insists they wear protective gear, that the equipment is used for the appropriate purposes, and that they have an emergency eyewash station. Jesse rolls his eyes at Walt's fastidiousness. He is back in class with the "prick" teacher, Mr. White.

Early on in his career as a cook, Walt makes mistake after mistake, costing him his nest egg more than once. In the final episode of the first season (Episode 1.7, "A No-Rough-Stuff-Type Deal"), first Jesse calls out Walt for picking a remote location for their meeting with Tuco Salamanca, and then Tuco calls him out for being so stupid. When Jesse tries to convince Walt to let him handle the business side, and reminds Walt that working with Tuco was his dumb idea in the first place, Walt squirms and says, "I will admit to a bit of a learning curve" (Episode 2.5, "Breakage"). After Combo is killed, Skinny Pete tells Jesse that everybody knows Jesse did not kill Spooge (a fact Jesse led everyone to believe), and refuses to sell anymore, citing the danger after pushing out the territory borders (Episode 2.11, "Mandala"). However, it was Walt who did not realize that expanding their territory would create fatal problems; Jesse warned him in Episode 2.7 ("Negro y Azul"). Walt does not understand the way this world works. Saul comments that Jesse and Walt are terrible at selling drugs, and suggests they bring in somebody who knows what he is doing on the business end (Episode 2.11, "Mandala"). Even after Walt takes over as kingpin in Season 5 (ostensibly learning something from working with Gus), Walt again reveals he is oblivious to how things actually work in the criminal world when he attempts to bargain for Hank's life with Todd's uncle Jack. Hank informs him it is a waste of breath since Jack has already made up his mind to kill him (Episode 5.14, "Ozymandias"). Hank is correct, and the white supremacist gang ends up taking most of Walt's money and his business. Walt constantly takes two steps forward and then one step back, as he slowly but surely falls deeper into the criminal world.

The first time Walt dons the black hat of Heisenberg is when he meets with Tuco alone (Episode 1.6, "Crazy Handful of Nothin'"). Jesse is put in the hospital (not for the last time) for doing Walt's bidding. Jesse attempted to expand their drug empire by reaching out to Tuco, the dealer in the chain of hierarchy above the newly deceased Krazy-8. This was at the request of Walt, who wants to make money faster, and knows this means they need to become the supplier, selling in bulk. Jesse tells Walt, "It's too risky . . . we are making money. Why can't you just be satisfied with the way it is?" To which Walt snarls, "Jesus, just grow some fucking balls!" In this partnership, Walt is not afraid to speak his mind to Jesse, and there is a constant power struggle between the two men, with Jesse frequently ending up on the bottom of the hierarchy, just as Walt does in situations with Hank. It turns out Jesse was right to be afraid, because Tuco takes the drugs and puts Jesse in the hospital. Walt decides to take matters into his own hands. Mr. White, chemistry teacher turned drug maker, is about to walk into a drug dealer's caged-in lair and demand the full amount for their drugs. He has seen the level of physical violence Tuco is capable of inflicting, and Tuco already has the drugs, so Walter has very little leverage. Due to the cancer invading his body, he also has nothing to lose. As he gets out of the car, he puts on the hat and slips into the persona of Heisenberg, a man who is not afraid, who has a plan, and is unwilling to take no for an answer. And, it works. When Tuco says no, Heisenberg blows up his office, and ultimately makes a deal to connect his fate even further with the crazy distributor.

The new persona of Heisenberg lets Walt become what Cranston calls "the emotionless, brave, risk-taking imaginary friend who looks out for Walt's best interests."[8] Although we officially meet Heisenberg in Episode 6, Walt's alter ego performs his first act of retribution in Episode 4 of the series (Episode 1.4, "Cancer Man") when he blows up Ken's sports car. We meet Ken at the Mesa bank, after he steals Walt's parking space. Ken is the type of guy who wants to command all the attention in the room and believes he is entitled to being first because he is a "winner" in life. It is survival of the fittest and everything in life is a competition. He blares his music, drives a red BMW convertible, and talks loudly on his Bluetooth headset, announcing to everybody at the bank that he makes a lot of money; his license plate reads "KEN WINS," and he excretes an arrogant machismo that is cringeworthy. While on the phone bragging about his $40,000-plus bonus and ability to get any job he wants, he zeroes in on an attractive blonde bank teller, loudly appreciating her body to the person on the other end of the line. When the person on the phone asks about another woman, Ken says, "Who? No, buddy—she's a cow. Stacy's a cow. We are talking major barnyard boo-hog. Roll her in flour and look for the wet spot before you hit that, man, you know what I'm saying? That kind of stink does not wash off." Ken is vulgar, misogynistic, and incredibly unlikable. He is Hank times a thousand, with zero positive qualities to balance out the macho self-importance, and immediately rubs Walt the wrong way. So, after a particularly bad day, where Walt has tried to explain to both Skyler and Walt Jr. that he thinks treatment is too expensive and Junior asks Walt, "Why don't you just fucking die already? Just give up and die," Walt runs into Ken again at a gas station and blows up his car, and it is one of the best episode endings in the entire series. Walter is not wearing the black hat for this moment, but he is Heisenberg as he walks away from the wreckage without any regret. This scene sets the tone for the extreme choices to be made by Walt/Heisenberg in the future.

There are turning points throughout the series that put Walt and Heisenberg in conflict with one another, where Walter White attempts to resist the appeal of the adrenaline-junkie risk-taker alter ego who says and does exactly what he thinks and does not submit to anyone. For me, there are two episodes that most strongly reveal this conflict within Walt: the episode where Jane dies, and the episode with the fly.

The One Where Jane Dies

The episode where Jane dies (Episode 2.12, "Phoenix") is fascinating to rewatch because it is such a clear turning point for Walt, where he becomes more Heisenberg than Walter White. Every fan of the show I have ever met—family, friends, students, and colleagues—cites that show as the most shocking in the series. Jane's death scene is an example of why Bryan Cranston won awards for his performances, and for this episode in particular which he submitted for consideration for the 2009 Emmy Nomination for Outstanding Lead Actor in a Drama Series. As Walt watches Jane die, Cranston's brilliant acting takes us through the character's thought process emotionally, without uttering a single word. About that scene, Cranston explains:

> There was a lot of discussion about that and how that would come about. And I had a lot of thought about that. I thought objectively about, "How I would want that scene conveyed" and then just let it go. So, I first wanted to respond in a humane way: a person was choking to death, so to stop it, so the impulse was to help. And then, he stops himself because he realizes this is the same person who was just black-mailing him and threatening to expose his whole enterprise and everyone's life would be turned upside down. . . . But then I look at her again and I said, "She's just a girl—she could be my daughter," and so you have an impulse again to do something. But then I think, "But she got Jesse on heroin and is going to kill that boy who I have affinity for." . . . So he's going back and forth trying to make sense of the whole experience and his act of ownership tells the story.[9]

That Walt decides to let Jane choke to death after accidentally shifting her onto her back illustrates his descent toward Heisenberg. Vince Gilligan reveals that he originally wrote that scene to have Walt give Jane a second dose of heroin, but his writers talked him out of that plan. As is, Sony questioned whether Gilligan wanted to have Walt culpable at all by not intervening, or what Gilligan calls Walt's "terrible sin of omission"; however, the writers knew it was important that Walt do something terrible at this point.[10]

The show writers intended for this scene to be a breaking point where fans began to recede from Walter, because he is becoming the monster. Actress Krysten Ritter, who plays Jane, says about the scene: "I remember thinking it was pretty fucked up that Walt would just let a young girl . . . die in front of him, but I certainly didn't realize that it would be such a pivotal moment for the show. . . . That decision was his turning point and there was no going back."[11] She continues in her interview to explain that she is still on Team Walt, and thinks she will be until the end.

And this comment speaks to the humanity that Cranston brings to Walt, in that he could let Jane die and still have the audience on his side. Another moment from the show had a similar effect, when the audience realizes Walt poisoned a child, Brock, in order to manipulate Jesse (Episode 4.13, "Face Off"). *New Yorker* writer Emily Nussbaum recounts conversations with her friends arguing that Walt is still not a bad guy, because he would have known just the right dose so as not to kill the boy. She continues, "The audience has been trained by cable television to react this way: to hate the nagging wives, the dumb civilians, who might sour the fun of masculine adventure. *Breaking Bad* increases that cognitive dissonance, turning some viewers into not merely fans but enablers."[12] Chuck Klosterman also uses the metaphor of "training" and argues, "We've all been trained to experience fiction through whichever main character we understand most deeply."[13]

Not all fans felt that way, however. In an interview with Vince Gilligan at the Edinburgh International Television Festival, host Charlie Brooker says he turned on Walt at this moment, and also indicates he was tempted to stop watching the series altogether. In the interview, Vince Gilligan says he and the other writers knew that was a potential risk when they made the decision to have Walt let Jane die. Gilligan continues to explain why Walt did it: "In his mind, she is going to ruin everything for him and potentially out him to his family. I'm not saying he is a good guy, he clearly is not, but he has a reason for what he does."[14] The moment Walt lets Jane die, we are not supposed to relate to him anymore. We know he cannot ever make amends to Jesse or Jane's father for her death. The scene with Jane's father, Donald Margolis (John de Lancie), at the bar earlier in the episode was a well-written creative choice, because, as much as we may understand that Jane was going to bring Jesse down a terrible road (and, in fairness, a road Jesse takes willingly), we have to hate Walt for this decision: there is no doubt what her death will do to her father and to Jesse.

What is interesting to me is that Bryan Cranston cites a much later episode in the series as the actual death of Walt and rise of Heisenberg. Toward the end of Season 4, when Walt makes the decision to disappear with his family, and then learns Skyler used all their money to pay Ted's IRS bill (Episode 4.11, "Crawl Space"), Walt realizes he is dead. He briefly allows himself to give in to an eerily gleeful delirium in the crawl space of the house, as the camera pans out and makes it look like Walt is in a coffin. Cranston says that in this moment, as Walt laughs maniacally, "Walter White is dead, and Heisenberg rises from the ashes,"[15] ironically, using the metaphor of a phoenix, which is the title of the episode where Jane dies. I see Cranston's point here, as a full-on turn to Heisenberg symbolizes somebody who has accepted his actions, and does not care who he hurts anymore as long as he reaches his goals. Episodes after Jane's death provide moments where Walt continues to grapple with his sins, thus indicating that he is not fully Heisenberg quite yet. The fly episode is one such moment.

The Episode with the Fly

Perhaps full-on Heisenberg comes later for Walt, but regardless, Jane's death and the tragic consequences for the entire community after the plane crash is something that Walt has to live with and, for a man with Walt's ego, something to rationalize. As Season 3 opens (Episode 3.1, "No Más"), we know that Skyler left Walt, and we see that he now knows that he talked with Jane's dad that night at the bar. He also knows the plane crash (which killed 167 people) was caused by her grieving father, who returned to work too early. The scene opens to Walt's disheveled house. Walt has been collecting newspapers covering the event, and the television is playing the news channel with coverage. An unkempt Walt sits in the backyard, lighting matches and throwing them into the pool. In one scene, he puts a pile of money in the grill, pours lighter fluid over it, lights a match, and throws it into the grill pit. After a brief moment where he watches the money burn, he panics as he realizes what he has done, and extinguishes it in the pool. Is he distraught over Skyler leaving him, or because he is responsible for 167 deaths? Does he blame his greed for causing the family turmoil, or in causing a plane crash?

Ultimately, Walt appears to clear his conscience by rationalizing his actions—a trick he performs countless times in the show. We see him do this at the assembly, as the students and teachers all try to make sense of the tragedy. Walt reluctantly takes the microphone and tries to point out the positive side to the situation, arguing that this plane crash was "just the 50th worst air disaster . . . actually tied for 50th," as his coworkers and students stare at him in disbelief. The assembly makes him confront his culpability in the situation, and he tries to make himself feel better by justifying the magnitude of the crash as small in the grand scheme of all airline disasters. He does this again later in the episode when he picks up Jesse from rehab, saying that he is not responsible for any of this (Jane's death or the plane crash), arguing, "I blame the government." Jesse, fresh from a counseling session where the therapist tells him that "self-hatred and guilt just stand in the way of true change," accepts his role in all that happened. In this moment, Jesse is far more self-aware than Walt.

What makes the fly episode (Episode 3.10, "Fly") important is that it allows the audience a glimpse at what is going on in Walt's head halfway through the series. Walt is a wonderful liar; Vince Gilligan calls it his superpower.[16] And because Walt lies to himself just as easily (through rationalization and justification of his actions), it is just as hard for the audience to make sense of his actions as it is for his family, both those in the know and those in the dark. The episode is almost a throwback to the dark humor of the first season, where Walt and Jesse act like cartoon characters beating each other with the fly-catching instruments as they run around the lab. The fly episode pinpoints the moment for Walt where he thinks he could have made everything work out the way he wanted it to. Jesse has been trying to help an obsessed and sleep-deprived crazed Walt catch a fly, and he finally drugs his coffee with sleeping pills to get him to calm down from his mania. A half-asleep Walt tries to figure out where things went wrong: "I mean I truly believe there is a combination of words . . . in a specific order that will explain all of this." Walt is trying to figure out how he got so far into the drug world, and lamenting his mistakes with the second cell phone, how he lost his wife and broke up his family. He says he has lived too long, and continues: "I know the moment. It was the night Jane died. I was at home and we needed diapers, so I said I would go. But it was just an excuse—actually that was the night I brought you your money . . . I stopped at a bar . . . walked in, sat down. I never told you." Walt reveals he had a drink next to Jane's dad: "Think of the odds of my going in, sitting down at that bar, next to that man. . . . He said never give up on family . . . and, I didn't [looks at Jesse]. I took his advice." However, he pinpoints his decision to leave his house as the beginning of the end: "I should never have left home, never gone to your house. . . . If I had just lived up until that moment, and not one second more . . . that would have been perfect."

Walt eventually accepts that the fly is not going to come down. Jesse, showing a soft spot for Walt in that moment, finds him a chair and gets the ladder: "I'm going to get that bitch." Walt looks up toward Jesse on the ladder and comes dangerously close to telling him about Jane. He says, "Jesse, I'm sorry." Jesse says, "Sorry for what? Being a lunatic?" Walt clarifies, "Sorry about Jane." Jesse pauses, "Yeah, me too." Walt continues, "I mean I'm very sorry." Jesse shrugs. "It's not your fault. It's not mine either. It's no one's fault. Not even hers. We are who we are. Two junkies with a duffle bag full of cash. You said we both would have been dead within a week. I miss her though. I do." And then, Jesse kills the fly and we watch it bounce in slow motion dead to the ground. Jesse is thrilled, as he turns to Walt in triumph; but Walt has fallen asleep. Jesse wheels him over to the sofa and tucks him in, as Jesse completes the cook on his own.

There are many different ways this pivotal episode in the series can be read, but the interpretation I prefer is that Walter White realizes he is on the road to Heisenberg, and he feels guilt about that, wishing he had died before that change occurred. He also understands that he has done a terrible job of keeping all the balls in the air. Instead of accepting responsibility, the drugged Walt tries to figure out where he could have fixed the situation, how he could have controlled it better so that it would not be such a mess. He wants to know when he could have died and still left his family with a positive image of him. He pinpoints the night he let Jane die. He is sorry that he hurt Jesse, but he is also sorry he did not do a better job of controlling his image.

The redness of the room, the location of the lab below the surface of the earth, and the Sisyphus of perpetual torment, where Walt gets close to killing the fly and then misses, all symbolize that Walt is in hell. But more than that, the devil is both the father of lies and the lord of the flies. Walt is in his own personal hell as he tries to figure out where he went wrong, but he is becoming the devil, the monster that Gilligan promised us from the beginning of the series. In his drugged state, the master liar is trying to figure out what his silver tongue could say to Skyler to make it all better. He does not see that his lies have gotten him to this point. Donna Bowman argues that both the fly episode and Jane's death follow the model of a "Greek tragedy, and in Greek tragedy, there is no exit to the maze. We are cued to understand that these characters are trapped in the world they made for themselves, and to feel the pity and fear that comes from recognizing ourselves in them."[17] This scene allows us to see him try to make sense of the transformation to Heisenberg, but also to recognize that Walt is in hell, and he has dragged Jesse down with him.

The fly episode ends with Walt warning Jesse that he will not be able to protect him if he is in fact stealing the overage from Gus. Jesse asks, "Who's asking you to?" This is a big question for the entire series and one that reminds us of Walt's ego. Who is asking him to do this for the family? Certainly not Skyler; she actively does not want him to do it. He takes it upon himself; Walt wants to be the one in charge, to help, to make it better, and he wants credit for succeeding. Similarly, the night Jane died, he was taking on helping Jesse (who, since his ouster from home, has become Walt's alternate family) and ends up ruining his life by killing his girlfriend instead. Maybe he did know better than Jesse, and the two would have shot all the money up their arms (their decision to use the night Jane died suggests this is the case), but he needed to let Jesse figure it out on his own.

A CYCLE: "GROWTH, THEN DECAY, THEN TRANSFORMATION!"

In the opening quote for this chapter coproducer Melissa Bernstein says, "To the rest of us, it felt like, by the middle of the series, Walt had crossed over, had made too many bad choices. But Bryan never let go of Walt—he felt so strongly that there were pure motives there."[18] It is difficult to discuss the evolution of Heisenberg, because it means Walter White becomes a monster, and Bryan Cranston did a wonderful job of showing the complexity of human nature, by making so many fans want to see the monster succeed. Cranston reminds us that "a more interesting complex character is someone who I'm not sure . . . is good or bad. I'm uncertain. And, that is what I think strikes the heart of [the psychopathic character] is that there is a mixture. It's really what human beings are."[19] Walter White is a reminder that we make choices, life gets messy, and the line between right and wrong frequently blurs.

In the beginning of the series, Walt's goal with making meth is to leave money for his family. Whether his motives are pure—whether they are based on love and concern for his family, or on ego and envy—is a riddle that goes unanswered up until the last episode. Even then, based on the choices he makes, it is hard to have a definitive answer. Although he admits to Skyler at the end of the series that all of this was about him, and not the family, he still manages to provide for the kids' educations, and to save Jesse from the misery of his enslavement by Todd and the neo-Nazis. The last shots of the series, as Walt walks through the lab, gently touching the equipment as if it is an old and dearly missed friend, reminds us that the distinction between Heisenberg and Walter White is a messy one.

3

DOES WALT WANT TO DIE?

His world has always been exact, and he enters into a world that is out of order and chaotic and dangerous—but it's also the first time he's had this kind of excitement. Even when he's dying, there are those moments where he gets that adrenaline rush, and he feels really alive.—Bryan Cranston[1]

Walter White comes alive when he finds out he is going to die. Instead of immediately telling his family that he has cancer, he decides to make money. After his family finds out, instead of trying to fight the cancer, he resists treatment and accepts, not his fate, but the science of the situation. He understands his odds, based on the chemistry of the human body. He recognizes the severity of his diagnosis for what it is: a death sentence. Walt does not make plans to try to stop his death, but instead to leave his family better off than they are now. The cancer is a ticking time bomb inside his body, and it gives him a renewed purpose in life. Although he finds himself in danger of being killed multiple times throughout the series, including twice in the first episode alone, Walter both cheats and courts death in his chaotic journey.

Walt was dying long before he received his cancer diagnosis. In Season 3, when Skyler separates from Walt and chooses to leave everyone else in the dark about her reasons why, Hank and his wife Marie (Skyler's sister) speculate that Walt must have had an affair (Episode 3.2, "Caballo Sin Nombre"). Hank says, "Look, a guy like Walt? Nice guy. Decent. Smart. Let's face it: underachiever—dead-end life. He gets cancer, time is running out. He steps out." Hank's impression of Walt is that he is not living his life to the fullest. Precancer Walt is mild mannered, nice but weak, and Walt felt that way, too, until he knew he was dying and there was nothing to lose. But there is a difference between not worrying about dying and wanting to die, and there are moments in the series that play between these two ideas, creating a question of whether Walt wants to die. In this chapter, I attempt to provide some answers to an overarching question about Walter throughout the series: Does he have a death wish?

ARROGANCE AND HUBRIS

In the middle of the second season, (Episode 2.8, "Better Call Saul"), after Hank returns home from El Paso awash in the emotional wreckage of having witnessed half his team blown up by a turtle bomb, he is sent home from work by his supervisor. At Marie's request, Walt enters Hank's bedroom, and he suggests Hank talk to a therapist about everything that has happened in the past year. Hank is still dealing with killing Tuco, and now he has witnessed the depravity of the cartel firsthand; it is a lot to take in, especially for a macho rock of a man, who is typically the one solving other people's problems. Hank initially resists Walt's attempt at advice, telling him that therapy would be career suicide, and then, annoyed to be receiving advice from Walt, argues that Walt cannot possibly understand what he is going through, citing their different fields of experience. Walt tells Hank he has spent his whole life scared of what might happen, but ever since his cancer diagnosis, he sleeps just fine, because "fear is the worst enemy." Hank looks at him, realizing he is right. Fear is holding him back. Walt tells Hank to get up out of bed. This quick glimpse inside Walt's head suggests he is not afraid to die, but it still does not reveal if he wants to live.

As I detailed in the previous chapter, prior to the cancer diagnosis, Walt is subdued and somewhat resigned to his life of mediocrity—just getting through the monotony of the day. We quickly learn how much this new world wakes him up. Being close to the danger, or more specifically, to death, is a sexual turn-on for Walt. The first instance of this is after he kills Emilio (and has injured Krazy-8), when he comes home to Skyler and has sex with her: he slips into bed, caressing her face, and then flips her over (Episode 1.1, "Pilot"). She is surprised, and then pleased and willing, as we hear her moans of pleasure to fade out the episode. The front-to-back position is particularly animalistic and primal. After the act is complete, Walt does not talk to her, answer her questions about his absence, or even really acknowledge her as a partner. He enters the bathroom and passes out naked on the floor, where he spends the night. The blocking of this scene suggests that his brush with death does not awaken a desire for Skyler because he realizes how much he loves her, but instead, seems to fulfill a need to expel the adrenaline it gave him, and to be in control. In this first episode, Walt is held at gunpoint by Emilio and Krazy-8, and narrowly avoids getting killed as they try to shoot their way out of the noxious RV. Then, when he thinks the authorities are coming to arrest him, he puts the gun to his own head and pulls the trigger. Walter White would have died that day if not for the gun jamming. The gun fires into the ground immediately following his attempt. His relief when the police cars zoom past him is evident, and he realizes how close he came to death. His first action upon returning to his family is to have sex with his wife.

This desire is much more significant and disturbing in the opening episode of Season 2 (Episode 2.1, "Seven Thirty-Seven"), when he rapes Skyler. Now, fans of Walter who just responded to my last sentence by saying, well, it wasn't exactly "rape," yes it was. She said no. Multiple times. In fact, she adamantly states she does not want to have sex because Walt Jr. will be home any minute (not to mention the fact that she is wearing a green mud mask—who doesn't feel their sexiest after layering a green mud mask on their face?). Walt does not listen to her as he pulls her underwear down. He keeps going without her consent. Skyler says, "No, enough, stop it, STOP IT!" As she wrenches free, the refrigerator door holds remnants of Skyler's mud mask where Walt shoved her face into the door. Walt slinks off to the backyard, either ashamed or frustrated, or both; however, this is clearly not something he has ever done before, as an angry Skyler immediately attributes his behavior to his cancer diagnosis. She comes out to the backyard, wiping off the mask, and tells him, "I know you are scared, and angry, and frustrated, and I know none of this is fair. But, you cannot take it out on me." Although this scene represents a rape, it is frustratingly residing in that gray area because we are not supposed to hate Walt here. The truth is, we are privy to information that Skyler is not, and ultimately, this scene does not cast Walt as a bad guy. It should, because it hints at what is boiling just below the surface, but the audience knows Walter just witnessed Tuco beat No-

Doze to death (Episode 1.7, "A No-Rough-Stuff-Type-Deal" and Episode 2.1, "Seven Thirty-Seven"), and both he and Jesse believe Tuco is going to kill them for knowing too much information. Walt is in a daze as he walks into the house; he walks up behind Skyler, inhales the scent of her hair, and then chooses to relinquish control of himself.

This scene has always disturbed me, particularly for the fact that I do not hate Walter after it happens. Maybe it is because Skyler forgives him so readily, or because I know the situation Walt just witnessed with a man dying a violent death, and is now in a psychologically unstable state. I can make a million excuses for Walt's behavior, but it is unacceptable, and yet, normalized in the course of this story. Gilligan wants us to see the transformation of a monster, but he and the writers (along with Cranston) make Walt so relatable that it is hard to see this scene for what it really is. The rape scene is helpful in demonstrating the slippage of who Walt was, and who he will become, but it also offers a reading of how Walt hugs the borders of impulsiveness, as he gets deeper into the drug world. Why is Walt giving in so easily to his impulses? Perhaps he is attracted to the thrill, an adrenaline junkie just trying to get his fix as he inches closer to death, without ever crossing over the line of no return. Bryan Cranston said of Walt, "Even when he's dying, there are those moments where he gets that adrenaline rush, and he feels really alive."[2] One of the themes of the series is addiction, and not everybody's vice is drugs. Drugs are not a draw for Walt, but adrenaline might be, because it wakes him up out of his slumber.

Freud's theory of the human psyche offers an interpretation of addiction that I think can be helpful in understanding Walt's reckless behavior throughout the series. Freud argued that the human psyche is made up of the id, ego, and superego. The id is the pleasure center, the impulsive site of desire. The superego is the moral center of the brain, where we are hyperaware of guilt, expectations, and morality. The ego moderates between these two areas to provide a balance between both pleasure and restraint. The ego can be helpful in avoiding truly harmful situations, or it can be like the Eddie Haskell of the brain, convincing you that the compromise is not as bad as the abandoned pleasurable behavior, even if it is still a terrible idea. Walter White has many moments of reckless abandon throughout the series, giving in to his id impulses, relying on an ego that tips the scales closer to the id than the superego; however, when it comes to his own death, he always goes right up to the line, even nudges his toe over it, but never chooses to cross it completely.

I posit that when Walt tells Jesse that he is awake after getting his cancer diagnosis (Episode 1.1, "Pilot"), and when he explains to Hank that he is no longer afraid (Episode 2.8, "Better Call Saul"), it is because he accepts the fact that he lost control of his life, but not his legacy. And this is where his arrogance comes into play. To me, the difference between arrogance and hubris is that the former implies pride or conceit without ability, whereas the latter is found in an individual with the same level of pride but also the capability to achieve one's ends. Walt's meth is 99.1 percent pure (Episode 1.4, "Cancer Man"); he is the best chemist on the illegal drug market. The chemists working with the DEA claim they would not be able to replicate his purity. Walt not only brings his scientific precision to the drug world, but he also contributes his talent as an exceptional chemist. His insistence that he not take money from Gretchen and Elliott Schwartz is arrogance, but Walt's hubris about his ability to make pure meth, and what that entitles him to, is what gets him in trouble. This is when he chooses to die a hero rather than a victim, and becomes obsessed with being the one to provide for his family.

Hints of this occur early in the series. For example, in the episode where Walt tells Hank, Marie, and Walt Jr. that he has cancer (Episode 1.4, "Cancer Man"), it is the first time that his control over the situation slips away. Skyler loses her emotional restraint after Walt tells the story of how the two of them met. She sobs at the dinner table, and tells the family to ask Walt why she is so upset. Walt has no choice but to tell the rest of his family about his diagnosis. Skyler does not tell his secret, but she does force Walt to reveal his information before he had planned to do so. The family is obviously upset, and Hank and Marie try to help Walt and Skyler work through the situation. Skyler accuses Walt of forcing her to keep it a secret, and then Marie and Skyler make a plan for how to tackle the cancer head-on. Skyler tells Walt, "Walt, don't you see? Everybody just wants to help you. We are a family. We get through these things together." Walt does not want to get through it *together*, though. He made an individual plan already and it requires that he be a hero after his death. Walt is silent as Marie tells Skyler that he will need a second opinion, and offers to refer him to a doctor she works with at the hospital. Skyler looks relieved. Hank then turns to Walt and says, "I hope this goes without saying . . . whatever happens . . . I want you to know that I'll always take care of your family." Walt visibly reacts to this declaration with frustration because he is taking care of his own family, and that is important to him (his arrogance demands it), but he quickly recovers and nods solemnly to Hank. The entire time, Walt barely speaks, and this creative choice by the writers emphasizes the lack of agency Walt has now that he has lost control of his secret and others co-own the information.

The famous "intervention scene" further emphasizes Walt's deliberate reticence regarding treatment (Episode 1.5, "Gray Matter"). The intervention is a classic example of the underlying humor throughout the series, and it serves to characterize all the main members of Walt's immediate and extended family. Skyler, Walt Jr., Hank, and Marie sit in the living room and share with Walt their honest feelings about his choice to let the cancer go untreated. Skyler goes first, stating, "I understand that it is hard for you to accept help. Maybe it is the way you were raised. But, honey, it's okay to lean on people now and again. You need this treatment and nothing can stop you from getting it, except you." As Walt tries to interrupt Skyler during her plea, she stops him and says he cannot speak until he is given the talking pillow (a couch pillow that helps regulate the process of the intervention, à la the conch in *Lord of the Flies*). Walt sits quietly while almost his entire family tells him that he needs to get treatment. Walt Jr. calls him a "pussy" for being afraid to get treatment and cites his own struggles with cerebral palsy as a contrast to his father's fatalism and cowardice. Hank utilizes two hypermasculine metaphors of gambling and baseball to suggest that Walt is giving up if he does not get the treatment. Hank even acknowledges that Walt's resistance to Elliott and Gretchen's offer to help is about pride, but suggests Walt take the money anyway. It is interesting that both Walt Jr. and Hank tie their comments back to his masculinity (or lack thereof, in their perceptions).

It is Marie who ultimately recognizes Walt's loss of voice in the process and suggests that he should not have to get treatment if he does not want to. Hank then asks, "Can I get the pillow back? Because I agree with Marie on this one." Skyler is furious with this turn of events, and Hank, doing a complete 180, says, "What? Maybe Walt wants to die like a man." They start arguing and Walt whistles loudly. He gets up, grabs the pillow, and begins to explain his decision about treatment: "What I want—what I want, what I need—is a choice." He continues to explain that his treatment gives him an option, at a time when he does not have any control: "Sometimes I feel like I never actually make any of my own—choices I mean. My entire life, it just seems I never . . . had a real say about any of it. This last one, cancer—all I have left is how I choose to approach this." Walt continues, explaining that treatment would allow him to survive, but he wants a better quality of life, and he wants his family to remember him as more than a patient: "That is how you would remember me. That's the worst part. So, that is my thought process Skyler, I'm sorry . . . I choose not to do it."

This statement is incredibly powerful. The entire family is moved to tears, or in Hank's case, as close as he comes to tears. Walt indicates in this speech that he does not want to die, but since he is going to die from this cancer, he wants to do it on his own terms. And, then, the next morning, Walt wakes up and sees the stack of books Skyler is reading, about babies and cancer. With tears in his eyes, he smells her lotion. He gets out of bed. In the kitchen, Skyler barely speaks to him. Walt leans on her back, puts his arms around her pregnant belly, and gives in: "All right . . . I'll do the treatment . . . it's going to be okay." Literally, within a few minutes of viewing time, and overnight in the storyline, Walt backtracks and does not make his own choice at all. He completely overrides the powerful statement he made about not being a victim, and not wanting to burden his family. Why does he give in here? Was last night the real Walt, or was that his cover story? The truth is he does not want to spend money on the treatment, when he knows he is going to die, because he wants to leave his family with a nest egg, not debt. When Walt agrees to treatment, he makes the decision to both get treatment and continue to cook.

And thus begins the vicious cycle for Walter White: a cycle that transforms him into the monster Gilligan promised us. Walt's goal in making drugs is to make a lot of money for his family. The cancer treatments cut into that profit. Now, if Walt had agreed to take the money from Elliott and Gretchen for the treatment, which is what he tells Skyler he is doing (Episode 1.5, "Gray Matter"), or, if he had taken Skyler's suggestion and asked Hank and Marie for financial help (Episode 1.4, "Cancer Man"), then he could have continued to make drugs and accrue his nest egg. His arrogance about taking charity completely negates his goals and thrusts him deeper into the drug world as he attempts to recoup his loss.

A DEAD MAN

Does Walt's recklessness stem from his arrogance or does he have a death wish? Throughout the series, there are a few key scenes that play with this idea. There is one scene in particular in the series that is difficult to read. To be more specific, it can be interpreted in a few different ways, and each reading offers a different answer to the question of whether Walt wants to die. In the middle of Season 2 (Episode 2.9, "4 Days Out"), Walt's cough gets worse; he now hacks up blood. After completing the treatment, he gets a PET/CT scan to see if it had any effect on the tumor. As he walks out of the scanning room, he sees his own X-rays and notices a sizable mass near his lungs. Fearing the end is near, Walt immediately reaches out to Jesse, who is in love and not interested in spending a long weekend cooking. Walt lies and tells Jesse the methylamine is going to go bad, so they need to cook right away. It becomes an incredibly long weekend, as one disaster after another strikes: the car battery dies (thanks to Jesse), they run out of water (thanks to Jesse), and Skinny Pete gets lost trying to rescue them (thanks to Skinny Pete). Jesse witnesses Walt's bloody phlegm and puts two and two together; he took care of his cancer-

Walt and Jesse stranded on a cook. *AMC/Photofest © AMC*

stricken aunt prior to her death, so he knows coughing up blood for a lung cancer patient is not a good sign. As Walt and Jesse lie defeated on cots in the RV, Walt says he deserves it, as he has not helped his family but just "managed to worry and disappoint them." Jesse does not want to hear that talk; he tells Walt to stop being a crybaby and to act like the scientist genius he is to get them out of this situation. Reinvigorated, Walt "Mac-Gyvers" their way home. When Jesse drops Walt off at the airport, the two men share a touching moment where Jesse reassures Walt, "Whatever happens, your family will get your share." It is an important scene, because as much as the two men fight and seem to hate each other at times, there is a true trust between them, and a lot of compassion on Jesse's side for Walt's situation.

However, all of their hard work and touching moments turn out to be in vain, when Walt and the family get the surprising news that the tumor has shrunk by 80 percent. Walt is visibly shocked, and the family is elated with the good news. Moments later, we see Walt in the restroom, splashing water on his face. He looks up to grab a paper towel, sees his reflection in the metal of the dispenser, and proceeds to beat the device off the wall. This is the moment that can be interpreted in a few different ways. What is the psychological catalyst for Walt's meltdown?

Does he think he needs to give up his new field of work because now it is unnecessary, and that disappoints him? He found a career he is very good at, and he feels powerful in his new role. Making meth and illicit cash thrills him. Perhaps, Walt is trying to figure out what all his hard work and risk have been for, if he is not going to die, and his family will not be in need of large quantities of cash. By the same token, being a chemistry teacher was painfully dull compared to building a drug empire, and Walt's remission now puts his happiness in jeopardy. We see some evidence to support this interpretation in the very next episode (Episode 2.10, "Over") when Walt drives himself crazy chasing fungus in the foundation of the house. In lieu of being able to cook (he and Jesse have ended the partnership), Walt obsesses over the foundation of the house, in a manner similar to his obsession in the "Fly" episode (Episode 3.10). This can be read as a metaphor, as he is focused on the foundation of the family house, but missing the minor details where his wife is heading toward an affair with her boss. It also serves to illustrate what happens when Walter has lost his purpose of helping the family by breaking bad. The foundation gives Walt something to obsess over as a distraction from doing what he really wants to be doing, which is cooking. Either way, his reaction in the bathroom in the previous episode (Episode 2.9, "4 Days Out") can be read as disappointment that he has to return to normal.

Does he need the thrill of being close to death to keep going in life? This interpretation relies on the adrenaline junkie theory. His new diagnosis means he is going to live. If death is what made him come alive, then what is the absence of that death going to do for him? He cannot possibly go back to his old life, but the fact that he is in remission now puts a major hole in the story he has been telling himself about why he needs to break bad. Morally, he is a criminal who puts drugs on the street; he lies to his family, makes illegal money, and, ultimately, puts his family in danger. And now, he is told he will live. The prospect of living, of getting a new lease of life, terrifies him as he can no longer place himself in risky situations with the rationalization of "Well, the cancer's going to kill me anyway." This new diagnosis ruins his life.

What does it say about Walt that the paper towel dispenser was reflecting his own image as he dented it beyond recognition? Arrogance is compensation for a person's subconscious self-perception of inadequacy. It is frequently coupled with deep-seated self-loathing, or at the very least, insecurity. Walt is incredibly arrogant but also filled with self-loathing; part of him thinks he deserves to die and part of him wants to die. The plan he has created keeps getting blocked by twists of fate. This interpretation of Walt's reaction in the bathroom suggests Walt wants to die. The other two readings above mean that he wants to live with the time bomb, but he does want to live. He is protecting his image and enjoying the ride. He is on a journey that should have a conclusion, but perhaps not yet. In this third interpretation, Walt needs to die, but he is not willing to commit suicide (as we saw in Episode 1.1, "Pilot"), so cancer is an easy out and buys him time to live. What were the kids saying in 2011? YOLO? Walt only lives once, but he lives best when he knows he is near the end of his life, so he does want to die.

A second, equally ambiguous scene that suggests Walt has a death wish occurs right after Gus extends Walt's contract another year (Episode 3.9, "Kafkaesque"). Jesse makes a comment that gets Walt curious about what happens after the three-month contract with Gus is completed. Walt did not tell Gus about his DEA agent brother-in-law, and consequently he seems to be a little unclear (and nervous) about where he stands with Gus. Walt drives out to Gus's chicken farm where Gus and Walt sit across the table from one another. Walt indicates he asked to see Gus in order to "clear the air." Walt tells Gus that he has figured out his game to set the American and Mexican government against the cartel and get the market all to himself. Walt says, "I know I owe you my life. And, more than that, I respect the strategy. In your position, I would have done the same." Gus nods slightly. Walt wants to know what happens when the three-month contract ends. Walt tells Gus he does this for security for his family. Gus offers him $15 million for a year of work, asking, "Would that be agreeable?" As Walt drives home, he begins pushing the gas pedal to the floor, going well over a hundred miles an hour. He then closes his eyes and lets the car drift into the next lane. A few terrifying seconds pass and a trucker leans on his horn, causing Walt to swerve and narrowly escape death. Breathing heavily, Walt carefully pulls back out on the road. Why did he do this? Does he feel a sense of empowerment from the adrenaline rush of facing Gus alone? Does he feel as though he met his goal? Why does he need $15 million when he estimated that $737,000 would be sufficient? Does this moment remind him that he has nothing to lose at this point?

THE END: DEATH WISH

I do not mean to ask more questions than I answer, but the *Breaking Bad* narrative is rich and open to interpretation. Ultimately, Walter White only clearly has a death wish at the end of the series, when he knows he is closer to death than ever before, and he decides he is going to stick it to Gretchen and Elliott one last time. At the end of the series (Episode 5.16, "Felina"), he is already dying from the cancer that is spreading and making him weaker with each passing day. He knows that saving Jesse's life is not enough to make up for the torture he put him through by turning him over to Todd's gang, so he seemingly offers his life up to Jesse as retribution, when Walt asks Jesse to kill him. However, Jesse turns him down, tells him he is not going to do anything he says ever again, and Walt is not allowed such an easy out. We realize in the final scene that Walt was already dead, having been shot by one of his own bullets. Maybe he asked Jesse to kill him because he wanted to go quicker, or maybe he wanted Jesse to have some sense of vengeance. We will never know. And this is why the question of whether Walt wants to die is central to so many conversations about Walt. His arrogance and hubris suggest he does not want to die, but perhaps he does in the end, on his own terms and after making sure his family is set financially. If his goal to live was about leaving a legacy, then he certainly succeeded and could finally die.

Part II

Breaking Bad and Culture

Jesse and Walt on a cook. *AMC/Photofest © AMC*

4

MORALITY, LEGALITY, AND EVERYTHING IN BETWEEN

And as one might expect, when someone embarks upon a whole new way of thinking, a whole new way of behaving, there are stutter steps and there are mistakes made. And a lot of those early episodes, in particular, involve Walt bringing his old world and the way he would make decisions and the way he would come to conclusions in a scientific fashion, you know, from his old life, bringing those ways of thinking in those ways of behaving into this new life. And, of course, that leads to moments of awkwardness and comedy.—Vince Gilligan[1]

Shows about a drug-distributing everyman are nothing new. It is not even the first show of the decade; think *Weeds*, with a premise similar enough to *Breaking Bad* that Vince Gilligan said had he known *Weeds* existed, he never would have pitched his show to the network.[2] In popular culture narratives, the turn to drug making and distribution is most frequently a means to an end: Walter White wants to make money. Whether his intentions are to use the money to take care of his family, or to leave a legacy to assuage his rampant underlying insecurities (or both—it's complicated), *Breaking Bad* offers an answer to the question of what people might do if they only had a short time left to live. Some might plan to spend that time eating cookie dough, alternating uncontrollable sobbing with binge-watching every remaining show on their "to watch" list; others, like Walt, have loftier goals.

One of the themes of the show is the balance between illegal and immoral behavior, and the underlying question of whether it is acceptable to break the law if it is for a good cause. During the final season, Scott Meslow of the *Atlantic* argued, "*Breaking Bad*, more than any other drama currently on television, is set in a moral universe."[3] Like any well-written work, the show constantly uses situations where the characters have to make choices, one typically more legal or more moral than the other. But *Breaking Bad* does not exist in a silo. American culture is built upon questions of legality versus morality. Is it okay to steal if you are starving? What if your child is starving? When does life begin? When can we take it away? Is killing someone who killed another person legal? Is it moral? These are questions of illegality versus immorality that come up in various political, social, and philosophical discussions, and *Breaking Bad* enters that conversation through the lens of drugs. Vince Gilligan says this is one of his favorite aspects of the show: "We try to come up with as many water cooler moments as we can per episode . . . moments in which people can honestly argue about [what a character does]. . . . I love fomenting arguments."[4] Many of those moments deal with the morality of decisions made by characters throughout the series.

Even within summaries of the show, the tension of illegality versus immorality is emphasized. Take, for example, the show synopsis on the back of the DVD collection of the series:

> Emmy winner Bryan Cranston portrays Walter White, a family man who turns to crime after a lung cancer diagnosis unravels his bland but simple life. Recruiting former student and small-time drug dealer Jesse Pinkman (Emmy winner Aaron Paul) to be his partner in crime, Walt rises to the top of the meth trade, leaving a trail of bodies in his wake. But he can't keep his dogged DEA agent brother-in-law Hank Schrader (Dean Norris) off his trail forever. Will Walt get away with it all, or die trying?[5]

Walt does not originally turn to crime simply to make money, but instead, very clearly, because of the prospect of dying. Walt's son has cerebral palsy, and his wife is expecting an unplanned, later-in-life baby; his family has some significant struggles ahead of them. However, Walt only decides to break the law after he finds out about his cancer diagnosis. Nothing can be more moral than a husband/father wanting to protect his family; especially, when he knows he will not be around much longer. And yet, his method for raising the money is illegal and requires him to flout the job of his hardworking brother-in-law. Additionally, Walt's involvement with Jesse, as well as the necessity to take days to cook the batches of drugs, also requires him to lie repeatedly, an immoral act. The deeper he goes into this new world, the more sinister acts he commits, and each event drives him further from moral intentions. Yet he constantly rationalizes his decisions by insisting that he is trying to provide for his family. In this way, the show teeters back and forth with ideas of illegality and immorality, resulting in some fascinating scenes and dialogue.

While the characters understand that certain actions are illegal, they frequently justify their behaviors in a way that values morality above legality. Walt never says that he thinks meth should be legal; in fact, he rarely seems to acknowledge or is confronted with the effects of his product on the people who use it. It is Jesse who gets deep and dirty in the back alleys, motel rooms, and junkie homes with the users of the product. Walt sees an opportunity to make money and provide for his family at the prospect of his demise, so the morality of that action outweighs the illegality of what he is doing to make the money. However, Walt had another option to take the money from his former partners Elliott and Gretchen Schwartz, who both offered a completely legal path to leave money for his family and have his cancer treatments paid for. Gretchen even insists, "That money belongs to you" (Episode 1.5, "Gray Matter"). Instead, Walt chooses to break bad, which ultimately allows the viewers to debate his motives. His ego, manifested as the desire for power and money, is worth more to him than the law, and eventually, we come to realize, worth more than anything or anyone in his life. *Breaking Bad* consistently plays with these boundaries between legality and morality in a way that asks viewers to think about larger cultural discussions within contemporary society, and question what boundaries might become blurred if they, too, had a death sentence.

The primary focus in this chapter is on decisions that force the characters to straddle the border between illegality and immorality. In the first and second seasons in particular, there are specific moments between characters that bring this tension to the forefront and establish it as a theme for the entire series.

DIALOGUING THE DEBATE

Breaking Bad could have been called *Gray Matter* because of the way the writers blur the lines between right and wrong; nothing is black and white. The plot is set up to inherently require the writers (and viewers) to explore this tension. For example, Hank versus Walt quite literally calls into question illegality versus immorality simply due to the conflict between Hank's job and Walt's new job. The series also pits characters against one another in a way that makes these conversations all the more interesting. There are moments within the dialogue where the characters each take a side and discuss what the viewers might be thinking or talking about as they watch the show.

"You Don't Want to Find Out"

One of these moments occurs between Walt and Skyler when they discuss Marie's shoplifting habit. In Episode 1.7 ("A No-Rough-Stuff-Type Deal"), Marie gives Skyler an expensive white gold and crystal tiara at the baby shower. Little does Skyler know that Marie stole the tiara and Skyler is almost arrested when she attempts to return the expensive and impractical gift. This quirk of the Marie character is interesting in itself (and one that is first revealed to the audience in Episode 1.3, ". . . And the Bag's in the River"), but the subplot also provides an opportunity to understand what is going on in Walt's head. In the episode, Walt comes home from allegedly attending a healing sweat lodge offering homeopathic treatment for his cancer (i.e., the place he lied about going so he could spend the weekend cooking meth with Jesse) and Skyler fills him in on her almost arrest. Walt is genuinely shocked that Marie stole the tiara, but he has been keeping a pretty big secret from Skyler as well, so he tries to justify Marie's/his behavior by telling Skyler, "People sometimes do things for their families." Skyler incredulously repeats what he has just said, and asks, "That justifies stealing?" Walt asks Skyler what she would do if she found out he was stealing: "Would you divorce me? Would you turn me in to the police?" Skyler, looking him dead in the eyes, says, "You don't want to find out," as she smiles and kisses him. Walt smiles and seems to retreat emotionally, looking away in contemplation. This is the first time we see Walt's choice to violate the law challenged by one of the people he thinks he is benefiting.

The implication in Skyler's words is that she would do much worse than divorce or turn him in; she does not pick one or the other of the choices he offers her. In fairness, Skyler is dealing with a much-changed Walt, who disappears for hours on end with no explanation. A Walt she believes has started buying and smoking pot on a regular basis and is keeping something from her, even if she does not know what it is. These suspicions have primed her to issue a warning to her recently reclusive husband. In the Season 2 finale, when she does get confirmation that he is lying to her and finds out about his sudden financial windfall, she leaves him and takes the kids with her, or at least attempts to. Thus, we do know eventually what her plan would be should she find out. However, in Season 1, as Walt asks his "hypothetical" questions to Skyler, this moment forces him to recognize that the justification he has given to rationalize the illegal acts he commits—it is for his family in the long run—is not necessarily as ironclad as he seems to think. The question is no longer simply, would you commit illegal acts to help your family? It becomes, is it moral to commit those illegal acts if your family does not want you to? Walt is going deeper down the rabbit hole; he has killed people, caused an explosion, and just spent a weekend making even more meth for the insane drug boss, Tuco, further entrenching himself in this new world of crime. And now, his wife has just confirmed that she does not want him to make illegal choices, no matter what.

This moment also asks the viewers to make a decision: Do you side with Walt or Skyler? Is it understandable to take illegal action to benefit those you care about, or not? Throughout the series, for reasons that will be detailed in a later chapter, Skyler White is not well liked by viewers. One reason is that she is one of the antagonists in this plot, obliviously thwarting Walt's goals at every turn. If she got her way, the show would be about the mundane life of a high school chemistry teacher. Walt is the star of the show, but, especially in these first few seasons, he is the protagonist and the one we root for, even if we see a glimpse of the spiral of doom that is in front of him. By Episode 1.7 ("A No-Rough-Stuff-Type Deal") in the first season, Walt has committed atrocities, and yet, the audience still roots for him. All of his horrific moments have been framed as protecting himself or others, particularly his family and Jesse.

Walt, Skyler, and Walt Jr. at the pants store. *AMC/Photofest © AMC*

Sometimes a Cigar Is Just a Cigar. . . .

Episode 1.7 especially sets up the viewer to sympathize with Walt. In the beginning of the episode, at the shower for a baby who he does not anticipate being alive to get to know, there is a moment when he talks to the camera that Walt Jr. and Marie are using to document the day. Walt tells the baby, "I think about you all the time," and the people at the shower react with a collective "aww," as do the viewers who are privy to more information about how much he wants to protect his family. His actions are for his family; they are for this little baby who may never know her father. Whether we would make the same choices he has, we are set up to understand the motivation to those actions, and the conflict that those choices cause. Skyler seems to adamantly place legality higher than morality within her value hierarchy, which causes her to unwittingly diminish Walt's sacrifices up to this point. It makes it hard to side with her, even if she is the far more rational character.

Earlier, in the same episode, Hank and Walt have a discussion about legality and illegality centered on the Cuban cigars Hank brings to the shower.

Walt: Now, I was under the impression—that these were illegal. Hmm?

Hank: [laughing] Yeah, well, sometimes forbidden fruit tastes the sweetest.

Walt: It's funny, isn't it? How we draw that line?

Hank: Yeah? What line is that?

Walt: What's legal—what's illegal. Cuban cigars, alcohol. [pointing to the whisky bottle] You know if we were drinking this in 1930, you'd be breaking the law. Another year, you'd be okay. Huh, who knows what will be legal next year.

Hank: You mean like pot?

Walt: Yeah. Like pot—or whatever.

Hank: Cocaine? Heroin?

Walt: I'm just saying it's arbitrary.

Similar to Skyler, in the first few seasons, if Walt is the protagonist, then Hank is an antagonist; Hank and Walt cannot both succeed in this story. However, the character of Hank is far better liked by viewers than is Skyler. There are many interpretations for this disparity from viewers, but I would argue one reason why Hank does not inspire the same level of vitriol as Skyler is because we have seen another side to Hank that tempers his hard-lined "bustin' the bad guys" persona. Hank is crass and loud; he has been rude and controlling with his subordinate, Gomez, and even made racist jokes about the people he is in charge of taking down; however, we have also seen that he loves his wife, he cares a lot about Walt Jr. and, in his own way, looks out for the relationship between Walt and his son. As viewers, we have also witnessed the consequences to some of Walt's actions so far, so we cannot entirely write off Hank's perspective that some drugs are illegal for a reason. Especially as this final episode of the season plays out, and we see Tuco beat the crap out of his lackey, No-Doze, with no provocation.

One of the points Walt makes in this exchange is that the boundary between legality and illegality is arbitrary, but Hank reminds us that Walt's viewpoint is a rationalization of the new world he is becoming a part of when he says to Walt, "You know you can visit lockup and hear a lot of guys talk like that." Walt talks like a criminal. There are very few other jobs that can understand the world of drugs like Hank's and therefore, his side of the debate offers a level of authority from his expertise as a DEA agent. Walt attempts to call out the capriciousness of the legal system, but Hank shoots down that idea by showing the hierarchy of drugs. Alcohol and cigars are much different beasts than cocaine, heroin, and especially meth. It is clever writing, because it forces the viewers to acknowledge the errors in Walt's thinking, or at least concede that he is rationalizing his own behavior, and that we might be complicit in this acceptance. Why are we rooting for him to succeed, when he is committing murder, furthering an addictive drug problem, and lying to his family?

Moments like this encourage viewers to think about whether Walt is somebody who we necessarily want to see succeed. Specifically about this episode, Vince Gilligan says, "[Walt] doesn't see how dangerous this is and by the end of this episode, I think he is starting to see just how deadly this situation can become . . . and, yet, now, it may be too late."[6] Later episodes showing a murkier side to drugs (Episode 2.6, "Peekaboo," is a particular tearjerker) much more blatantly reveal the problems with what Walt and Jesse are adding to the world with their purest of meth; however, only seven episodes in, with Walt written as the protagonist, this is where the writers encourage us to question Walt's logic and intentions, if we have not done so already.

The cigar discussion between Hank and Walt makes for interesting television because it can be analyzed in any number of ways. In addition to the blatant discussion about drugs and legality, there are some underlying implications about morality that can only surface in a conversation between these two men. Since the first episode, there has been a clear hierarchy of masculinity that has created a point of tension between Walt and Hank. At the surprise birthday party for Walt (Episode 1.1, "Pilot"), Hank is loud and boisterous, his ultramasculine behavior foiled with the much more submissive Walt. When Walt rides along with Hank on the drug bust, he is relegated to the backseat of the car, wearing a particularly bulky bulletproof vest, and Hank demeans him each time he asks a question that appears to have an obvious answer. In addition, Hank takes on a more fatherly role to scare Walt Jr. straight when Marie mistakenly assumes that is whom Skyler is talking about smoking pot. Although he does so at Marie's request, there is tension when it comes to Walt Jr. that bubbles up in later episodes. At the baby shower, Hank's initial reluctance to give Walt a cigar due to his lung cancer indicates a level of knowing better than Walt, but his acquiescence also suggests that he sees the other side. This episode lets us question whether Hank might understand why Walt made the choices he did to sell drugs, even if we know there is no way he could condone it. Two episodes previously (Episode 1.5, "Gray Matter"), during the intervention Skyler organizes for Walt, Hank says that he understands why Walt has refused to undergo treatment: "Maybe Walt wants to die like a man." And we find out later that he has made an allowance in his moral code for Marie's problem with stealing. This moment lets us question what he would do if he knew Walt was making meth, and more importantly, *why* he was doing it.

We know at the conclusion of the series that he does not make the same allowance for Walt's behavior. Obviously, Marie's kleptomania is a pathological issue, whereas Walt has committed a series of aggressive and terrifying criminal acts, many directly hurting Hank emotionally and physically, so he is less inclined to forgive. At this moment, though, the initial exchange about whether Walt should have a cigar lets us wonder if Hank might understand Walt's choices. If he forgives him this behavior due to having the disease, where does that forgiveness end? The potential for Hank to forgive Walt again casts Skyler as the unforgiving, cold-hearted shrew; even the abrasive legal hound dog Hank seems as though he could be more understanding of Walt's situation than his own wife. It turns out that is only in theory, but this episode raises the possibility early in the series. It is this complexity around morality, and the "arbitrary" boundaries, that make the discussions among the characters so enticing to watch and analyze.

MORAL RELATIVISM

To take a more philosophical tack in understanding the legal/moral balance, the series allows viewers to explore ideas of moral relativism through Walter White in particular. Condemned by conservative

American politicians and the religious Right as a leftist mind-set that ruins traditional values, moral relativism defined late twentieth-century American culture with a "live-and-let-live" sense of morality.[7] A philosophy of moral relativism is frequently attributed to situations where people take advantage of other people by justifying their actions. *Breaking Bad* aired in 2008, the same year as the housing market crash where millions of people were affected by the greed and rationalization of bad decisions made by Wall Street. The economic crisis that followed the bursting of the housing bubble caused a lot of discussions about legality and immorality, as the government bailed out lenders without forcing accountability. Additionally, the country was in the midst of a health care crisis, where people were going bankrupt to pay for limited health insurance coverage. The philosophy of moral relativism provides a framework to understand a narrative where a law-abiding citizen becomes a drug kingpin, and what kinds of bad decisions might have been rationalized along the way. More importantly, *Breaking Bad* explores how those decisions could possibly seem logical in the moment.

The conversation between Hank and Walt in Episode 1.7 about the arbitrary nature of legality contrasts Walt's moral relativist perspective with an absolutist perspective from Hank. Absolutists view decisions, actions, and behaviors as either right or wrong; the world is black and white with an ethical code basically built into this thinking. If killing someone is wrong, it is always wrong, no matter the circumstances. For Hank, specifically in this particular conversation with Walt, drugs that cause as much damage as meth need to be illegal no matter what. This mind-set from Hank makes sense when his job is to catch drug makers and dealers. He cannot afford to have anything other than an absolutist stance when it comes to the world of drugs if he wants to be good at his job, and he is very good at his job.

On the other side, moral relativism views actions and behaviors as more right or wrong, depending on the situation, person, or culture in which it exists. Writer Helen Rittelmeyer argues that the antihero is dead, and the rise of true villains tells us something about the decline of moral relativism.[8] Similarly, Jonathan Merritt, contributing writer for the *Atlantic*, points to popular culture as a gauge of the cultural mind-set regarding morality, arguing that society is moving away from moral relativism where "modern audiences do not wonder if Voldemort or the Joker is actually justified, right, or moral."[9] However, the popularity of shows like *Breaking Bad*, *Mad Men*, and *House of Cards* suggests that perhaps the line is not as clear as we like to believe. Walt is the epitome of moral relativism, because he is constructed as someone we root for even though he is deeply flawed, or perhaps because of his flaws. Moral relativism is a mind-set that Walt engages in the second he makes the decision to break bad as a means to provide for his family. And it is the framework he draws upon when he continues to cook meth instead of accepting the money from Elliott and Gretchen. Walt consistently makes decisions throughout the series from this viewpoint.

One of the first and most blatant examples of Walt's mind-set of moral relativism is when he decides whether to kill Krazy-8. In Episode 1.1 ("Pilot"), Walt and Jesse are both threatened with death by Krazy-8 and Emilio. Walt convinces them to keep him alive long enough to make another batch of meth. Under the guise of teaching them his method, he creates an explosion of phosphine gas to kill them both while he escapes. Krazy-8 miraculously survives and becomes a prisoner, locked in Jesse's basement. Walt and Jesse immediately determine that he needs to die, and they flip a coin to decide who will kill him. Walt loses the coin flip and must kill Krazy-8. Although he and Jesse agree that Krazy-8 needs to die, it takes Walt two episodes to complete the task.

In Episode 1.2 ("Cat's in the Bag . . ."), Walt tries to build up to killing Krazy-8. He smokes a joint and brings Krazy-8 food, water, toilet paper, and a bucket for a toilet. He clearly has not made up his mind about killing him if he brings supplies designed to keep him alive. Krazy-8 even recognizes the conflict in Walt telling him he could have just poisoned his food and killed him quickly if he really wanted to do it (Episode 1.3, ". . . And the Bag's in the River"). Walt already killed Emilio, and thought he had killed Krazy-8 as well, so it raises the question, why does he struggle to make this decision to kill him again? The answer to that question can be found in his science lesson. In the first part of Episode 1.2 ("Cat's in the Bag . . ."), Walt talks to his chemistry class about the concept of "chiral" elements, which in science refers to mirror images, "identical, and yet opposite." These can be physical traits, molecules, mathematical equations or models—anything that is a mirror image, but not identical. Walt gives the students the example of chemical compounds where one iteration can produce a drug that reduces morning sickness, like thalidomide, and the mirror image of the same isomer of the drug can produce one that causes "horrible birth defects"; one side good, one side bad. This discussion can be read as a foreshadowing of Walt's progression to Heisenberg, and even more broadly to the characterization of the antihero, but specifically in this episode, early in the series, chirality indicates the conflict within Walt about killing. He is a murderer and confronted with the need for another murder. Later, when Walt and Jesse realize Krazy-8 is still alive, Walter White is responsible for killing him because Jesse reminds him the "coin flip is sacred" (Episode 1.3, ". . . And the Bag's in the River"). Is this murder the one that makes Walter White bad? The conflict within Walt serves the purpose of walking us to the line with him. Even if we know he has to kill Krazy-8, we want it to be hard for him to accomplish.

The discussion of chirality also relates to ideas of moral relativism. A combination of elements in one compound can create something positive, but the same combination in a different compound can create something negative, thus making any discussion of good or bad relative to the situation in which the elements occur. In the previous episode, when he originally killed the "two" men, he had a gun on him and seemed to react in the moment to save his own life, and potentially Jesse's as well. This time, Krazy-8 is a captive, chained by a bike lock to the pole in the basement. Krazy-8 defied the odds by escaping death the first time, and now Walt has time to think about his decision, rather than react on instinct. Killing Krazy-8 now is cold-blooded murder. Does this kind of murder make him a bad person, whereas the previous murder and attempted murder was self-defense? Or has he already become the mirror image? In this case, he knows that if he does not kill Krazy-8, his family will surely die. It seems obvious that he has to kill Krazy-8, because if Krazy-8 wanted him dead before, attempted murder and locking him in the basement is not doing anything to soften his feelings toward Walter. However, the writers make the audience feel the weight of Walt's decision in the next episode, when we see how badly he does not want to do it.

In Episode 1.3, (". . . And the Bag's in the River"), Walt tries to gear himself up to kill Krazy-8. Walt makes a list of pros and cons. A pro/con list can only exist in a world of moral relativism. The idea that a decision is not easily determined as yes or no, and that there might be both benefits and drawbacks to an action, relies on the philosophy that the world is not black and white. On Walt's pros/cons list, the pros side of the list is longer, including one point that not killing Krazy-8 is the "moral thing to do." On the cons side of the list, the only item he has written down is that if Krazy-8 is allowed to live, he will kill Walt's family. Walt ultimately kills Krazy-8 because it is not about the number of items on either side, but the weight of those items; one con can outweigh seven pros.

The list reveals how Walt approaches morality, as a scientific process that can be boiled down to pros and cons. It also suggests that he does think about morality, just in relative terms. Although too early in the series to understand where Walt will go, the scientific approach is what allows Walt to justify and rationalize his actions in later episodes when he repeatedly insists that he did what he had to do. The focus on justifying his actions as only purposeful killing is most clear when he shoots Mike Ehrmantraut because he wants a list of names that Mike will not give up. Walt sounds genuinely apologetic as he tells a dying Mike, "I just realized that Lydia has the names and I can get them from her. I'm sorry, Mike. This whole thing could have been avoided" (Episode 5.7, "Say My Name"). Mike's death was not necessary, and Walt realizes it too late. Walt's supposed goal with all of his immoral decision making up to this point is to keep his family safe, and that pro always tops the list and helps him rationalize his immoral actions.

A second scene in Episode 1.3 (". . . And the Bag's in the River") that highlights why this show is so brilliant is Walt's discussion with Gretchen. It continues the scientific allegory with Walt detailing the elements that make up the human body. In a flashback, Walt calculates the levels of carbon, oxygen, iron, calcium, and so forth, and pronounces, "There has got to be more to a human being than that." Gretchen argues that the human body is not just made up of science; you have to account for the soul. A young Walter responds to Gretchen, "It is only chemistry here." But, to some degree, his hesitation in killing Krazy-8 is about the soul. If Walter White is chiral, then killing Krazy-8 may make him the bad combination of elements. Walt goes out of his way to find reasons not to kill Krazy-8, even allowing himself to be convinced that Krazy-8 will not retaliate if he just lets him go. Krazy-8 tells Walter that this line of work does not suit him and he should "get out before it's too late." In some sense, the audience has to acknowledge the truth of what Krazy-8 is saying: Walter White is not very good at being bad, initially. Scott Meslow reminds us that "*Breaking Bad* operates by the rules of science; every action causes an equal and opposite reaction."[10] As Walt makes decisions that sink him deeper into this new world, the reactions keep him from ever being able to climb back out. When he realizes Krazy-8 stole a shard of the broken plate, he understands that he has to kill him, yelling, "No, no, no!" We knew this was coming; the audience has seen Krazy-8 sizing up the situation. Like Walt, we want to believe that if he lets Krazy-8 free, Walt can walk away to go back to his old life. But he can't and he doesn't; he's gone too far to walk away now. He goes back down to the basement, pretends to unlock Krazy-8's chain, and strangles him to death yelling sorry throughout the gruesome ordeal. He cries while he commits the murder. This dichotomy between Walt's actions and emotions is important to note, because I would argue it is one way to explain how the writers get the audience to root for Walt early on in the series even though we see some incredibly ugly sides to him. In the beginning, he does not seem to want to hurt people, but when forced to, he does so reluctantly and emotionally. For the audience, this episode tells the viewers they are not always going to like what they see, and there are not going to be easy ways out for Walt.

NO HEROES, JUST HUMANS

Walt is not the only character to face difficult choices, rationalizing and justifying behaviors to get what he wants. The beauty of this show is that every single character is complex in some way, and the writers use both dialogue and visual elements to detail the complicated inner workings of some truly memorable characters. The scene between Hank and Marie in Episode 1.3 (". . . And the Bag's in the River") is an early example of the adeptness of the writers to jar viewers out of complacency. Marie is in a shoe store on her cell phone, when she tells Hank (what she thinks is true) about Walt Jr.'s use of marijuana. Hank is on the job, lining up criminals, screaming, "Sit your ass down! *Comprende?!*" He turns back to Marie on the phone and calmly says, "I'm back, babe. What's up?" He makes time for her, tries to make her happy by agreeing to talk to Walt Jr., and then smiles into the phone, asking, "Hey, where's my sugar?" Marie makes a kissing noise at the phone and they hang up. On Hank's side, there are men in hazmat suits cleaning out a meth lab with the perpetrator junkies lined up against the wall in handcuffs. He is loud and tough, ultramasculine, but that is juxtaposed with the love he shows toward his wife. This moment is oddly sweet. They seem to have a great rapport and balance.

And then, we are jarred out of the moment when we immediately find out that Marie steals. Does she do it because the store clerk was rude, and Marie is punishing her like a customer-service-rating vigilante? Are Hank and Marie having financial problems? Or is this a compulsion? We thought we knew what to expect from Marie, but she steals the shoes just moments after decrying drug use; we do not know Marie. It is a very smart moment, because it peels back layer upon layer, revealing the tensions lying just beneath the surface of all the characters, not just Walt.

Some of the more interesting tensions happen within a single character. For example, we see Hank seemingly strike his own balance between moral rules and the law when he deals with Marie's shoplifting habit. In Episode 2.1 ("Seven Thirty-Seven"), Skyler reveals to Hank that she almost got arrested returning the tiara that Marie stole:

Hank: Yeah, if I thought you were going to return it, I would have . . . never . . . you know.

Skyler: You knew about this.

Hank: We—we are working on it. She's got this therapist, Dave, and I mean, Dave is really good—

Skyler: —Dave is, yes—

Hank: —but it's an ongoing process, Sky. And, we've got to be understanding, you know and we've got to, you know, we've got to support the shit out of her.

He is a law enforcement officer. No, Marie is not making and selling drugs, but she is violating the law and he knows about it. He has decided to work on it with her, get her help, and "support the shit out of her." Interestingly, this is exactly what Walt is talking about with Skyler in Episode 1.7 ("A No-Rough-Stuff-Type Deal"), when he asks what she would do if he were the one stealing. He is asking if Skyler will stick by him. He wants to know if she loves him enough to forgive him for doing something illegal if he had a moral purpose behind it, like helping his family. She is not ready to do this in the first few seasons, but Hank is doing this for Marie, and he has even more of a stake in recognizing and not reporting illegal activity than does Skyler.

These complicated details are what make the show so good, and are really the crux of tension throughout the series. It creates foils between characters, but more importantly, explores why good people might do bad things. While individual episodes illuminate the thought process of the tension, the series as a whole seems to explore moral relativism as people adapt to ideas, feel their options limited, or assess the situation. Even Skyler changes and adapts, ultimately making a series of immoral and illegal choices herself.

The use of scientific discussions contrasted with the idea of a soul is a persistent theme: proof and theory versus faith and morality. Humans can be broken down to just the chemical elements, but that list leaves out a great deal of information. Gilligan and the other writers of the show have found a way to combine the principles of science and morality to explore the inner workings of human beings. This exploration helps us understand not just Walt, but every character in the series.

5

JUST SAY NO?

Drug Use and Abuse in *Breaking Bad*

The idea of keeping illegal drugs out of the hands of little kids is a sound [one]. But I don't pretend to have any answers about how things could suddenly, instantly, magically be better overnight.—Vince Gilligan[1]

To live outside the law, you must be honest. That dictum has become the only erudite way to think about fictional drug dealers. As straight-up TV villains, their time has passed. Now they're just complicated versions of hard-working entrepreneurs.—Chuck Klosterman[2]

Breaking Bad aired at a time when marijuana was still illegal in all states, and debates raged about the success or failure of the "war on drugs." The exploration of drugs, drug making, and the reasons people might turn to the use and distribution of drugs is highly relevant in contemporary culture. In the cultural landscape, ideas about drug use and distribution are deeply personal and intimately intertwined with politics, religion, and life experiences. Writer Chuck Klosterman argues that the increased prevalence within fictional narratives of the main protagonist as a drug maker or dealer is a result of viewers who were "born in the 1970s [trying] to reconcile the dissonance between what they were told in the 1980s and what they actively experienced in the 1990s."[3] Walter White and the depiction of meth in *Breaking Bad* join a culture that already accepts characters who reside firmly in a world of drugs.

Much has been written in the popular press about the depiction of drug use in *Breaking Bad*, with the *New Yorker* writer Patrick Radden Keefe calling it "uncannily accurate" when it comes to the use and production of methamphetamine.[4] Gilligan and crew utilized the expertise of DEA agents and scientists to provide realistic settings and story details. Unlike *Weeds*, which deals with marijuana, a drug that has now been legalized in some states, *Breaking Bad* is about selling meth, a drug that the Office of National Drug Control Policy warns "can cause addiction, anxiety, insomnia, mood disturbances, and violent behavior. Additionally, psychotic symptoms such as paranoia, hallucinations, and delusions can occur."[5] The report continues to emphasize, "The psychotic symptoms can last for months or years after methamphetamine use has ceased." Meth is not about helping people mellow out, deal with anxiety, or combat the side effects of chemotherapy drugs. It is a hard-core drug, and one that is a widespread problem in America.

At the start of *Breaking Bad*, the prevalence of meth labs was steadily increasing in the United States. Acknowledging the real-life inspiration, Vince Gilligan states that a news article pointed out to him by series writer Tom Schnauz inspired the story. It was "about a meth lab some-

Jesse lights a joint at Saul's office. *AMC/Photofest © AMC*

where that was getting a bunch of neighborhood kids sick."[6] The lab was set up in an RV, and Gilligan and Schnauz joked about that being their next move if they did not get writing jobs soon. The idea of resorting to an RV meth lab began Gilligan's wheels spinning. The use of meth was an important decision for the purposes of plotting in the series, but it also reflects the culture that already exists prior to and outside of the fictional world.

Throughout this book, I take the perspective that television reveals something about the culture we live in, and acts as both a mirror and a creator of reality. In this chapter, I explore an overarching question about the series: Is *Breaking Bad* antidrugs? I begin by demonstrating how the series uses the representation of drugs to delve into broader discussions about class and economic opportunity, or lack thereof. The interconnection between the world of drugs and socioeconomic status is an underlying theme throughout the series. Additionally, the dialogue within the narrative acknowledges the complexity of America's drug problem, an issue, which Vince Gilligan says, "I don't pretend to have any answers about how things could suddenly, instantly, magically be better overnight."[7] I detail the conversations between characters that seem to present various sides in a debate about drugs. I then describe how *Breaking Bad* depicts the use of drugs, the degree of "junkie" on the show, and how it frequently highlights the terrible effects of drugs on family relationships. I conclude by suggesting the series cues viewers to question traditional ideas about the drug problem in America.

CHAMPAGNE TASTE ON A BEER BUDGET

At its heart, *Breaking Bad* is a story about a pauper aspiring to become a king. The Whites live in a simple home. The three-bedroom, one-bathroom house has become worn and dated in the almost sixteen years since they purchased it, with a leaking, rusty water heater and faded wallpaper. In Episode 3.13 ("Full Measure"), we get the benefit of seeing it brand new via a flashback to a pregnant Skyler (this time with Walt Jr.) as she shows Walt around the home she wants to purchase. Walt tries to convince Skyler to stretch the price range and get a bigger house. He wants more than they can currently afford, asking Skyler, "Why be cautious? We have nowhere to go but up." At this point in the series, the viewers are privy to almost three full seasons of Walt being wrong about this projection for his future wealth. The story itself, of a lower-middle-class man refusing to be kept down by a system that keeps him in his place, taps into ideas of economic determinism. Walt chooses to transcend the social class in which he resides: a socioeconomic system that requires people to rise up within certain (legal) boundaries. With the timing of the 2008 recession, the audience ate up this story. Even though Walt had the opportunity to legitimately earn money with Elliott and Gretchen, via the tidbits of information Walt doles out, we are led to believe they did something to screw him over so we do not blame him for wanting to provide for his family without their help, even if he must do so illegally.

Walt's decisions are based on money and ego, but the insecurities behind those goals existed for Walt prior to his cancer diagnosis. In an AMC Q&A, Jessica Hecht reveals the backstory to Walt and Gretchen's romantic relationship prior to Walt selling his shares in Gray Matter.[8] In a nutshell, Walt met Gretchen's family and their wealth intimidated him so he ran for the hills. We get a tiny hint about this revealing backstory in Episode 2.6 ("Peekaboo") when Gretchen is torn about how to handle the fact that Walt lied to his family by telling them Elliott and she were paying for his treatment. Walt meets Gretchen at a restaurant to discuss the issue and immediately bristles at what he perceives as her condescension. He angrily informs her, "I don't owe you an explanation. I owe you an apology." Bryan Cranston comments about his thought process during this scene: "Gretchen was kind of placating, and maybe he took it as condescension, 'Oh, we're happy to come to your rescue.' And he doesn't want her to be smug with him."[9] Walt's anger ramps up in the scene as he belittles Gretchen for "build[ing] your little empire on my work." He continues, calling Gretchen a "rich girl, just adding to your millions." Finding out later in the series that Walt was not cut out by Elliott and Gretchen, but instead willingly sold his shares in the company, puts this scene into perspective (Episode 5.6, "Buyout"). He made a mistake, based on feelings of inadequacy about his social status, and he blames Elliott and Gretchen for having the wealthy life that he always dreamed of.

Material possessions become an important theme within the series. In Episode 1.4 ("Cancer Man"), Walt blows up Ken's red sports car. Walt is cast as the underdog in the showdown with Ken (a tension that Ken is not even aware of). Walt is the lower-middle-class schlub who cannot afford his cancer treatments, and Ken is bragging about his $40,000-plus bonus. As an obnoxious member of the upper-class earning bracket, Ken has to suffer, so Walt hits him where it hurts most: his shiny status symbol. It is particularly telling that when Walt becomes the new drug kingpin after Gus's death, his first major purchase is a brand-new Chrysler 300, plus a Dodge Challenger for Walt Jr. (Episode 5.4, "Fifty-One"). He leases both to keep in line with the Whites' cover story, but the car signifies success for Walt, and a way to show the world he has money.

In Episode 1.5 ("Gray Matter"), Jesse tries to get a sales job with a legitimate company and the owner informs him that his high school degree qualifies him to spin the sign in front of the building. It is assumed that Jesse starts his drug habit in high school, and we know that he was not a strong student, getting an F in Walt's class. He did not go to college, and this scene emphasizes that it is hard to find good jobs without a college degree. This leads to a life of crime. Jesse can make more money selling drugs than he can living a lawful life. In Episode 2.5 ("Breakage"), Jesse shows his friends/drug distributors around his new apartment, describing where the flat-screen TV will go and how he plans to fill the space. Later, in Season 3 (Episode 3.5, "Más"), Skyler starts to reconsider her stance against Walt's drug money when she realizes how much she appreciates the finer touches of Ted's fancy home, including the heated tile in the bathroom.

Popular culture draws on ideas about wealth and status from the time in which it exists. Fictional narratives from the 1980s about wealth and greed fit along the lines of *Wall Street*'s Gordon Gekko, whose material possessions were admired by the impressionable Bud Fox. The message of *Wall Street* is that although Gekko gets caught, he will simply bide his time and come out a winner, whereas Fox will never work in finance again. Over time, the message shifted to an idea that those who worked hard enough could achieve financial success. After the recession of 2008, in *Breaking Bad* we see wealth accumulated by people on all levels of the economic spectrum from Elliott and Gretchen to Ted Beneke, to Jesse Pinkman and Walter White. Outside the series, the health care system, the legal system, and the economic system of America failed people in the middle class and below. The ability for those within the lower-middle class to pull themselves up by their bootstraps was laughable in the face of government systems that kept them in perpetual debt. Drugs exist within a cycle. The more drug problems in a neighborhood, the lower the educational achievements for members of that community. The lower the educational background, the lower the economic status, and the more likely there will be a drug problem. *Breaking Bad* does not hit us over the head with this rhetoric, instead developing a compelling narrative based on social facts and character motivation. The series allows viewers to reflect on the interconnected system of drugs and money, and over-whelmingly accept a main character who cooks meth in an attempt to get a bigger slice of the financial pie.

DIALOGUE ABOUT DRUGS

Commenting on why he chose meth as the drug of choice in the series, Vince Gilligan notes that "meth makes perfect sense, story-wise, for *Breaking Bad.* Unlike marijuana or cocaine, it's a completely synthesized drug that needs a chemist and . . . I liked the idea of Walt being good at chemistry and having a unique set of skills that would allow him to cook the best meth available." He continues, "And it's also just a nasty, terrible drug that destroys people and whole communities."[10] While Gilligan's comment certainly indicates that he considers drugs destructive, *Breaking Bad* avoids a strict antidrug stance. Instead, Gilligan and his fellow writers use the characters in the show to acknowledge the layers of dialogue that exist about drugs in our culture.

The dialogue between characters sometimes functions to highlight contradictions within the mind-set of those involved in the drug world. For example, twice in the series, Jesse judges mothers who use drugs. The first instance of this is in Episode 2.6 ("Peekaboo"), when Jesse tells Spooge's Woman (yes, that is how actress Dale Dickey is credited) she needs to take care of her son. The little boy is filthy, hungry, and lonely, and Jesse tells her she needs to be a better mother. Spooge's Woman agrees, if she can "just have a little taste" of meth. Eventually, Jesse is so preoccupied with the little boy that Spooge's Woman knocks him over the head, saying, "Call me a bad mother, I'll show you a bad mother, bitch." As audience members, we cannot ignore that the house is disgusting and the little boy is clearly suffering from neglect. Spooge's Woman is a terrible mother. However, Jesse contributes to this little kid's sad world when he puts meth in the hands of the boy's parents, and he never acknowledges this culpability. Jesse does this again in a conversation with Andrea in Episode 3.11 ("Abiquiu"). After Jesse and Andrea have sex, she asks about the "blue stuff" he had been going on about at the twelve-step meeting. Jesse tells her to think about Brock and asks, "What kind of mom gets wasted with a little kid to take care of?" The hypocrisy of Jesse the junkie acting as if having children should magically cure addiction and the underlying problems that lead to drug dependency illustrates how addicts always thinks their habit is not as bad as other users'. It also reveals how out of touch Jesse is with the consequences of his own actions when he met Andrea at the meeting as a way to sell drugs to people trying to get help.

Culpability is an underlying theme in the series. In the last chapter, I detailed the conversation between Hank and Walt at the baby shower (Episode 1.7, "A No-Rough-Stuff-Type Deal"). After listening to Walt expound his views on the "arbitrary" decisions about what drugs are legal and what are not, Hank explains, "Sometimes there is stuff that is legal that shouldn't be. I mean friggin' meth used to be legal. Used to sell it over every counter in every pharmacy in America. Thank God they came to their senses on that one, huh?" Walt can rationalize every murder he commits, but Hank reminds him that there is a difference between meth and alcohol. There is a difference between meth and marijuana, in the production of it, the addictiveness, and the side effects.

Regardless of the danger, some members of society believe that adults can make their own decisions, and the government does not have a right to violate personal freedom of choice. Gilligan utilizes the character of Gale Boetticher (David Costabile) to voice this opinion. Walt asks Gale why he got into this business, and Gale responds, "There is crime and then there is crime. I'm definitely a libertarian. Consenting adults want what they want and if I'm not supplying it, they will get it somewhere else. At least with me, they're getting exactly what they pay for" (Episode 3.6, "Sunset"). It was a clever choice to have this conversation occur between Walt and Gale. Walt is impressed by Gale's ingenuity, appreciating the invention of a coffee machine that produces the best cup of coffee. Gale understands chemistry and asks intelligent questions without any prodding from Walt. He is an intellectual, quoting poetry and discussing philosophy in a way that challenges Walt intellectually. Gale is everything Jesse is not, including enamored with Walt's genius. Gale's ideology provides another way for Walt to rationalize his culpability in providing a product that produces heinous results. Outside of the fictional world, Gale's comment articulates one philosophy within a contentious debate about freedom and choice, when it comes to drugs and other liberties.

The writers of *Breaking Bad* are particularly adept at staying true to the characters' motivations and tendencies throughout the series. In a narrative about a good man going bad, it makes sense to have dialogue quietly debating the main character's contribution to a terrible drug problem in the United States. This is especially important when the protagonist is the Great Justifier Walter White, with many fans remaining on his side until the bitter end.

DEPICTION OF DRUG USE AND ABUSE

Drug narratives have veered away from the Afterschool Special message of "Just say no" that was the mantra of all little kids' 1980s elementary upbringing, and the fodder for eye rolling from teenagers for decades. The idea that a drug dealer was lurking around every corner, just waiting for an innocent kid to be alone, or that a friend might take something and try to fly out her bedroom window (and, assuming I was sleeping over, I might have to talk her off the ledge), produced an unhealthy level of anxiety surrounding drugs. As preteens, we laughed at Jessie Spano's breakdown from caffeine pills (so did Screech if you can believe Dustin Diamond's recounting of the scene in Lifetime's *The Unauthorized Saved by the Bell Story*); however, we also had contingency plans should anybody offer us a joint at a party. Or, the D.A.R.E. bear told us it might be called a "roach"? Looking back as an adult, I realize the manipulation of those fears, when nobody offered me anything stronger than a cigarette until I was in graduate school. Chuck Klosterman argues, "An entire generation had been programmed to fear the very same drugs they came to recognize as mostly innocuous."[11] The hit-you-over-the-head cautionary tale and redemption story were the premier narratives when it came to drug abuse, until the mid-1990s when the hit film *Trainspotting* came to the United States. Not a celebratory tale of drugs by any means, as the scene with the baby is still hard to think about decades later, *Trainspotting* offered a more realistic look at addiction to a hard-core drug like heroin and entered at a time when the conversation about drugs was changing.

Breaking Bad similarly accomplishes a realistic depiction of the drug world, while still emphasizing that methamphetamine is not a drug to experiment with. The portrayal of drug abuse in *Breaking Bad* revolves primarily around Jesse's story, as he is the druggie who comes from this world. It appears that part of drug dealing is drug using, when Tuco insists Jesse take a hit of the meth, and then takes one himself (Episode 1.6, "Crazy Handful of Nothin'"). The scene is reminiscent of the 1991 film *Rush*, except Jesse is more willing than Jennifer Jason Leigh's character, Cates. Jesse is referred to as a "junkie" throughout the narrative, frequently by Walt, but also by Gustavo Fring and Hank. Jesse's relationship with drugs follows a realistic telling, as he is off and on the wagon repeatedly throughout the two years the story unfolds. *Breaking Bad*'s convincing depiction of drugs does not valorize the users, even as it accurately (if you believe the *New Yorker*) depicts the drug world. When asked about whether creative work can be blamed for inspiring real-life events, Gilligan comments, "It's up to the writer to know the difference between a dark story that is basically instructive and a cautionary tale."[12] In Gilligan's series, the depiction of the highs and lows of drug use, as well as how drug abuse strains family relationships, is front and center, causing the narrative to function as both a mirror and creator of reality.

The Highs and the Lows

Klosterman argues that drug narratives from the nineties stoked the flames for understanding why audiences are eager to cheer on a drug dealer main character in contemporary television.[13] He notes, "It was still wrong to lionize drug use, but it was no longer necessary to demonize 'drug culture.' You could actually *like* drug culture, and you could like the people who lived inside it."[14] This is a particularly interesting comment considered in context of the grotesque physical portrayal of many of the junkies in *Breaking Bad*. Wendy the hooker (Julia Minesci) is gaunt with straw-like bleach-blonde hair, and she is the first physically altered junkie we meet. She subsists on food out of vending machines and root beer, focusing her hard-earned john money on buying drugs instead. In Episode 1.3 (". . . And the Bag's in the River"), Hank has Wendy show Walt Jr. her teeth in an effort to scare him straight, when he thinks Jr. is smoking pot. A much more disturbing image of junkies comes as a duo with Spooge (David Ury) and his Woman. These two are the ones who rob Skinny Pete at knifepoint and steal his cash (Episode 2.5, "Breakage"). Spooge's Woman's cackle is terrifying, and they are both jumpy from needing a fix. They are covered in sores on their scrawny arms; their faces are loaded with boils. David Ury comments, "I remember the first day in 'Breakage' we were in downtown Albuquerque and I came out of the make-up trailer and was walking across the parking lot and the set security guard said, 'Sir, you cannot be in here.' That's when I knew the make-up folks had done their job."[15] The realistic portrayal of many of the junkies throughout five seasons of *Breaking Bad* presents images that could easily keep viewers from ever wanting to try methamphetamine.

Jesse is also supposed to be a junkie, but in the show, he is a good-looking guy (no matter how many saggy jeans or Xzavier sparkle shirts they put him in). He does not have the scabs and bruises of the other junkies on *Breaking Bad*, and he does not look as bedraggled as Skinny Pete or Badger, who are the next-best-looking junkies in the series. Vince Gilligan notes the lack of realism with Jesse's appearance as one of his only regrets about the show: "I wish Jesse's teeth had been a little more realistic, a little more messed up. Aaron Paul has perfect teeth, and Jesse Pinkman, on the other hand smoked a lot of meth, and that smoke eats the enamel right off of teeth."[16] There has to be some creative license because, frankly, watching somebody like Spooge help Walt cook meth is not something audiences would enjoy. Part of the appeal of Jesse is that he has so much going for him, if he would just stop getting in his own way, and some of that potential resides in the fact that he is handsome.

In addition to the cautionary visual images, Jesse has a well-established habit of using drugs to deal with emotional turmoil, which never ends well for him. In the premiere episode of the series (Episode 1.1, "Pilot"), the first thing Jesse wants to do after seeing the results of Walt's cook is to try the "glass-grade" meth. Walt tells him, "No. You only sell it, you don't use it." Walt is talking to a drug addict in this moment, and he recognizes early on how important it is to set rules against using the inventory for personal habits. In the next episode (1.2, "Cat's in the Bag . . ."), Jesse sneaks to the bathroom to grab a hit of meth after cleaning up Emilio off the floor (and ceiling). Walt catches him and they physically fight over the drugs. Later, Jesse turns to both pot and crystal to deal with his guilt when Combo dies (Episode 2.11, "Mandala"). He tells Jane, "One of my guys got murdered and it's my fault because I put him on the corner." He tells her to leave because she is eighteen months sober, but she stays and falls off the wagon when she joins him.

Jane's drug of choice is heroin, and she functions as a gateway to the drug for Jesse when, in Episode 2.11 ("Mandala"), she describes the feeling as "ecstasy." Jane shows him how to use it, and we see Jesse floating above the room as he succumbs to the euphoric feelings of the drug. Unfortunately, it is during Jesse's heroin blackout when Walt needs his partner the most, a situation that calls into sharp detail what Gus told Walt: "You can never trust a drug addict." In Episode 2.12 ("Phoenix"), Jane coaches Jesse to prepare the heroin himself, teaching him with comments like "Not too much . . . now the cotton." She tells him to put the needle "flat against your skin so it doesn't wiggle around too much." The scene indicates how realistic it is for somebody like Jane, eighteen months sober with a father who actively helps her with her recovery, to get back into drugs.

It's a Family Matter

One of the saddest conversations about addiction occurs when Jane's father, Donald Margolis (John de Lancie), finds out she is using again (Episode 2.12, "Phoenix"). Jane misses the support group meeting and her dad, suspecting something is wrong, waits outside and watches her leave Jesse's house. He barges into the home and back to the bedroom, where he sees the drug paraphernalia on the bedside table. Infuriated, Donald throws Jesse around, yelling at Jane, "You are going back to rehab today—now!" A desperate Jane tells her father, "Look, as it so happens, we were just talking about that now." Her dad responds in a mocking tone, "Yeah?" He has heard this before. Jane tells her father, "I backslid, okay? What, you think I'm proud of this? I didn't do it on purpose." Her dad says that perhaps the only way to help her is to turn her in, as he calls the police. Donald says, "I've tried ten years of love and understanding. Maybe what it takes is you drying out in a cell." Jane calls him "Daddy" and agrees to go to rehab "first thing tomorrow." Her dad refuses and insists, "Today." A tearful Jane then works in some subtle manipulation, saying, "Last time I went to rehab all my houseplants died, because you didn't water them. Dad, please?" He finally acquiesces and says he will pick her up tomorrow.

Jane's father never sees her alive again. Jane immediately convinces Jesse to let her blackmail Walt for the money. Prior to using again, Jane appeared to be a voice of reason for Jesse, somebody who had gotten her act together and was on a better path. She had the recovery story the audience wanted to see for Jesse. As soon as she starts using again, she becomes manipulative and controlling, lying to her father and scheming for Jesse's money. Jane's story illustrates the incredible power of drug addiction, when, after eighteen months of sobriety, she "backslides." It also highlights the push against the family members who fight to get the addict clean. Jane lies to her dad repeatedly when she starts using again and becomes defensive. She is at the same time devastated to disappoint him, but furious that he is disappointed with her. Her plan is to get Jesse's money and go to rehab on her own terms, "not because anybody is telling us to."

The dialogue between Jane and Jesse once they get the money from Walt is tragic, and for anybody who has an addict in his or her life, a realistic portrayal of how the mouth says one thing, but the urges say another. Jane insists, "First, we've got to get clean. . . . We do this for us, right?" Jesse agrees, and Jane continues, indicating the money, "All this here, we are not going to just shoot this up our arms, Jesse. We're not." She is convincing, and voices what they both know they need to do logically: get help. Jesse nods, "No, no, no, no—we're better than that." Jane confirms, "We're way better than that. All this here—I say we flush what we've got left and we start tonight." The two then stare at the heroin. Jesse, quietly: "Yeah, we can do that. Definitely." They cannot do it, and they do not do it; and, of course, that is the end of Jane.

In addition to seeing a glimpse of an addict's thought process, where they think they can quit anytime, the same episode reveals the surrounding family's frustrations in dealing with addiction from the sidelines. Walt was not trying to swindle Jesse out of his share of the money. He was angry with him for causing him to miss the birth of his daughter, Holly, but he also recognized Jesse's drug problem was even worse than when they started together, when it kept him from being a viable partner. Jesse comes to Walt's classroom when he realizes that the drugs were not stolen, but instead sold by Walt to Gus. Jesse wants his money, insisting he is clean and he "didn't even like" heroin. Walt tells him, "If I gave you that money, you would be dead inside of a week." Walt insists Jesse pee in a cup, throwing him a beaker: "If you are clean, I will give you every last dime." Walt angrily calls him a "junkie" and then calls Jane his "junkie girlfriend." Jesse whips the beaker at Walt's head, where it shatters loudly on the wall behind him. Walt is shocked, staring at Jesse who rarely retaliates physically. It sets Walt up to later believe Jane is serious when she says she will turn him in, because in that moment, Walt knows how much Jesse loves Jane.

The scene with Jane's dad in the bar articulates what it means to have a child who struggles with addiction. We see brief examples of this in Jesse's relationship to his parents earlier in the series, where they resort to the tough love approach. Addiction specialists note that this approach rarely works: "We have this idea that if we are just cruel enough and mean enough and tough enough to people with addiction, that they will suddenly wake up and stop, and that is not the case."[17] Offering parenting advice, Jane's dad counsels Walt to "just love them. They are who they are." Walt tells Donald a story about his "nephew," referring to Jesse. This is the first time in the series that Walt has acknowledged, even couched as a lie, how much he cares about Jesse and considers him family. Later, in the series, we get similar glimpses. For example, in Episode 4.10 ("Salud"), a drunk and drugged-up Walt cries to Walt Jr. about sending Jesse to his death. As he is falling asleep, he asks Walt Jr. how his birthday was, and then accidentally refers to his son as "Jesse." Again, right after sharing a touching moment with Walt Jr. in Episode 5.12 ("Rabid Dog"), he calls Jesse to convince him to contact him because he wants to explain himself. Hank tells Jesse that message indicates Walt cares about him, saying, "Look at how far he will go to try to convince you he's not such a bad guy." Jesse responds that yeah, Walt loves him when he is "not ripping me off, or calling me an idiot, or poisoning people that I know . . . Mr. White's gay for me." However, he does not realize that Walt is terrible to all his family members, always trying to "help" them but ultimately putting them in grave danger. He seems to consider Jesse a son, so when Donald Margolis tells Walt that he "can't give up on them. Never. What else is there?" and Walt goes back to Jesse's house, he genuinely intends to not give up on Jesse. Unfortunately, he kills Jane instead, hurting Jesse tremendously. This is perhaps the biggest lesson about the addiction narrative in *Breaking Bad* and the broader discourse about drugs: it cannot be controlled and eventually you have to let people make their own choices.

AMERICA'S DRUG PROBLEM

What does it say that the scariest characters in the series are not the drug users? Walt smoked pot once in the Episode 1.2 ("Cat's in the Bag . . ."), as he tries to gear up to kill Krazy-8. We never see Gus use drugs, and his disdain for "junkies" suggests he sees it as a character flaw at best. Todd Alquist and the neo-Nazi group are never shown smoking anything harder than cigarettes. *Breaking Bad* accurately portrays the inability for drug addicts to maintain functional financially productive lives at the top of the social stratum. At the same time, it acknowledges how the system seems to be stacked against those on the lower end of the spectrum, sometimes leaving otherwise law-abiding citizens with no other choice but to break bad.

The realism of the drug business is purposeful, with Gilligan utilizing DEA and scientific consultants to get the details right. The first few seasons depict the major drug front-runners in America as the Mexican drug cartel. In *Breaking Bad*, the American operations are small-time cook sites primarily run by junkies. Emilio and Jesse are making small batches at a time (Episode 1.1, "Pilot"). Walt warns off the men in the parking lot in Episode 2.10 ("Over"), but they are not capable of making mass quantities. Even Jesse and Walt are limited by access to methylamine and the size of a lab that can fit into an RV. And then Gus comes along—he has cartel connections, but his megalab operation is run in the United States. Critic Patrick Radden Keefe argues that this is an inaccurate reflection of drug labs, because the United States currently regulates the chemicals necessary to make meth, making it "much easier to shift production to Mexico or Guatemala, as the major drug cartels have done, where mega-labs (that dwarf Walter's) churn out meth for export to the U.S. Meth is still cooked in this country, but generally in smaller 'shake and bake' batches."[18] The writers' choice to bring the megalabs home to America (first with Gus's laundry lab, and then with the neo-Nazis' lab) was most likely a decision to keep the environments interesting; however, it also challenges our ideas about assuming megalabs do not or could not exist in the United States.

The enslavement of Jesse by Todd at the end of Season 5 is also an interesting twist in the narrative. Being kidnapped to Mexico and forced to cook at a lab is a fear referenced multiple times in the series. The threat is first referenced in Episode 2.2 ("Grilled") when Tuco kidnaps Walt and

Jesse, and he says he plans to take Heisenberg to cook for the Mexican cartel. It becomes a threat once again when Gus flies Jesse down to Mexico with him to cook Walt's recipe (Episode 4.10, "Salud"). Up until Season 5, within the drug world on *Breaking Bad*, the cartel is depicted as the group the cooks want to avoid being enslaved by. When the show makes Jesse a slave in his own backyard, it brings the threat closer to home. It is easy to imagine the drug problem as originating from far away; it is foreign and untouchable to the average American viewer. But when the writers of *Breaking Bad* make Jesse a slave in Albuquerque, they reinforce the idea that drugs are not primarily a foreign problem.

As a fan of Jesse, I hope that his ordeal with the neo-Nazis was punishment enough, and he can just enjoy freedom after living like a caged animal for months. As Walt contends in Episode 5.11 ("Confessions"), Jesse has "a whole lifetime ahead of [him] with a chance to hit the reset button." Although both Vince Gilligan and Aaron Paul say they hope Jesse finds his happy ending in Alaska, realistically in a drug addiction narrative like this, we know one option for Jesse is that he will turn to drugs to deal with the demons of his enslavement.

The series mirrors reality by providing (mostly) realistic details about the effects of drug use and abuse, but also creates a reality when the dialogue encourages people to discuss or at least consider the debate about drugs, choice, and family dynamics. The depiction of drugs as a complex and deeply rooted system is not about a popular television show using its platform to address big issues, but instead a creative series acknowledging the world in which it exists. In keeping with the goal to represent the gray shades within cultural conversations, the series as a whole presents us with a collage, rather than a snapshot. *Breaking Bad* is not an antidrug story, but it certainly is not a pro-drug narrative. Instead, it offers a cautionary tale based in reality, offering the viewers the ability to come to their own conclusions.

6

MARKETING *BREAKING BAD*

A Sign of the Times

I am grateful as hell for binge-watching. . . . I don't think you'd be sitting here interviewing me if it weren't for Netflix. In its third season, Breaking Bad *got this amazing nitrous-oxide boost of energy and general public awareness because of Netflix.*—Vince Gilligan[1]

Many individual episodes, and sometimes a half-season or season-long arc, are indeed puzzles that we as viewers race with Walter to solve. But because of crucial choices not only in what Walter does, but more importantly in how he sees himself and those around him, the interstices between arcs and seasons marinate the show and its viewers in a character stew.—Donna Bowman[2]

When the first season of *Breaking Bad* aired in January 2008, the reviews were mixed and the viewers were sparse. *New York Times* writer Alessandra Stanley compared the show to AMC's *Mad Men* and, while admitting Cranston's acting was strong, argued it "lacks [*Mad Men*'s] originality and sparkle. This crime story is in many ways a bleaker male version of 'Weeds,' Showtime's comedy about a widowed soccer mom who sells pot to keep up with the Joneses."[3] The *Washington Post*'s Tom Shales enjoyed the show, but did not anticipate a ratings buster, suggesting a "'cult hit' still seems the most that the creators of *Breaking Bad* can hope for."[4] In the UK, the series did not air past its third season, with the *Guardian* dubbing it "the finest thing you haven't seen."[5] By the end of the seven-episode first season, *Breaking Bad* had earned some critical acclaim, with four Emmy nominations and a win for Bryan Cranston as Lead Actor, but viewership was weak at 1.5 million for the final episode.[6]

More than five years later, for the finale episode of the series, *Breaking Bad* viewership had increased to 10.3 million.[7] There were a number of contributing factors to this significant increase in eyeballs, aside from the outstanding writing, directing, and acting that led to its success. This chapter explores the marketing decisions surrounding *Breaking Bad*, which entered the media landscape at a turning point for television and social media engagement. I look at the effects of streaming services, primarily Netflix, which helped the series become more than a cult following. I also analyze the integrated marketing approach of AMC, who delivers podcasts, responds to fan feedback online and via the metashow *Talking Bad*, and develops robust supplementary materials in the form of Easter eggs geared toward the uberfans of the series.

RECORD FINALE: NETFLIX, BOOM!

CEO of Netflix Ted Sarandos says, "*Breaking Bad* creator Vince Gilligan personally thanked Netflix . . . for saving the show," because "ratings for the show . . . [started] climbing in Season 3, after it started its Netflix run, as it became wildly popular with Netflix subscribers."[8] Dubbing Netflix as a contributor to "the new world of catch-up TV," Richard Greenfield highlights the importance of creative series to attract fans on a variety of platforms.[9] Greenfield continues, "The creative quality of *Mad Men* and *Breaking Bad* allowed those show to find an audience on Netflix, who were then interested in watching live when the series returned." Thanks to Netflix, *Breaking Bad* experienced an increase in fans into Season 4, and by the end of that season, "which averaged 2.7 million viewers per episode," the series was "up 29 percent from the previous year."[10] Many Season 5 fans of *Breaking Bad* joined the AMC-watching viewers after bingeing Seasons 1 through 4 of the series on Netflix.

The term "binge-watch" reached the popular American vernacular by 2012, but the practice had been going on for years prior thanks to streaming services like Netflix that allow viewers to watch entire seasons in one sitting. *Time* writer James Poniewozik suggests, "Binge viewing is transforming the way people watch television and changing the economics of the industry."[11] Traditionally, television show plotlines are constructed around making time for advertisers. Streaming devices do away with the profitable, but annoying, commercial breaks. In doing so, the process of bingeing "breaks habits that have long supported the TV business, built on advertising and syndicated reruns."[12] Viewers are encouraged by the Netflix platform to binge when, "as a TV show ends and the credits begin to roll, an algorithm determines the moment when most previous viewers clicked off. At that point, the credits minimize and a pop-up menu prompts the viewers to play the next episode," sucking them into a marathon session before they can click away. Netflix vice president of "discovery and personalization" Todd Yellin contends that "viewers are taking cues from friends and family members who boast about their 'monomaniacal' TV sessions." Consequently, "the behavior 'spreads virally, and it's learned at a societal level.'"[13] Thus, word of mouth combined with clever encouragement from technologically savvy data mining creates opportunities for television series to become hits like never before.

Even more importantly, audiences are accessing narratives through a variety of mediums. Poniewozik details the various ways people watch television series in a contemporary television landscape: "live, DVR, with commercials, without, on big screens, on phones, spoiled, unspoiled, spread out over time, crammed into a few days, with DVD commentaries, with online communities and Twitter—and every one of them changes the experience."[14] Netflix analysts claim that "73% of Netflix viewers who started streaming season one of *Breaking Bad* finished every episode. The completion rate jumped to 81% for season two and 85% for season three."[15] Vince Gilligan notes that some fans experience the story "in a giant inhalation," and writers have to consider the bingers, as well as focus on "unspooling a narrative week by week, year by year" to accommodate more traditional viewers.[16] Netflix viewers' bingeing habits mean they are primed to appreciate highly serialized shows, thus giving a creative television series like *Breaking Bad* a steadily growing fan base into the final season and beyond.

BUILDING HYPE

AMC brilliantly markets its television series, building hype among fans
and potential viewers alike. The network has been lauded for its foresight
in bringing some of the most creative series to non-premium channel
audience members and capitalizing on a creative revolution in television.
However, its marketing decisions are all about the money (Heisenberg
would approve). Case in point, Season 5 of the series was split into two
halves (eight episodes each), which aired a year apart. It was essentially
two short seasons that AMC got to bill as one final extended season. As
Bloomberg Businessweek writer Joshua Brustein comments:

> Dragging out the seasons for as long as possible gives the company
> extra leverage in negotiations with carriers, which need to carry the
> most popular shows. Also, by making the final 16 episodes one long
> season rather than two shorter seasons, AMC has been able to trumpet
> to viewers that it is in Breaking Bad's "Final Season" for the last 14
> months.[17]

AMC pulled this same move with *Mad Men* for the final season. Not
all critics and fans were happy with this duplicitous labeling of two seasons as one. Writer Jeff Jensen at *Entertainment Weekly* contends,
"*Breaking Bad* has also shown us that the long intermission between
halves has a cost to the narrative. It kills momentum and makes demands
on the viewer that can diminish their enjoyment of a show at a time when
they should be enjoying it the most."[18] As viewership ramped up on
Netflix, AMC wanted to capitalize on all budding fans who might tune in
for the weekly network viewings of the series. As the series finale loomed
closer, Netflix CEO Ted Sarandos revealed, "The most-watched episode
of *Breaking Bad* on Netflix last night was the pilot . . . with all the
excitement of what's happening right now (as the show nears its close),
people started watching the show from the beginning."[19]

It takes a well-written, creative show to keep fans interested in waiting
out the long break. *Breaking Bad* is a unique combination of "plot-driven
in microcosm and character-driven in macrocosm."[20] It offers something
for viewers who love a character analysis and it also appeals to viewers
who are concerned with plotting a well-told story. And viewers love to
dissect various elements of the series. In multiple interviews, Vince Gilligan expresses pleasure at how involved fans become with Walt's world,

parsing out the details and clues to create interpretations about the characters and storyline. Gilligan notes, "I view people interpreting *Breaking Bad* and *Better Call Saul* very closely as the highest form of flattery."[21] He continues, "I will admit that a great many of the interpretations that people have of both shows involve details and conclusions which—frankly—I never had in mind. But my opinion is that these shows, once on the air, belong to you the fans as much as they belong to me and those who act and work on the shows, so your reactions are just as valid as mine." Gilligan's respect for his viewers starts in the writers' room where he notes, "To assume the audience is less smart than I am would be really short sighted, really dumb. . . . Assume the audience is smarter than you are, and they will hold you in good stead."[22] The director, the actors, and the writers of *Breaking Bad* all appreciate the fans and join them as part of the cultural construction about the series in the popular vernacular.

This is perhaps the biggest key to the success of *Breaking Bad*, and AMC's other creative series like *Mad Men* and *The Walking Dead*. The writers, directors, and actors are actively engaged with the fans and critics of the show, and get deep into interpretations and conspiracy theories, all analyzing the beloved and hated characters, as well as key plot points in the narrative. There is a plethora of discourse out about the show from podcasts to videos, to articles and Q&A discussion board postings. The creators of *Breaking Bad* make sure they are part of the cultural conversation. They do not limit interpretations of the series, but rather encourage it.

Nowhere was this more clear than with the launch of *Talking Bad* in August 2013, a play on Chris Hardwick's hosted series *Talking Dead*, which analyzes the weekly episodes with special guest fans, actors, and writers connected with the show. *Talking Bad* was conceptualized as a way to pay homage to a fantastic series during the last eight episodes by

> spending time with fans, actors, producers and television enthusiasts, recapping the most recent *Breaking Bad* episode, and taking questions and comments from viewers. Fans may continue to engage with the after-show following the on-air conclusion, online, at www.amc.com for more videos, weekly polls and photo galleries of the guests featured on the series.[23]

AMC capitalized on fan discourse by creating a show that gave them interviews with the accommodating and accessible cast members and writers as well as allowed the viewers to share their interpretations and love of the characters. Geared toward the uberfan loyal viewers, the first episode of *Talking Bad* kicked off with 1.1 million viewers, following the first episode premiere for the second half of Season 5 for *Breaking Bad*, which had 5.9 million viewers.[24] By the finale episode, *Talking Bad* reached 4.4 million viewers.[25] It broke the fourth wall by actively inviting viewers to critique the fictional world and writing choices, and acknowledged fan excitement and intelligence regarding the storytelling and acting of the series.

In another astute marketing move, AMC and Vince Gilligan took advantage of Easter eggs planted throughout the series. When it comes to media, an Easter egg is a hidden clue or joke that only close viewers will notice. The egg is a treat for those who are most avidly engaged, and typically the uberfans of whatever media is being consumed. During the airing of the series, fans noted Easter eggs connecting *Breaking Bad* to popular culture references from *Pulp Fiction* to *The Godfather*. The songs that are played at key moments and movie clips that the characters watch during various scenes have also been analyzed for clues about Walt's state of mind, and even upcoming plot points. In a podcast about one of the final episodes (Episode 5.15, "Granite State"), Vince Gilligan learned of an egg the costume department planted when they put Jesse in Todd's shirt from the train heist episode (Episode 5.5, "Dead Freight"). *Time* writer Megan McCluskey explains the significance of this detail, stating, "Well, it's apparently the same shirt that Todd was wearing when he shot [Drew Sharp]. This moment was significant . . . as it showed Todd's true nature and led to Jesse's final breaking point with his meth-dealing mentor." Vince Gilligan was delighted to learn about this egg, since he says, "That's the kind of shit, that we're proud of ourselves for coming up with the perfect detail in the writers' room, and that was such an ironic thing that makes perfect sense."[26]

AMC also used these Easter eggs to cleverly create online marketing material to enhance the audience's connection to the series. When Jesse gets kicked out of his aunt's home in Episode 2.4 ("Down"), Jesse tries to crash at his friend Pete's house and the two sing the song "Fallacies." This song comes up again in Episode 4.5 ("Shotgun"), while Jesse waits for Mike to finish the last pickup; he softly sings the song while drumming on the dashboard. An Internet search of "Fallacies" will lead to a music video for the band TwaüghtHammër. The lead singer of the band is

Jesse's friend Badger, Pete plays bass, and at one point, Jesse was the band's drummer, but he does not appear in the music video. TwaüghtHammër is also listed on Jesse's MyShout page, which Skyler looks up in Episode 1.2 ("Cat's in the Bag . . .") when she suspects Walt is lying to her about his connection to his former student. To generate hype for the second season of *Breaking Bad*, AMC created mini-episodes and one features an interview with the members of TwaüghtHammër as they talk about wanting to become famous. Too bad they were all a bunch of druggies.

AMC geared its marketing efforts around creating engagement with the series and developing a loyal fan base that continues today. In addition to releasing podcasts with Vince Gilligan and giving fans access to high-resolution images, which allowed for the easy creation of memes online, the marketers also built microsites based on plot points in the narrative. A microsite is a web page separate from the main website that marketers use to create an experience for the user. For example, e-commerce marketers might create a "BacktoSchool.com" microsite to build hype in July or August for kids to purchase school clothes and accessories. The goal is to make it engaging but also less promotion focused, thus couching the goal to sell merchandise with entertaining content. AMC created two microsites based on plot points and characters in the show. The first is BetterCallSaul.com, which is a fake website for Saul Goodman's legal business. The second is SaveWalterWhite.com, the website Walt Jr. (a.k.a. Flynn) created for his dad in Episode 2.12 ("Phoenix"). It features the same images and copy they used in the episode itself, and the links direct the user to various articles and sections of the AMC website. It is a clever integration of marketing with a fan experience that only adds to the richness of a multilayered narrative.

THE POSTERS: VISUAL EASTER EGGS

Traditional promotional mediums have become anything but traditional in the creative age of contemporary television. Coming out at the start of each new season, avid fans deconstruct the poster art for clues giving information about possible upcoming events in the narrative. According to A.V. Club writer Donna Bowman, "The much-discussed thematic posters for each successive season are less about setting the tone for what's going to happen, and more about suggesting possibilities for *who Walter will be.*"[27] With a show about the evolution of the main character from man to monster, Bowman's comment rings true, but audience members were also trying to decipher hints about which loose ends were going to be tied in the upcoming season. For the most avid of fans, the posters function as Easter eggs hiding in plain sight. Writer Laura Bennett argues, "Over the past few years, AMC, Showtime, and HBO have become increasingly adept at milking the hype around their shows with poster art that can be endlessly parsed."[28] This is the beauty of creatively written shows; they are not only enjoyed in the moment, they also become part of the cultural conversation that happens at the water cooler and beyond.

The Season 1 poster is a delightful nod to the dark humor that permeates even some of the most gruesome of scenes (I am thinking of the Emilio slushy incident from Episode 1.2 ["Cat's in the Bag . . ."] in particular). When the poster came out, the goal was to get people interested in a show nobody knew anything about. Cranston was coming off the popular but different in tone *Malcolm in the Middle*, and the plotline of a man dying of cancer spending his last days making methamphetamine was a tough sell. The Season 1 poster conveys everything we need to know about Walter White and his story. It involves chemistry, as symbolized by the red fog coming from the RV, the gas mask behind his left foot, and the choice to use the periodic table symbols in the logo of the show. Walt is out of his element, as witnessed by the fact that he does not wear pants and his shirt is disheveled, wrinkled and sticking half in and half out of his underwear. He is a man who wears tighty-whities, lace-up loafers, and a mustache and haircut that says he is middle aged. These elements make him look vulnerable; however, we also see a man who has nothing to lose, which is conveyed by the forward-facing stance, and direct eye contact with the viewer; his thumb is poised over the safety hammer of the gun in his right hand. It is intriguing and oddly humorous, and designed entirely to get people to want to tune in.

As the seasons continued and viewership ramped up, by the time the Season 5 posters came out, fans were deconstructing the art for hints about the upcoming season. Vince Gilligan comments that he refused to tell even his closest friends the ending of the series, noting, "I've never comprehended this idea of spoilers, the folks who line up to get the last Harry Potter, and turn right to the last page of the book as soon as it's in

Poster art from Season 1—the now iconic image of Walter White in his tighty-whities looking like he is ready to take on the end of the world. *AMC/Photofest ©AMC*

their hands."[29] However, Gilligan and the writers of *Breaking Bad* finished Season 4 with a literal bang and viewers were hungry for any clue of what could possibly be in store for the conclusion to Walter White's story. For most fans, the posters provided anticipation rather than spoiling.

Announcing the start of the first half of Season 5, AMC's poster features Walt sitting in the middle of a warehouse surrounding by bins of blue meth and blocks of stacked bills. For the version announcing the airdates of the season, the words "All Hail the King" are written across the top in a particularly ominous choice of color and font: mustard yellow Geogrotesque Medium. The poster (and everything about the show) was discussed at length on the discussion boards of Reddit trying to guess what Season 5 had in store for Walt and the other characters in the series. One member comments on the machine gun inconspicuously propped up in the background by the blue meth,[30] and the other members on the board try to figure out if it is intended for Hank or someone else. A clever

Part-one Season 5: "All Hail the King." *AMC/Photofest © AMC*

comment from the same thread on Reddit notes Walt's "throne," asking, "Is this a nod to *Game of Thrones*' ad campaigns? If so, I like how the 'Iron Throne' of Albuquerque is a lawn chair." The part-one Season 5 poster art symbolizes the empire Walt builds as well as nods to the underbelly of the drug world with the lawn chair and dim warehouse. Walt wears the uniform of the cook, but the posture of the leader. In the contemporary television landscape, "TV culture has become so obsessive, so attuned to any sign of what's to come, that even its off-screen manifestations are subject to exacting scrutiny."[31] What this changing landscape indicates is that the creators have to be deeply involved with the marketing materials so as to keep fans engaged with upcoming seasons.

The appeal of deciphering the seasonal poster art is due in part to Gilligan and the writers' claim not to know the ending of Seasons 4 and 5 when they began writing. They let the stories develop organically, "writing their way into and out of dead ends" as the narrative unfolds.[32] Gilligan notes that this is particularly effective in a television medium because "you're telling one story for so long that you have the time to adjust the story, over many episodes and many seasons, as you learn more about your actors. No other medium allows for that."[33] Thus, audience members and viewers can approach the season as a puzzle to be solved, anticipating the necessary payoffs and loose ends that will be tied up.

No puzzle is more enticing than the poster for the second half of Season 5. Walt faces the camera directly, with fists clenched at his sides, wearing the watch Jesse gave him for his fifty-first birthday. The sun is directly over his left shoulder, partially obscuring his face. The same yellow font from part one's poster tells us "Remember My Name," "echoing the famous 'Say my name' scene from the first half of *Breaking Bad*'s fifth season."[34] While some critics viewed the poster with anticipation and hope for a satisfying finale,[35] others tried to suss out the potential hidden meanings. Judy Berman at *Flavorwire* focuses on the use of the word "remember" as opposed to "say," proposing that the "bright, white light that forms an off-center halo around Walt's head, could also imply what fans have been speculating since the beginning of the show: *Breaking Bad* is going to end with Walter White's death, ostensibly sometime after his 52nd birthday at Denny's."[36] *Atlantic* writer Richard Lawson speculates that the fact he is not looking into the light means Walt is not dead yet, suggesting, "Maybe he's telling us to remember his name because he's going to kill us and he wants us to tell the Devil he's on his

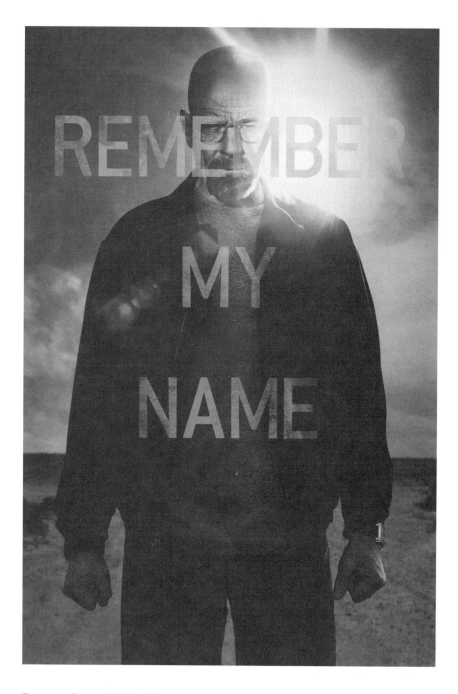

Part-two Season 5 Walt: "Remember My Name." *AMC/Photofest © AMC*

way when we get there."[37] AMC's head of marketing, Linda Schupack, says, "AMC sets out to make its posters 'richly layered' and 'a metaphor for what the season is going to be about.'" The posters are made not only to get viewers to watch, but also to get fans talking in "an attempt to capitalize on the culture of buzz by providing ample grist for the social media mill to get them building hype for the show."[38]

At the conclusion of the series, the demand from Walter White in the seasonal poster art appears ironic, as he finally gives up his fateful need to leave his family (and the general world) with a desirable image. The fictional world will remember the name of "Heisenberg," but it will be as the unassuming drug kingpin who skipped town while his wife and kids took the brunt of the punishment for his actions. Or it could be read as foreshadowing the confidence and determination a dying Walt rustles up at the very end of his life, as he seeks vengeance against all those who wronged him and sets his family up for financial stability. Even at the conclusion to the season, the poster art remained open to interpretation and conversation, and this is the value of a creative series and smart marketing campaign.

THE UNIVERSE CONTINUES ONLINE

The buzz continues years after *Breaking Bad* has officially come to an end. The success of Vince Gilligan and Peter Gould's spin-off series, *Better Call Saul*, has helped maintain the discussion, when characters from *Breaking Bad* are poised to make an appearance at any moment as the two series share an overlapping fictional world. Fans were thrilled to decode a clue in Season 2's *Better Call Saul* that hints Gustavo Fring is going to make an appearance in Season 3 of the series.[39] More than that, the world of *Breaking Bad* continues in the online space as more people find Easter eggs or visit SaveWalterWhite.com.

At the conclusion of the series, the *Breaking Bad* Facebook page had 6.5 million followers.[40] At the time of this writing, they have more than 11 million followers. In an age of streaming, it is not unusual for a series to pick up fans years after it goes off the air; however, the snowball effect of viewership and fan engagement with *Breaking Bad* offers some unique takeaways for understanding the value of a creative integrated marketing approach. The robust marketing of AMC and the willingness of Gilligan, his writers, and the cast and crew of the series to engage with fans can serve as a lesson to marketers and creative showrunners for years to come.

Part III

Being *Bad* in Walt's World

The cast of *Breaking Bad* from the second part of Season 5: Walter White Jr. (RJ Mitte), Skyler White (Anna Gunn), Marie Schrader (Betsy Brandt), Hank Schrader (Dean Norris), Walter White (Bryan Cranston), Jesse Pinkman (Aaron Paul), Saul Goodman (Bob Odenkirk), Todd Alquist (Jesse Plemons), and Lydia Rodarte-Quale (Laura Fraser). *AMC/Photofest © AMC*

7

BAD ASS MAMA
Skyler White

Vince Gilligan, the creator of Breaking Bad, *wanted Skyler to be a woman with a backbone of steel who would stand up to whatever came her way, who wouldn't just collapse in the corner or wring her hands in despair. He and the show's writers made Skyler multilayered and, in her own way, morally compromised. But at the end of the day, she hasn't been judged by the same set of standards as Walter.*—Anna Gunn[1]

It starts when we can't stand to see her trying to make sense of what she cannot see going on; it has continued into a culpability that is as severe—through compliance and survival—as her methlord husband's. We must watch all of this, a strong leading woman, imprisoned in her own home—an equal to a villain, yet subject to his whims— waiting for a shift in the tides of fate. Maybe this is it, though: the terrible relatability we feel with her lack of life choices. That, because we are Skyler, we hate Skyler—and this is our character issue.—Ethan Richardson[2]

The cast of *Breaking Bad* is heavily male dominated, with Skyler White and her sister, Marie Schrader, as the two most prominent female characters in the series. Like all the characters in the show, Skyler White is complex and makes a number of immoral and, at times, illegal decisions of her own throughout the five seasons. Unlike the other characters in the series, many fans of the show hate Skyler. We are not talking about a general dislike or annoyance, where some fans do not care for Marie's love of purple or find Hank obnoxious. This is also not a case where Skyler is a character who fans love to hate, with an understanding of how good the bad character is for the series. For Skyler, the level of public vitriol is unprecedented with fan-created Facebook pages titled "I Hate Skyler White" (30,309 members) and "Fuck Skyler White" (29,089 members); fans also took to the AMC message boards to voice their strong opinions against the character to ask that she get killed off.

As Anna Gunn acknowledges in an op-ed piece for the *New York Times* titled "I Have a Character Issue," Skyler is not the only hated female character on television in the past decade. She mentions similar anger against *Mad Men*'s Betty Draper and Carmela from *The Sopranos*. In her article, Gunn offers an explanation for the venomous loathing of Skyler (a loathing that inexplicably transferred to the actress herself) arguing that show creator Vince Gilligan wrote a woman who would not be afraid to speak her mind and stand up against her husband. She continues by stating that the attitude toward Skyler articulates society's dismissal of strong women: "Could it be that they can't stand a woman who won't suffer silently or 'stand by her man'? That they despise her because she won't back down or give up? Or because she is, in fact, Walter's equal?"[3] Vince Gilligan agrees with Gunn, arguing, "People who have these issues with the wives being too bitchy on *Breaking Bad* are misogynists, plain and simple." He continues, "People are griping about Skyler White being too much of a killjoy to her meth-cooking, murdering husband? She's telling him not to be a murderer and a guy who cooks drugs for kids. How could you have a problem with that?"[4]

I understand where both Gunn and Gilligan are coming from, and upon reading the comments on the boards, I agree that many of the most vocal fans are misogynists and most likely fueled by the protective anonymity of online posting. However, I am not convinced that Gunn's "character problem" comes down to fans not being open to strong women on the screen. As a feminist and scholar who makes a living studying strong women, I also find her generally unlikable (although less so upon my fifth viewing of the series), especially in the first two seasons, and I find it fascinating that this is not what Vince Gilligan and the other writers intended for her character. For me, it is not the acting, as I feel that Anna Gunn acts her role as brilliantly as everybody else in this talented cast.

In this chapter, I focus an internal lens on the show to peel back the layers of Skyler White, a character whose storyline primarily resides in the traditional private sphere of the home, and yet is someone who violates her own moral codes as she gets sucked into Walt's world. Because the dislike of Skyler happened very early in the series, I primarily focus on Seasons 1 and 2, but use her characterization in Seasons 3, 4, and 5 to show the growth that may have come too late to save her in the eyes of fans. I start from the understanding that many fans do not like her character, and I attempt to offer explanations for this response that do not come down to a simple hatred of watching strong women.

BOYS ONLY CLUB

In *Breaking Bad*, Vince Gilligan creates a male-focused world from the start, pitching the series to the studio as "a story about a man who transforms himself from Mr. Chips into Scarface,"[5] a study of how a good man goes bad, and violently bad at that. This male-centered storyline includes many men on the periphery. In addition to Walt, Jesse, and

Skyler White, the final episode. *AMC/Photofest © AMC*

Hank, the bad guy antagonists, lackeys, and fixers are also almost all men. Tuco, Saul, Gus, Mike, Todd, Gomez, the Cousins: the show is a sausage fest. This fact does not diminish the quality or enjoyment of the narrative, but it does create a male-centric focus for the series.

Gilligan is a talented and astute creative force in Hollywood, making a name for himself as a writer and producer on *The X-Files* (1995–2002) and screenwriter for the films *Home Fries* (1998) and *Hancock* (2008), long before *Breaking Bad* aired. In interviews, he appears perceptive about human motivation; humble about his talent; grateful to the actors, crew, and his audience; and overall, charmingly good natured and kind. Like Steve Carell or Meryl Streep, he is the kind of person who ends up on the "Celebrity I'd Most Like to Have Dinner With" list. It is with this caveat that I now say: Skyler White is painfully underwritten in Seasons 1 and 2, and because she is one of the few women in this male world, this lack of depth becomes a gendered issue.

The Boys Only Club genre of narratives that permeate critics' lists of best writing and loyal fan followings like *Mad Men*, *True Detective*, *The Sopranos*, and almost anything by Quentin Tarantino appeals to audience members, male and female alike, with gritty scenes and dialogue balancing humor with charming arrogance. Women exist, sometimes as key players in the plotline, but the main story is frequently about a man trying to understand his inner demons and violently battle exterior monsters. In the first few seasons of the series, Skyler White is written as a one-note character whose primary focus is telling Walt what he should be doing and constantly suggesting he fails as a partner by shutting her out. In interpersonal communication, this is the concept of demand-withdraw, where one partner (typically assumed to be the woman) demands attention, communication, and/or time and the other partner (typically assumed to be the man) withdraws as a result of the demands. If one partner withdraws, this creates a sense of wanting to know what is going on and increases the demands from the other partner. It is a vicious cycle that frequently results in dissatisfaction for both partners in the relationship.

A demand-withdraw pattern emerges early in the premiere of the series, but the effects of the combination of demand from Skyler and withdraw from Walt is most prominent in the second episode of the series (Episode 1.2, "Cat's in the Bag . . ."). Walt and Jesse try to deal with their culpability in the death of Emilio and the upcoming (re)murder of Krazy-8. Skyler is understandably concerned about where Walt disappears to, especially because she does not yet know he has cancer. She confronts Walt, telling him he owes her the truth about what is going on and an explanation for why he shuts her out. It is at this moment that Walt utters the line, "What *I* need, is for you to climb down out of my ass." In one sense, if my husband were disappearing without word and not answering my phone calls, I would be incredibly frustrated and probably not half as calm as Skyler about finding out what is going on (I am very demanding). On the other hand, I know to what lengths Walt has gone in order to leave a nest egg for his family, so Skyler's demands appear particularly taxing when he has just killed a man and needs to kill another one in order to protect her. In this moment, it is not just Skyler's question that weighs on Walt, but also the fact that he has to keep this huge secret. He feels a sense of responsibility against a ticking clock and he grapples with a moral dilemma so intense he is mishearing the word "murder" when students ask him questions about the midterm. We see the tension in Walt's body (thanks to the incredibly talented Bryan Cranston) as Skyler demands an explanation. It is a funny moment, because Walt's response is so unexpected. Even though we see how keyed up Walt is over having to kill Krazy-8 and deal with Jesse's bumbling ignorance, all while juggling Skyler's expectations, we still expect him to come up with another lie and attempt to pacify her concerns. Instead he gets verbally aggressive and snaps, the even-keeled acquiescing façade of Walter White the husband slipping a bit. Even though logically, we might understand why Skyler is frustrated, as viewers we are privy to Walt's side of the story. Skyler's persistence in combination with her lack of knowledge is frustrating for Walt and, by extension, for us; it makes it hard not to side with Walt in this moment.

Skyler does not just demand or "nag" as some vocal fans have argued (one of the nicer claims against the character). She acts on some of her assumptions, which creates some humorous moments but also places her in a position to cause trouble for Walt. In Episode 1.2 ("Cat's in the Bag . . ."), Skyler investigates a mysterious phone call and finds out Walt is connected with Jesse. Skyler assumes she has figured out Walt's secret and confronts Jesse directly. She threatens to tell her DEA agent brother-in-law if he sells Walt any more marijuana. Where is Skyler's Winnie the Pooh sweatshirt and mom jeans? Did she leave the fanny pack in the car? She comes across as a naïve prude, unaware of how the world really works, and treats Walt like a child, telling his friend, "No, you can't play with him anymore." It is written and directed as a humorous scene with the very pregnant Skyler surprising Jesse as he drags a dead body across his driveway, which he then spends the majority of the conversation hiding from her view. Visually it is funny, but the context is humorous as well because her assumption has so undervalued the consequences for Jesse and Walt. It is well written and beautifully acted by everyone involved, but it does not do anything to make the audience like Skyler and reinforces the fact that she is not part of the Boys Only Club. Her anger about Walt smoking pot cements her as the ultimate killjoy, and reinforces the demand-withdraw pattern that perhaps hits too close to home for many viewers. Walt and Jesse are dealing with manly issues like murder, meth, and mayhem. And all Skyler can do is demand his attention and wag her finger at the fact that her husband is smoking marijuana.

This is one of the main problems with Skyler White in the first few seasons: she always says no to Walt. In one way, the characterization of Skyler as the rigid, do-the-right-thing wife makes sense. Skyler's character needs to evolve just as much as Walt's throughout the series. In the first season alone, she adamantly does not want Walt smoking pot, even after he reveals his cancer diagnosis; she consistently devalues Walt's pride by suggesting they ask other people for money—first Hank and Marie (Episode 1.4, "Cancer Man") and then Gretchen and Elliott (Episode 1.5, "Gray Matter"); she stages an intervention to convince Walt to go through with a treatment he does not want (Episode 1.5, "Gray Matter"); and she refuses to acknowledge that Marie's stealing habit may not be black and white (Episode 1.7, "A No-Rough-Stuff-Type Deal"). Depicting Skyler as a goody-goody and unwaveringly moral from the first episode foreshadows how angry she becomes when she finds out Walt is lying to her and making money illegally. It is a glimpse at her moral code, but in addition, the stricter it is in the beginning of the series, the more leeway it gives the writers to articulate her transformation. In the same way that Gilligan is exploring how a good man goes bad, he also reveals how that man's partner is affected by the transformation, making a good woman go bad. Unfortunately, the deck was stacked against Skyler early in the series. Viewers need some glimpses of something other than "no" to get us to agree to care about her transformation. In this case, the writers may have taken too long to allow Skyler some complexity.

Skyler White becomes far more interesting as the series continues, resisting Walt, giving in to Walt, resisting Walt, helping Walt, and then, ultimately, resisting Walt. The series features turning points for all the characters, where they face a choice and there is no turning back. For Skyler, one of the most revealing turning points is toward the end of the series when she suggests they get rid of Jesse (Episode 5.12, "Rabid Dog"). Skyler has not only accepted her fate with Walt but is an active participant who hides the money, blackmails her brother-in-law, and helps Walt figure out his options, including murder. In this case, both Saul and Skyler are on the same page about killing Jesse, but Walt is the one who says no. This is perhaps the most revealing glimpse of the new Mrs. Scarface, where Skyler is more of a monster than Walt, lacking a conscience as she suggests Jesse needs to die. For a while, Skyler becomes the mob wife her lawyer warns her about in Episode 3.5 ("Más"), looking the other way as her husband provides for the family through any means necessary. In this episode, she goes even further by becoming a willing participant in the Boys Only Club. However, this only lasts for a short amount of time because Skyler cannot remain a complicit player in this world of men.

TRADITIONAL ROLES

Skyler is eventually written out of the Boys Only Club because her story is centered within the home, a traditionally female-focused location. Toward the end of the series, Vince Gilligan comments that he does not understand why viewers go against Skyler to side with Walt: "She's got a tough job being married to this asshole."[6] This quote reinforces Skyler's role as Walt's wife, where her job is to be married to the monster. It also suggests something about the way the writers approached her plotline in relation to Walt; Skyler represents the home, which encompasses the children and the marriage. In gender research, men are viewed as having a voice, place, and location outside the home, in the public sphere. Women are traditionally viewed as having a voice, place, location within the home (the private sphere), where they tend to be the primary caretaker of children, partner, and home care (even if they also work in the public sphere). In Episode 1.1 ("Pilot"), Skyler is visually and circumstantially domesticated. We learn she recently quit her job to stay home and work on her writing career (a bygone plot point by Season 2); we see her make a birthday breakfast for Walt complete with veggie bacon spelling out

"50"; and, she is pregnant, which could not symbolize her role as a mother any more clearly. She is the nurturing caretaker for her family, virtually barefoot and pregnant in the kitchen the first time we meet her. If we interpret Skyler's role within the context of the home, then there are a number of consequences to this characterization that may suggest why she is so hated by many fans of the series.

The first consequence of centering Skyler's story within the traditional role of the home is that her main goal is to protect her children and keep the home life in harmony. Walt's goal within a traditional male role means he takes on a dangerous job that requires lying, miscommunication, and lack of availability (emotionally and physically). All of Walt's actions affect the home and, thus, create incompatible goals between Skyler and Walt. Skyler's plotline makes her role the catalyst for a lot of the family drama. In the first season, she protects Walt's health by making him turkey bacon (Episode 1.1, "Pilot"); she believes communication is the key to a healthy marriage (Episode 1.2, "Cat's in the Bag . . ."); she confides in Marie with a "hypothetical" story about Walt's drug use (Episode 1.3, ". . . And the Bag's in the River"); she breaks down crying at a family dinner shortly after she finds out Walt has cancer (Episode 1.4, "Cancer Man"); she stages an intervention with the family to convince Walt to fight to live (Episode 1.5, "Gray Matter"); she convinces Walt to attend cancer family counseling sessions (Episode 1.6, "Crazy Handful of Nothin'"); and she is responsive to her husband when he wants to have sex, even if that occurs in the backseat of a car, at a school, while she is pregnant (Episode 1.7, "A No-Rough-Stuff-Type Deal"). All of her plotlines early in the series are centered within the home and on the family drama, maintaining the health (both physical and emotional) of her loved ones.

Season 2 reveals a new Skyler, unhappy with her marriage and not speaking to her sister, suffering from the stress of everybody's problems and the lack of a present partner. When Walt is home, he barely speaks to her, and in one very troubling scene (Episode 2.1, "Seven Thirty-Seven") he sexually assaults her in the kitchen. In light of this, Skyler can be understood as a woman who is at once enacting and resisting the traditional female role in the domestic sphere. One of the best Skyler monologues in the series occurs in the first episode of Season 2, when Hank comes over to attempt to convince her to take Marie's calls, and admits he knows about the stealing. He says they need to support Marie, and Skyler says no:

> I need support. Me. The almost 40-year-old pregnant woman with a surprise baby on the way. And, the husband with lung cancer who disappears for hours on end, and I don't know where he goes and he barely even speaks to me anymore. With a moody son, who does the same thing. And, the overdrawn checking account—and the lukewarm water heater that leaks rusty-looking crap and is rotting out the floor of the utility closet and we can't even afford to fix it. But, oooh—I see! Now, I'm supposed to go, Hank, please, what can I possibly do to benefit my spoiled kleptomaniac bitch sister, who somehow always manages to be the center of attention. Cause God knows, SHE'S THE ONE WITH THE REALLY IMPORTANT PROBLEMS!

In this speech, Skyler runs through the plotline of the family drama, highlighting all their issues. She indicates that her expected role as the rock in the center of the home is not possible—the problems are too big, and she does not have anybody supporting her. Hank awkwardly comforts a crying Skyler and offers to look at the water heater, a job he is more comfortable dealing with than her emotions.

Skyler's outburst and Hank's reaction are both important because they set up a conversation about traditional familial roles, which tend to place women in the private sphere, and men outside of the home in the public sphere. The entire crux of the plotline of *Breaking Bad* is a man who is about to die wanting to leave his family in a better financial situation. Walt works two jobs in the first episode of the series, one as a high school chemistry teacher and a second at a car wash where he cleans the cars of rich students. There are visual elements that reveal the family's lack of finances, with a modest house and drab furnishings, but the fact that this man has to work two jobs, with a special-needs son and a baby on the way, all suggest the family is experiencing financial troubles. In one particularly illuminating scene in Episode 1.1 ("Pilot"), Skyler is so preoccupied with a lack of money that she interrupts Walt's birthday hand job to celebrate when her online auction brings in more money than expected. One way to read Walt's turn to drug making is to understand that he wants to be better at his traditional gendered role as the breadwinner of the family. Skyler does not have a paying job, so Walt is the breadwinner by default; but he is not very good at it prior to making meth, and they struggle for money.

At the same time, in addition to being the breadwinner in a traditional gender role perspective, men are also supposed to be somewhat present in the household. In the monologue from Skyler about who has important problems, she focuses on the fact that they cannot afford to fix the water heater, and Hank's response is to help her by looking at the water heater, a traditional job for a man, and one that Walt should take care of if he were home more often. In a later episode in Season 2 (Episode 2.10, "Over"), when Walt tries to make amends with Skyler and repair some of the emotional damage he has caused with his lies, his first task is to replace the leaking water heater. He substitutes household maintenance projects for tackling the emotional repairs Skyler needs.

Walt's storyline is deeply intertwined with the traditional masculine role to provide for his family's financial needs. In Episode 3.5 ("Más"), Gustavo Fring reinforces this mentality with Walt as he tries to convince him to work for him, telling him a man's job is to "provide" financially for his family. Hank also repeats this rhetoric in Episode 5.5 ("Dead Freight"), telling Walt he is a great father and husband because he "provides" for his family. When Skyler attempts to serve Walt with divorce papers, he insists on paying money for the children, arguing, "You want me out, I'm out, but I will provide for my family" (Episode 3.6, "Sunset"). Regardless of the complicated reasons for why he needs to enact that role, we accept his goal and understand that this series is about seeing how he achieves it, for better or worse. In one way, we dislike Skyler because when she enacts a traditionally female role, it keeps Walt from enacting his traditional role. This offers one reason why the character of Hank is not hated as much as Skyler, even though he also actively (and frequently unknowingly) works against Walt's ability to enact a traditional male role in his household. We see Hank as simply doing his job, a role he embodies in the traditional male public sphere as well.

In Season 2, we start to see Skyler slipping from her traditional role through a variety of behaviors, even while she enacts traditional role rhetoric by claiming to try to help her family. As her character deals with the new, secretive Walt, Skyler makes choices in the storyline that go against her role as wife and mother and this makes her less likable. In Season 2 (Episode 2.4, "Down"), Skyler is frustrated by Walt's lies about the second cell phone. She stages an emotional shutout until Walt tells her the truth, which he never does, and she knows it, yelling at him to "shut up and say something that is not complete bullshit." Exasperated, the very pregnant Skyler smokes a cigarette. This should provide that glimpse of a chink in the moral armor; she has flaws and recognizes it when she glares back at the judgmental old woman watching her smoke. However, because she is pregnant and adamant about open communication and honesty with Walt, her sneaking of cigarettes comes across as hypocritical rather than an example of character complexity. She is hiding this habit, knows it is not good for the baby, and does it anyway.

A longer plot point of Skyler's hypocrisy is rooted in her relationship with Ted Beneke. Eventually, Skyler sleeps with Ted (Episode 3.3, "I.F.T."), and we can argue that she did not do this until after she had filed for divorce, or, to be more realistic, after Walt refused to leave the house, making her a prisoner in her own bedroom, but the relationship with Ted did not start there. In Episode 2.7 ("Negro y Azul"), Skyler takes a job at her former workplace, Beneke Fabricators, where she rekindles a flirtation with the owner, Ted Beneke. Marie, surprised that the very pregnant Skyler got a job, lets us know that the last time Skyler worked at Beneke, Ted tried to kiss her at a company party. Marie offers to help financially when Skyler suggests money is the reason for her return to work. This information serves a variety of purposes: one, Marie questions her desire to work for a man who acted inappropriately with her; and two, to plant the seeds of a history between Ted and Skyler so that when she does start to turn to him a few weeks later (or approximately two to three episodes later) for emotional support, it is not completely out of place. Skyler initially appears to resist Ted's advances, putting him off when he asks her to lunch after telling her he is divorced. With growing problems in her own marriage, she eventually opens up to Ted emotionally, crying about her frustrations, holding his hand, and, in the oldest trick in the book, knocking over her pen cup to make him come into her office to help her (Episode 2.10, "Over").

As this relationship with Ted blossoms, Walt finds out that he needs to have surgery to remove the remainder of the shrunken tumor and Skyler falters when Walt says he will do it (Episode 2.11, "Mandala"). After spending so much time in the first season trying to convince Walt to fight through the cancer, saying they will figure out the money, now that she has started working with Ted, she says they should talk about spending the $170,000–$200,000 on a necessary surgery. Has she completely given up on helping Walt live? It is this same episode where Ted makes a birthday request to have Skyler sing "Happy Birthday, Mr. President" to him in front of the entire office. She initially refuses, but then gives in, producing one of the most uncomfortable scenes in the entire series, which is saying a lot in a narrative filled with intensity and debauchery. Apparently Albuquerqueans are kind and not gossipy, because every time I see this scene I think that somebody in that office has to find this all very strange and uncomfortable. I look for that one coworker giving another coworker a knowing glance. Instead they all seem delighted by the banter. As a viewer, I cringe and groan, peeking from behind a pillow that I have jammed to my face. Skyler is headed down her own rabbit hole, and we can see that this love affair is not going to end well for anybody. This turn for Skyler should make her more complex, and thus more likable to the audience, but I would argue that her visibly pregnant body juxtaposed with her flirtations serves as a visual indicator of her hypocrisy. She is supposed to be the moral center of the home and she fails.

It is this back-and-forth with her roles in the private and public spheres that makes her story interesting to watch. Skyler does not succeed in the private sphere, partially due to a withdrawn partner, but then she is also not successful in the public sphere. She is a failure at her own job when she helps Ted cook the books (Episode 2.11, "Mandala"). Her affair with Ted brings trouble to the workplace when Walt shows up and wants to fight (Episode 3.4, "Green Light"). In the beginning of Season 3, Skyler does not live up to her marriage vows to stick by Walt for better or worse, actively working to break up the family, simultaneously enacting a traditional role (to protect her children) and resisting it (starting divorce proceedings). In light of this, Skyler can be understood as a woman who is at once enacting and resisting traditional female roles, which ultimately works against Walt realizing his goal to enact a traditional male role in the public sphere as the breadwinner for the family. Although Walt's decisions are dangerous and potentially harmful, they are rarely in direct conflict with his goal to make money. There may have been other options to get the money he needed for his family, but regardless of that, all of his actions are in line with someone who wants to build a nest egg. This is in direct contrast to Skyler who works to disconnect first herself from the home, and then the father from the home when she finds out Walt makes drugs. Therefore, it is possible that some audience members dislike

Skyler throughout the series in part because, whether she represents the home or public role, she then commits a series of hypocritical acts that go against her goals. Perhaps it is her failure at both roles that makes her unlikable.

LET'S FACE IT: SHE'S RIGHT

At this point, I would like to offer one more possible explanation for why Skyler White is so strongly disliked that does not necessarily come down to issues of misogyny, or even gender stereotypes. And that is, we want to root for Walt, but Skyler forces us to see the problems with him, and by extension with us. She is unlikable for that reason. There are multiple moments in the narrative when Skyler is right to say no, to "nag," to try to break free from a family that is led by Walter White. Skyler worries that Walt's new profession will bring danger to their home and it does. The first time is when Tuco kidnaps Jesse and Walt at gunpoint (Episode 2.1, "Seven Thirty-Seven"), literally bringing danger to the curb of the house. The next instance is even closer to home when the Cousins come to avenge Tuco's death (Episode 3.2, "Caballo Sin Nombre").

When the Cousins crawl onto the scene in the opening of Season 3 (Episode 3.1, "No Más"), we do not quite know what they represent, but we know it cannot be good. They place a sketch of Heisenberg complete with the black hat on the shrine of Santa Muerte—a known saint for killers and thieves—and then conduct a string of odd and violent behaviors as they make their way across the border. The Cousins steal clothing and pay off their debt with a car. They shoot an entire truck full of illegal immigrants and the driver, and then light it on fire. They are hunting down Heisenberg, but why do they want him? Is he their prey or their prize? When they visit Tuco's Tio Hector, and we see the anger in the older man's face as he reveals Heisenberg's real name to the twins and make the connection to Tuco, it is clear Walter White is in trouble.

At the end of Episode 3.2 ("Caballo Sin Nombre"), Mike narrowly avoids getting caught placing listening devices at the White family home. He climbs back in his car and watches as Walt carries his belongings into the house. Moments later, the Cousins pull up to the curb and get out wearing impeccable sharkskin suits, black gloves, and carrying an ax. They walk through the house. Mike can hear Walt in the shower via the listening devices he placed, and he quickly makes a call. The Cousins walk slowly down the hallway, noticing Holly's sonogram picture on the fridge and peering into her nursery. These domestic elements, signs of a baby and innocence, are juxtaposed with the malevolent danger represented by the two men. The Cousins make their way to the bedroom, hear Walt in the shower, and sit down side by side on the bed, facing the bathroom door. One of the twins rubs his thumb along the gleaming metal of the ax head as they wait. Walt continues to bathe and sing, as he obliviously focuses on his anger with Skyler and new resolve to stay in the family home against her wishes. While the shower water turns off, one of the twins gets a text message and shows his brother "Pollos" on the phone's screen. They look at one another. In the next shot, Walt opens the bathroom door to an empty room, save for his open suitcase. He notices some of his items have been disturbed and he looks around, gazing down the hall. The Cousins are gone.

I remember watching this scene for the first time with my husband. We turned to each other and burst out laughing at the tension that had built up watching those final three minutes of the episode, exclaiming, "It's so gooooood!" Walter White almost got his head chopped off with an ax and he had no idea. The Cousins do not play around. Up to this point, we have seen the violence they are capable of committing. They have now hunted Walt down, entered the sanctuary of his home, and patiently waited for him to exit the shower. You cannot get more vulnerable than wet and naked, and yet, they were going to let him come out of the bathroom first and realize he was dead meat. They are not just killers; they are soulless. It was exhilarating to see Walt so close to death, to see him escape, and to understand that he had no clue what had almost happened.

This scene sets up two important points when it comes to understanding Skyler's role in the narrative. The first is that she is absolutely right about keeping him away from the family, and especially the kids. Walter White just invited danger into their home. His choices have consequences, and if he did not realize this after watching Tuco beat No-Doze to death in the junkyard (Episode 2.1, "Seven Thirty-Seven"), or after being kidnapped to become a cook for the cartel (Episode 2.2, "Grilled"), then he cannot possibly fathom how dangerous his involvement in this world is for his family. What if it had been Skyler in the shower, or Walt Jr.? As the Cousins walk through the house, they notice signs of baby

Holly; would she have been allowed to survive the attack? We have seen what these men are capable of, which creates an understanding that Walt's family is not off limits. Skyler has made it clear to Walt that she expects him to stay away from the kids with this divorce; her intention is to protect them from the world he has gotten involved in. She did her due diligence in figuring out why he was lying. It is not an affair; she checked. He did not get the money from his mother; she checked. She remembers his connection to Jesse Pinkman and, being an intelligent woman, puts two and two together and assumes that he is a drug dealer. She finds out it is meth (Episode 3.1, "No Más") and makes a deal that she will not tell Hank if Walt stays away from her and the kids. She knows the danger. In the voice message that spurred his homecoming (Episode 3.2, "Caballo Sin Nombre"), Skyler threatens to file a restraining order against him if he continues to come by the house uninvited. In a gesture of asserting a particularly masculine power, Walt screams, "I've got your restraining order right here"; then he grabs his crotch, shouting, "Restrain this!" But clearly Skyler is right to be worried.

The second point this scene highlights about Skyler's role in the narrative is that Walt is so far in over his head that we cannot trust his judgment. His hubris has clouded the bigger picture for him and he has not yet become the drug kingpin that is his future. He does not understand the consequences to his actions, and although Walt is a character who should be fun to watch, he is not somebody we should necessarily want to see succeed. Gilligan did not write Walter White as a person to emulate. He wanted to explore the creation of a monster. In the first few seasons, the writers use Skyler's character to represent the voice of reason against the madness of the monster, the reminder that Walt is making dangerous choices. She needs to cue the audience that he is getting deeper and deeper into this world and at some point, maybe as early as when he cooks for the first time, there is no turning back.

In Anna Gunn's article, she suggests that Skyler is Walt's equal, but in what way? I have argued that she is the counter to Walt, but in the domestic sphere. It is not just that they both cannot succeed, but her desire to keep danger out of the home devalues his desire to provide. She enacts her traditional gender role but diminishes his traditional gender role, which goes against stereotypical domesticity. It is complex and makes for a fascinating watch, but it is also a plot conflict that does not work out in Skyler's favor. Once she realizes that Walt's goals go against her own, she attempts to keep him away from the family by kicking him out of the house and threating a restraining order. Try as she might, she cannot out-villain him, and yet she is the one, not Walt, whom people dislike.

The episode following Walt's near decapitation should make us sympathize with Skyler: Walt almost died and we know his family has been implicitly threatened. However, the first few times I watched this episode (Episode 3.3, "I.F.T."), I was delighted by Walt's antics, as he gets his way. Skyler comes home to find that Walt has broken into the house, and she tells him she will call the police. Walt attempts to pick up a crying Holly and Skyler blocks his path. Walt tells her to go ahead and call the police because "this family is everything to me. Without it, I have nothing to lose." Skyler wipes away tears as she asks the Albuquerque police to come to her home. What follows is an emotional game of chicken. While they wait for the police, Walt Jr. comes home and Walt offers to make him a grilled cheese. Skyler nervously tries to get Walt Jr. to go to his room, because she does not want him to see the police when they arrive. When they show up, Walt Jr. yells at her and Walt says, "Don't blame your mother." As the police separate them to figure out the dispute, Holly cries and Walt says, "I've got it, honey," knowing that she does not want him to touch the baby. Walt feeds Holly a bottle, one-handed, while he continues to answer the police officer's questions. Walt plays the perfect father, setting it up so that Skyler looks insane for calling the police. He does not lose his temper or show any of the aggression we witnessed in the previous episode as he grabbed his crotch or threw a pizza up on the roof in anger (Episode 3.2, "Caballo Sin Nombre"). In "I.F.T.," he leaves Skyler with only one option to get him out of the house and dares her to take it. When the police officer asks, "Is it possible that he's broken any laws that you are aware of?" she gives up her chance and Walt wins this first round. I did not connect with Skyler in this scene until I had a baby of my own. As I rewatched it with my two-month-old peacefully sleeping in his pack-and-play next to our couch, I seethed with rage at Walt's manipulation. After having my baby, one of the most shocking changes for me was this almost primal fierceness in my desire to keep him happy, healthy, and breathing. If I were Skyler, I would have had a hard time keeping myself from murdering Walt in his sleep that night (fair warning to my lovely husband). Walt is so frustratingly smug as he controls everything around him, forcing Skyler to be the bad guy in front of everyone.

Skyler wins round two, though—kind of. Later in the episode, Walt makes an impassioned plea for Skyler to accept his drug money and to accept him. She goes to work and has sex with Ted. Later, she comes home and Walt is busily making dinner. He has allowed Walt Jr. to have his friend over, and he tells Skyler how much better he feels after having been honest with her. He truly believes he has convinced her (or will soon) and his family will remain intact. Skyler watches him putter around the kitchen and waits for him to look up. She picks up the salad bowl, looks him square in the eyes, and says, "I fucked Ted."

I say that Skyler sort of wins the round, because she does so in the narrative. However, with fans, this moment just makes her look cruel. The "I fucked Ted" moment is debilitating for Skyler's character. It is a line that sucks the air out of the room. Walt deserves this punch to the gut for countless reasons: he lied to her repeatedly, he is controlling and manipulative; she has asked for the divorce and he has refused to grant it; he has made a fool of her in front of the police; and he is pitting the family against her, including her own son, the main person she is working to protect by not exposing Walt. Skyler is angry because he brings her drug money and refuses to acknowledge the danger that comes with it. So she sleeps with another man and describes it in such graphic language ("fucking" someone is very different from "making love" to someone) with the intention of hurting him. She then sweetly calls out to Walt Jr. and his friend Lewis that dinner is ready. Comedian Louis C.K. has a sketch in his comedy special *Louis C.K.: Chewed Up* about the difference between boys and girls, and by extension, men and women. Basically he acknowledges that a man may take a limb, or cause serious physical harm, "but he will leave you as a human being intact . . . women are non-violent but they will shit inside of your heart."[7] Skyler's decision to "fuck" Ted is a way to get Walt to leave, to accept the situation so that she can move on with her life and keep her children safe. At the same time, the calm intensity of the statement cuts to the soul. Because Skyler is not as likable in the first few seasons, when she makes this cruel, calculated move, we do not root for her. Walt may have damaged people, but he has left their souls intact. Skyler, on the other hand, has shit inside his heart.

Skyler's resolve about keeping Walt away from the family does not start to slip until she is drawn in by the allure of money (Episode 3.5, "Más"). We see her visit her lawyer, who point-blank asks her incredulously, "Are you asking my permission to spend this money?" In this episode, Skyler finally starts to buy into the idea that Walt might actually be making choices with the goal of helping the family, to which her lawyer responds that what she is saying is an "enormous load of horse-shit." This scene between Skyler and her lawyer is important for the progression of Skyler White's character arc. The lawyer becomes the logical character through which we are supposed to see Skyler's slipping moral conscience in contrast. Because Skyler treats the lawyer as a thera-pist in this scene, unloading details like the fact that she is sleeping with Ted, we get to see Skyler's thought process at work and understand some of her choices in a different light. At one point in their conversation, Skyler tells the lawyer that Walt was not a criminal when she married him, and the lawyer says, "Well, you are married to one now."

As is the case in all well-written narratives, the tension continues when, as soon as Skyler begins to consider letting Walt back into her life, Walt lets her go and signs the divorce papers. Skyler's turn from hard-and–fast, black-and-white morality, and our desire to see Walt succeed, puts her on his path but at the same time forces viewers to question why we want her there. Writer Ethan Richardson suggests that we hate Skyler because she makes us view ourselves and we do not like the mirror she holds up.[8] Richardson suggests it is her "lack of life choices" that we relate to, and we cannot stand to watch. She is the more relatable of the two, the one who gets sucked into Walt's world even after repeated attempts to resist it. Maybe we simply dislike Skyler because she was able to resist longer than we did.

IN THE END . . .

At the end of the series, it is possible that Skyler is allowed to live, even if it is not a great life, because she stops trying to protect her family from secrets. In one of the final episodes of the series (Episode 5.14, "Ozyman-dias"), Skyler finally exposes Walt to his son, and Walt Jr. sees his father in a new light and takes her side. She does so under somewhat false circumstances, because she does not fully highlight her own culpability in the situation, but she has attempted to escape the situation before and this is her chance. Both Skyler and Walt claim to make decisions to save the family, but Hank's death ultimately makes Skyler realize the family cannot be saved.

In the end, Skyler chooses her children by exposing them to the monster their father has become. In the final episode of the series (Episode 5.16, "Felina"), while she is punished for her role in Walt's activities by being ostracized by the community, she also gets the satisfaction of hearing Walt say this was about him and not his family. Walt admits, "I did it for me. I liked it. I was good at it. And, I was really—I was alive." Walt ultimately destroys the family he is trying to save.

If we see Skyler in a traditional feminine role, as the moral compass and center of the home, then perhaps Gunn is right in her article. The way she is criticized, where Walt is not, reveals a double standard from society. But it is not necessarily because the audience does not want to see Skyler as Walt's equal, or because they cannot stomach a strong woman. Instead, the writers have created a Boys Only Club where Skyler cannot compete. And when she does, because Skyler's role is so heavily centered in the home, her actions appear hypocritical. Her goals are to protect her family, specifically her children, but in attempting to beat Walt she commits adultery, and embodies the bad mom who smokes while pregnant and then leaves her infant daughter to go have sex with her boss.

In the end, Skyler is right. Walt ruins her life and the lives of their children. They will be taken care of financially, but only because Gretchen and Elliott have been manipulated to do so. Walt Jr. and Holly will live in a town that is suspicious of their mother and thinks their father is a monster. They will not have a father figure or extended family to lean on because Hank is dead, and Marie and Skyler will never be able to repair what they once had. Skyler was right, from the beginning.

In *Breaking Bad*, especially in the first few seasons of the series, Walt cannot succeed if Skyler succeeds. Although the concept of an antihero is muddied when dealing with Walter White, if we accept that he is supposed to be the protagonist, then we are conditioned through storytelling conventions to root for him. This is one way to understand the audience's anger toward Skyler, where she does not want Walt to succeed at being a drug dealer. But her resistance to and support of him ebbs and flows over the course of the series. Thus, the persistent dislike of Skyler White suggests deeper issues at the heart of what it means to be a woman in a man's world, both on and off the screen.

8

BREAKING DOWN THE BAD GUYS

I don't think Gus is a good man, but he's not an entirely bad man. He's infinitely pragmatic. When he does something awful, it's not with any pleasure or joy. He's out to accomplish a goal and make a point.— Vince Gilligan[1]

*Gus was amazing. Tio was brilliant (ding!). The Cousins, Tuco, Krazy 8, even Don Eladio in his two-episode appearance—all memorable, ruthless villains for Walt and Jesse. But Todd (*Friday Night Lights*' Jesse Plemons) is more dangerous than any of them.—*Shirley Li[2]

How does villainy work in a show about the creation of a monster? Critics frequently compare Walt to the "villains" of the show, because if we agree that Walt is evil by Season 5, it is interesting to analyze how he measures up to the bad guys in *Breaking Bad*. Writer John Hanlon argues, "Over the course of the series, Walt hasn't just become a villain—he's become a reflection of every villain he's had to face on his five-season journey."[3] *Breaking Bad* has some of the most pernicious antagonists on television, each more evil than the last. We thought Tuco was bad until we meet the sophisticated calm of Gus. Gus's level of control and punishment was terrifying until the white supremacists enslave Jesse, and the creepy Howdy Doody face of Todd becomes the stuff of nightmares. In this chapter, I give the bad "guy" antagonists of *Breaking Bad* their due space.

Fans and critics have theorized that each time Walt kills one of his enemies, he takes on one (or more) of their characteristics. I am not interested in breaking down that argument here, as it has been debated ad nauseam online and, while interesting, I see a few holes in the logic. What I do think warrants more discussion is that as Walt picks off his enemies, the vacancies allow him to more fully realize his potential. Walt as a young man sold out on the billion-dollar company Gray Matter too early, and he has been kicking himself for that mistake every day since. In Episode 5.6 ("Buyout"), Walt reveals to Jesse, "I look [the company value] up every week . . . I sold my share, my potential, for $5,000. I sold my kids' birthright for a few month's rent." This statement in Season 5, now that Walt has allowed his flaws to consume him and we see the evil more clearly, puts his Season 1 self in sharper context. There is no way the drab, slightly flabby Walter from Episode 1 could have imagined, let alone articulated, his desire to build an empire; Season 5 Walt can and does.

As quickly as he rose to power in the timing of his fictional world (one year), for the viewers it took four years of fighting bad guys to work his way to the top of the corporate ladder (so to speak), when he becomes the kingpin at the start of Season 5. Vince Gilligan comments that perhaps viewers like the bad guys because they are good at their jobs, arguing, "What is it people like about Darth Vader? Is it that he's so evil, or that he's so good at his job? I think it might be the latter."[4] The confidence and competence of a cruel antagonist is certainly appealing, but maybe not just to viewers. Gilligan's remark perhaps also highlights how the bad guys give Walt something to strive for. With the initial cancer diagnosis, "Walt has always had a clear motivation—but what he wants at any given time is less a reflection of who he is than it is a reflection of who his enemies are."[5] Analyzing the men (and one woman) who challenge Walter White's claims to power throughout his journey helps us to understand and interpret Walt's tragic transformation.

Although many critics and fans consider Mike and Hank as antagonists, I focus on five bad "guys" who were out to get Walt within a business context. Hank is an enemy based on ideas of justice and the law, but he is undisputedly a good guy. And even though Mike attempts and/or threatens to kill Walt on multiple occasions, he never embodies the evil that the other antagonists do throughout the series. If anything, I would say Walt was Mike's bad guy by Season 5. In a stronger case against analyzing Mike or Hank as antagonists, these two men's deaths were perhaps the hardest moments to watch in a series of heartbreakers. I am still not over Hank's death at the unworthy hands of the repulsive Uncle Jack, and Mike's death is a classic live by the sword, die by the sword moment, but I so wanted him to have a chance to run. In this chapter, I analyze five people whose deaths did not bother me (or most fans) in the slightest: Tuco Salamanca, the Cousins, Gustavo Fring, Lydia Rodarte-Quayle, and Todd Alquist. An exploration of these five characters helps to articulate how antagonism functions in a show centered on the protagonist becoming bad.

TUCO SALAMANCA

Bustle ranked the characters of *Breaking Bad* from least to most evil, and Tuco Salamanca finished at number two just behind Todd's uncle Jack.[6] Tuco placing second in a contest of the supreme evilness of the worst people in the five seasons of the series initially seems like a decision geared toward sparking conversation (or rage!) among fans of the series; however, Tuco *was* terrifying, because he was especially unpredictable and unreasonable.

Tuco initially represents how out of his depth Walt is in the drug world, as Jesse tries to explain how the hierarchy of buying and selling works. In the beginning of Episode 1.6 ("Crazy Handful of Nothin'"), Walt tells Jesse he wants to remain in the background as the chemist: "Out there on the street, you deal with that. As far as our customers go, I don't want to know anything about them. I don't want to see them, I don't want to hear from them—I want no interaction with them whatsoever." When Jesse sells the meth "one teenth at a time" and brings back only $1,300, Walt tells him that his lack of motivation is keeping them from making big money. He wants to know how they can sell by the pound. In comes the first mention of drug distributor Tuco. Jesse is reluctant to reach out, telling Walt "This guy is OG. . . . Look, he's upper level, man. He's not going to do business with some dude he doesn't know." Walt tells Jesse to grow a pair, and Jesse finds Skinny Pete to vouch for him with Tuco. He nervously walks into Tuco's cage (literally when he gets locked in via the pat-down waiting room). Our first image of Tuco Salamanca shows him picking his grilled teeth with a knife, the size of which Crocodile Dundee would be impressed. It is immediately clear he does not feel the warm and fuzzies for Skinny Pete. He tries the meth and screams, bursting from his chair with pleasure, and demands to know how Jesse got the "glass." His wild-eyed, frantic behavior is unnerving, and his intensity foreboding. They make a deal, but when Jesse demands the money up front, Tuco says no and then beats him violently as Jesse coughs up blood on the floor. Tuco screams over Jesse's writhing body, "Nobody moves crystal in the south valley but me, bitch."

When Walt finds out what happened to Jesse, he knows he has to challenge crazy with crazy. He not only wants the money, but it appears he also wants to make amends to Jesse. It is fitting that the first time Walt uses his alias of Heisenberg is when he introduces himself to Tuco. Werner Heisenberg is the father of the uncertainty principle, and nobody so far in the series has been more unpredictable or as volatile as Tuco. Case in point, when Walt demands $35,000 for the stolen drugs, and another $15,000 for Jesse's pain and suffering, Tuco nods as he puts out a lit cigarette on his tongue. Tuco's habit of laughing and then stopping short is frightening; there is no joy in that man's eyes. Walt (as Heisenberg) sets off an explosion in Tuco's office. A disoriented Tuco recognizes Walt's intensity and tells him, "You got balls. I'll give you that." Tuco seems impressed with Walt's level of crazy, and gives him the money.

After blowing up Tuco's office, Walt hightails it to his car and checks the money, looking at it greedily. He quietly screams in his car, shocked by what just happened, and thrilled with his success. Until Walt sees what Tuco is capable of, as he looks down on an unconscious Jesse lying in his hospital bed, he does not understand who he has to become in order to work in this world. However, at this point, the two men could not be more different. The unpredictability of Tuco's moods (to be fair, he is taking hits of meth as part of his job, so that is going to lead to instability) is no clearer than when he beats No-Doze in the junkyard (Episode 1.7, "A No-Rough-Stuff-Type Deal"). No-Doze made the mistake of telling Walt and Jesse to "just remember who you are working for," which Tuco takes as an indication that he is not powerful enough for Walt and Jesse to be scared of him without the reminder. Prior to this scene, Walt gets a little cocky with Jesse about his ability to handle Tuco. When Jesse is incredulous that Walt got the money, Walt does not inform Jesse of what he had to do to get Tuco to pay attention. Tuco beating his own associate to death is a slap in the face for Walt about the realities of why Jesse warns him off from working with Tuco, the "insane ass-clown dead-eyed killer."

As a direct antagonist, Tuco's time was cut short, only making it into four episodes of the series. This was not the original intention of the writers, according to Peter Gould, who states, "We thought that the character of Tuco was going to play all through season two, that he was going to be this enormously important opponent for Walt and Jesse."[7] Scheduling conflicts with actor Raymond Cruz required Tuco to meet his demise earlier than planned. Within the context of the storyline, "As soon as Tuco was gone, Walt craved the power created by the vacuum once occupied by his deceased enemy."[8] Walt and Jesse decide they will become their own distributors, moving up a rung on the drug world ladder. Unfortunately for Walt, Tuco's family connection goes deeper than he could have imagined.

THE COUSINS

When Tuco kidnaps Walt and Jesse, he explains his plan to Walt (Episode 2.2, "Grilled"). He is waiting for his cousins to meet them and then they are going to take Walt to Mexico so he can make the blue meth "24/7." Walt protests that he has a family, and Tuco makes it clear Walter does not have a choice in the matter. After Hank kills Tuco, Tio Hector Salamanca knows who is really to blame, and the family loyalties run deep. At the beginning of Season 3, the Cousins (Marco and Leonel Salamanca, played by Luis and Daniel Moncada, respectively) strike out to avenge Tuco's death, becoming an ignorant Walt's primary enemies. The Cousins offer an unnerving calm after the frenetic energy of Tuco. They do not speak until Episode 3.6 ("Sunset") and Luis Moncada, who plays Marco Salamanca, says remaining silent for five episodes made him nervous about finally using his voice, noting, "I hope my voice matches this badass killer."[9] Quiet becomes terrifying, and silence is a primary villainous trait used frequently throughout the series. A calm quietness is unsettling to the bad guys' underlings and victims alike. From Tio Hector and the Cousins, to Gustavo Fring, *Breaking Bad* does a particularly good job with scenes that have limited or no dialogue.

Technically, Hector was more of an antagonist in his pre-wheelchair life, but because he is the central patriarchal figure for both Tuco and the Cousins, I have to note how powerful his facial expressions are in conveying evil. Mark Margolis, who was nominated for an Emmy for his primarily silent role as Tio Hector, comments, "Acting is doing. In life, there are many things we do without speaking."[10] I chose not to give Tio Hector his own section because in relation to Walt, his antagonism is far more peripheral to the story. We find out Tio Hector conditioned the twins in their vengeance as young boys with cruel lessons about valuing family above all else (Episode 3.7, "One Minute"). He warns his beloved nephew Tuco of Walt and Jesse's plan to poison him, and he is the one who gives the Cousins Walt's name; however, in Season 4, we come to realize that Hector is Gustavo Fring's antagonist more than Walt's.

In chapter 7, I detailed the moment Walt first comes closest to his death, when the Cousins wait with an ax on his bed while he takes a shower (Episode 3.2, "Caballo Sin Nombre"). It is Gustavo Fring (via Mike) who saves Walt's life in this moment, and proceeds to hold the Cousins off as long as he can. As they wait impatiently for approval to kill Walt, we learn a great deal about their methods of murder, which consequently reveals the Mexican drug cartel's depths of depravity. They are the hit men who take out Tortuga (Danny Trejo), a cartel member turned DEA informant who loses his head with a machete (Episode 3.3, "I.F.T."). They torch a truck full of immigrants they gunned down seemingly because one young man recognized the sign of the cartel via their skull-capped boots (Episode 3.1, "No Más"). The Cousins are terrifying. Gus calls them "animals" in Episode 3.4 ("Green Light") and based on what the viewers have seen, this seems a fitting descriptor; they do not flinch at the level of horror they inflict on others. They are scary antagonists for Walt, who is primarily ignorant to their existence, but they also represent a bigger symbol of the world he has joined. In addition to setting up the appeal of sociopath Todd Alquist for Walt later in the series (another animal who reacts on instinct), more immediate to the Season 3 storyline, the Cousins give us a glimpse of what the next rung of the ladder brings for Walt.

GUSTAVO FRING

Gustavo Fring is the most complex member of the bad antagonists squad, with deep connections and a history with the Mexican drug cartel that goes back more than twenty years. He is the antagonist we spend the most time getting to know in the series as his character enters at the end of

Gustavo Fring. *AMC/Photofest © AMC*

Season 2 and meets his demise at the end of Season 4. When Walt kills
Gus, critics wondered who the new bad guy would be: "After going out
with a literal bang last season, *Bad* faced the challenge of finding a

worthy villain to replace the placid terror that was Esposito's buttoned-up Gus."[11] Gus made a formidable opponent for Walt, and because the writers did not know if they would have a fifth season to write, he was always the potential end to Heisenberg. What makes Gus the most complex antagonist in the series is the combination of his professionalism, unnerving ruthlessness, and sympathetic backstory.

Professionalism

Saul Goodman initiates the first connection between Gus and Walt in Episode 2.11 ("Mandala") when he suggests Walt and Jesse need someone to help them with their business. Saul tells Walt that Gus "sounds a little like you," meaning he is "cautious and low-profile." However, unlike Walt, Gus knows how to successfully run a drug empire. He initially refuses to work with Walt, citing Jesse as the problem: "I don't think we are alike at all, Mr. White . . . you have poor judgment. . . . You can never trust a drug addict." Walt's connection to Jesse makes him look unprofessional and inept in Gus's eyes. Walt gets the picture when Jesse's high causes him to miss the birth of Holly; however, then Hank beats Jesse to a pulp, and Jesse threatens to turn Walt in as soon as he gets busted (Episode 3.7, "One Minute"). Walt then has to convince Gus he needs Jesse, who shows up to the lab as Walt tells Gale Boetticher he has to leave (Episode 3.8, "I See You"). A baffled Gale wants to know why, and Walt fumbles through lame excuses like they just have "different rhythms." As if to punctuate Walt's lies, Jesse shows none of the respect Gale does toward Walt when he loudly asks, "What's up? Partner." He then walks around the lab uttering orgasmic-like shouts of happiness, exclaiming, "We should have ditched that RV months ago. It's all like shiny up in here." The intelligent, diligent, science-loving Gale stands open mouthed watching his replacement. The message is clear about Walt: he lacks the ability to vet his associates like Gus does, especially when it comes to Walt's unlikely loyalty (or obligations might be a better word depending on the season) to Jesse.

There are a number of visual cues where Gus's professionalism is immediately put into sharp contrast with the instinctive and ruthless behavior of other members in the drug world. In Episode 3.3 ("I.F.T."), Gus calls a meeting with Juan Bolsa, to whom the Cousins report in the cartel hierarchy. Gus sets up the room and pulls the plastic off a minitray of fresh veggies. He repeats this gesture for the next cartel meeting in Episode 4.7 ("Problem Dog") as well. This courtesy is about showing respect, with small gestures that separate him from the hotheaded animals he despises. Gus is the epitome of politeness with Juan Bolsa, as well as with Tio Hector and the Cousins, as he indicates the attempted murder of Walter encroaches on his territory, and he therefore should have a right to bless the execution. After the cartel members leave, we can tell by Gus's face that he did not respect any of the men in that room, but the ceremonial acts and language are important. When Walt informs Gus that Jesse plans to kill his men in retribution for using Tomás to kill Combo, Gus again sets a meeting (Episode 3.12, "Half Measures"). He requires the street thugs and Jesse to shake hands before leaving the room, attempting to symbolize an ironclad deal among criminals. One reason for his obsession with professionalism is the tight hold he has on the façade he presents to the rest of the community.

Giancarlo Esposito comments that he was able to identify who his character was based on one note from Gilligan in the script: "He wrote on the stage direction, 'hiding in plain sight,' and I just went, 'Wow. How many people in our world hide in plain sight that we know, but they're not really who we think they are?'"[12] With his understated suits and 1998 Volvo V70, Gus is the unsuspecting millionaire next door. As a business owner and a contributing sponsor to various legal events in the Albuquerque area, Gustavo Fring embodies the image of an active community member. After his death, this is perhaps the hardest pill for Hank's boss ASAC George Merkert to swallow, when he tells Hank in disbelief that he had Gus over to his home for barbecue and still makes "the foil packet" for his fish like Gus taught him to do. The shock felt by Merkert to find out that Gus was "hiding in plain sight" provides a glimpse of how Hank might feel when he finds out his own brother-in-law is the Heisenberg he has been tracking for more than a year. An article in the *New Yorker* highlights Gus's depiction as particularly accurate, noting, "Flashy drug dealers in the Scarface mode make for enjoyable movie villains, but in real life they don't tend to last long in the business. Quiet businessmen like Gus, on the other hand, often thrive."[13] As a cultural commentary, the contrast between the ruthless Gus that we come to know throughout two seasons, and the polite fast-food manager that the rest of the fictional *Breaking Bad* world knows, suggests that the face of drugs in America may not be what it seems.

Unnerving Ruthlessness

Although Gus runs his illegal operation like a professional business, he is not afraid to get dirty, and when he does, he is ruthless. The scene when he kills Victor with a box cutter is a turning point for most audience members in terms of seeing Gus as an evil man, instead of just a bad guy (Episode 4.1, "Box Cutter"). The horror on Walt's, Jesse's, and even Mike's face when Gus slices Victor's throat mirrors that of many viewers'. Vince Gilligan has commented that he had to look away in the editing room for that scene. Esposito says he was "absolutely shaken" when he first read the box cutter scene. He says he "had to find a way into the scene, and realized that 'Gus has a family to take care of. This is how a man provides—if you have to do something, do it with no remorse and no looking back.'"[14] The shocking part is not that Gus kills someone. We know he wants Walt dead, and Jesse dead, and it is only a matter of time before we actually see him murder someone personally. No, it is not even the fact that the killing was abrupt and a painful way to die, but the fact that it is Victor he kills.

He needs to send Walt and Jesse a message. It is terrifyingly methodical and seemingly comes out of nowhere. When he walks into the lab, Gus proceeds to carefully take off his suit coat and tie and meticulously covers up in the work suit. The whole painstaking time, Walt desperately tries to save his and Jesse's life. As we watch Walt schizophrenically switch verbal tacks as he tries to convince Gus to keep them alive, we wonder: Is Gus really going to kill one of them? How will they get out of this dungeon with Mike standing right behind them? Is Gus just trying to scare them? It is the complete lack of emotion as a confused Victor bleeds out, with Gus staring at Walt the whole time, that is chilling. Victor had no warning, and clearly no fear that he was Gus's target. The lack of emotion makes Gustavo more terrifying than Tuco, but they share the same trait where they are willing to kill their associates/underlings for perceived insubordination. Esposito reflects on this quality of Gus, and how he had to convey a cold demeanor as power:

> I just drop myself to the point where I become devoid of feeling. The moments when Gus is really demonstratively powerful and frightening is when his eyes go dead. I use my breathing to just take me down to a level where I'm hearing what you just said, but what you're saying is

not pleasing to me. You're not giving me the answer I want. And I'm going to look at you with dead cold killer eyes until you do. [15]

Gus knows Victor was seen at Gale's apartment (Mike confirms this with Victor earlier in the episode), but it was also about Victor stepping out of line. Walt reflects on this interpretation in Episode 5.3 ("Hazard Pay") when Mike informs Walt that they will be paying off Gus's men even though he is no longer around. Walt watches Mike walk away from the garage and says to Jesse that maybe Gus killed Victor because he overstepped his bounds and "took liberties he shouldn't have." Vince Gilligan says it was important that Gus not take pleasure in killing, but that he does it only when he has to "make a point." [16] The fact that Gus's provocation for murder is practical, leaving emotions at the door, is as terrifying as Tuco being entirely subject to the whims of his emotions and moods. When the antagonists kill members of their own crew with seemingly no provocation (Tuco and No-Doze) or no warning (Gus and Victor), it means nobody is safe.

Sympathetic Backstory: Vengeance

The most disturbing aspect to Gustavo is that there are moments when it is hard not to root for him. The pool scene in Episode 4.10 ("Salud") and the aftermath in Episode 4.11 ("Crawl Space") is a prime example of this dissonance. Gus, with his customary formality and professionalism, brings a hospitality gift when he meets with Don Eladio, who forces him to give up part of his business. Gus does not want this alliance for a variety of reasons, one of which is he has to share control of his business and profits, and two, as we know from Episode 4.8 ("Hermanos"), twenty years prior, Don Eladio murdered Gus's dear friend and partner Max. The relationship between Gustavo and Max is intentionally vague with Tio Hector's comment that Gus and Max like what they see as he pees in the pool immediately followed by kissing noises, the major hint that the two are romantically involved. Vince Gilligan says the relationship is "open to interpretation," [17] but regardless, there is no ambiguity about the fact that Max meant a great deal to Gus. Watching Gus forced to see his friend bleed into the pool after his death was painful. It is the first time we see a burst of emotion from Gustavo, as he sobs for his lost partner. Gus uses the alliance to exact his revenge on Don Eladio for the murder of somebody he cared for deeply (Episode 4.10, "Salud"). He is willing to poison himself and possibly die to seek his retribution. It is hard not to appreciate his confidence and foresight. When we find out he also prepared to save both Mike and Jesse should things go wrong, it makes Gus slightly endearing. I root for Gus to succeed in this moment. As Gilligan hopes, Gus is not redeemed as a good man, but this move suggests he is not entirely bad, either.[18] Esposito says, "If you feel sympathy for Gus and understand who he is, then I have done my job."[19]

When Gus poisons the members of Don Eladio's inner circle at the pool, it is for love of family, whether that comes in the form of a dear friend or a lover. This is a goal that Walt claims to understand. This fuller picture of Gustavo Fring comes late in his character's life. Is his story at the end conveyed with the intention of getting us to sympathize with him just as he wants Walt dead the most, or to make us realize that all he does is for love as well, which can be interpreted as understanding the consequences to motives that are similar to Walt's? Regardless of intention, the pool scene foreshadows how far Walt will have to go in the finale of the series to seek his own retribution.

LYDIA RODARTE-QUAYLE

After Gus's death, the viewers become privy to the complex system needed to run a drug empire. We learn that Gus built an intricate network to keep his business running smoothly and this is again important information to help the viewers acknowledge how far Walt has come in one year of his life. It is also crucial to revealing how underprepared Walt is to run his own empire. Mike tells Walt that Gus spent years building his distribution channels and making the necessary cautious connections. In Episode 5.3 ("Hazard Pay"), Mike says, "Walter, just because you shot Jesse James, don't make you Jesse James." In this moment, Mike wants Walt to bear the weight of responsibility the one on top has for those beneath him. He tries to teach Walt that he has to look out for the people who help the network run smoothly on the ground level. Up to this point, Walt's instinct to solve problems is to kill, not unlike his soon-to-be associate Lydia Rodarte-Quayle.

When we meet Lydia in the beginning of Season 5, she is reminiscent of Walt from Season 4. Lydia stupidly puts out a thwarted hit on Mike

Lydia Rodarte-Quayle and her Stevia. *AMC/Photofest © AMC*

when he refuses to kill Gus's trusted inside men (Episode 5.2, "Madrigal"). Her desperate reaction is similar to Walt's response after watching Gus kill Victor with a box cutter. In Episode 4.2 ("Thirty-Eight Snub"), Mike calls Walt who is walking toward Gus's door with his illegally purchased gun to tell him he is watching him. Mike says, "Go home, Walter." Lydia's anxiety and neuroticism are palpable. Laura Fraser calls her character a "clean-cut, bonkers sociopath,"[20] but she is also intelligent and astute, keeping herself alive with Walt by reading him like a book. In Episode 5.8 ("Gliding over All"), Lydia reasons out the situation and finds herself a loose end in Walt's world. She talks her way out of being killed by recognizing Walt's greed for both money and power. She tells him to use her to expand into a global empire and says he will double his current profits. Lydia suggests the Czech Republic, where his product will succeed because buyers there have never seen his level of quality. In this one move she appeals to his vanity by acknowledging the superiority of his Classic Coke meth, and also his desire to make a fortune. Lydia then moves in to stroke his ego further when she envisions him as an empire builder; she says she pitched it to Fring and he said yes. She knows what drives Walt, and he agrees to the relationship. When she walks away from the table, we see that Walt was hiding the ricin vial under this hat and that she was correct, he had planned to tie up her loose end. When Walt retires from the meth business, Lydia continues to work with the neo-Nazis, and in the finale episode, she orders Todd to kill Walt (Episode 5.16, "Felina"). Lydia serves as a reminder that the position at the top of the power structure is tenuous at best, with those desperate to stay alive always willing to take full measures.

Outside of the series, Season 5 can be read as a challenge to the easy idea that drugs are a problem in the United States directly because of our southern neighbors. The personification of Madrigal, largely via the face of Lydia (sorry, Herr Schuler—you didn't make it past the opening credits of Episode 5.2, "Madrigal"), reminds the viewers that drugs are not only hustled via the seedy underbelly of illegal immigration and drug cartels, but also in the squeaky-clean halls of large corporations. Her ultrafeminine appearance also makes her stand out in the Boys Only Club of *Breaking Bad* and highlights how common it has become to assume men run the show when it comes to drugs. When Jesse tries to convince Mike not to kill Lydia (Episode 5.4, "Fifty-One"), Mike tells Jesse, "Now you are being sexist. Trust me. This woman deserves to die more than any man I've ever met." Her brand of badness is wrapped up in a beautiful package, and the portrayal of white-collar wealth and status was purposeful. In Episode 5.10 ("Buried"), Lydia hires the white supremacists to kill Declan's group and she shows up in Louboutin heels, which cost upwards of $600 a pair. Laura Fraser discusses the importance of that little detail, arguing:

> [The Louboutin heels] were real, and we were playing them for real, because it's part of the morally-bankrupt measure of Lydia. She's unable to bear the sight of this massacre she ordered—the shoes are the bloodshed red she's responsible for. It's representative of faceless corporations where no one's ever accountable for any of their actions.[21]

When Todd's group shows up at Declan's site, Lydia cowers at the sound of the bullets ringing out overhead. Todd tells her it is safe to come up, and she looks up at him from the bunker and says, "I don't want to see." Todd tells her to close her eyes as he leads her through the carnage. To her, this is business. Prior to the execution, she informs Declan and his chemist that her Czech Republic buyer has higher standards than the 68 percent purity he's producing. She wants him to use Todd, whose first two cooks were at 74 percent. Declan declines and Lydia mutters, "I really wish you would give him a chance," just as the men above the bunker tell them there is a problem. For Lydia, her decision to order a murder is about business, and the fact that she cannot stomach the visual consequences of her actions symbolizes the lack of human connection between the corporation and the workers.

TODD ALQUIST

The contrast between Lydia's suit-and-heels-wearing corporate involve-ment is starkly contrasted with her connection to Todd Alquist, Uncle Jack, and his white supremacist group, who are "the tattooed monsters you might have expected to lord over a meth empire in a less complicated show than *Breaking Bad*; people whose capacity for blank brutality makes them awful even before you see their Swastika tattoos."[22] I primar-ily focus on Todd, because he is the first face we meet and the most complex member of the group, simply because he is unassumingly scary. If I saw Uncle Jack at the grocery store, I would not be surprised to find out he had murdered people, but the depths of the boyish Todd's deprav-ity scarred my soul.

If Gale Boetticher was Walt's perfect lab assistant, then Todd Alquist is Heisenberg's. Todd does not question Walt's decisions, he shows re-spect for authority, and best of all, he does exactly what needs to be done without regret. The train heist episode (Episode 5.5, "Dead Freight") is the best demonstration of these qualities. As they are planning the heist, digging the hole for the container of methylamine, Todd asks how it is going to work, and Walt turns it over to Jesse. Jesse smiles, a little placating with the dumb Todd, as he explains the plan. The writers em-phasize the ignorance of Todd to harken back to Jesse in the beginning of the series. Todd shows Jesse and Walt nothing but admiration, ingratiat-ing himself to them with compliments on their genius. Todd eventually becomes Walt's new Jesse, but one who does not have the same con-straints of kindness, or a conscience of any kind. During the heist, Todd does an excellent job, pulling off his end of the plan and jumping from the train at the last minute. It runs like clockwork, until Drew Sharp shows up on his dirt bike and we see who Todd really is as a person. *Entertainment Weekly* writer Shirley Li argues:

> Todd is the worst of all the villains, [because he's] not a calculating villain. He's reckless and unreasonable, and that makes him do unexpected, terrifying things. Did he think twice before shooting Drew Sharp? Did he consider the moral ramifications of sending his uncle's gang to coordinate the murder of 10 prisoners? Does he know what "consequence" means?[23]

The most chilling and early example of this is when Todd, Mike, and Walt take care of dismantling and disposing of Drew Sharp's dirt bike (Episode 5.6, "Buyout"). Both Walt and Mike look sad and resigned, as they see Drew's small hand poking out of the mound of dirt in the back of the truck. They approach the situation methodically, handling the cleanup before punishing Todd. A furious Jesse cannot even bring himself to be in the garage as the "fix" is under way, and an oblivious Todd writes off the incident as "Shit happens, eh?" Jesse punches him hard, for himself and for all the viewers.

I have never met any fan of *Breaking Bad* who is sympathetic toward Todd, and I think that is why there were so many viewers still on Walt's side at the end. Compared to Todd's creepy sociopath tendencies, Walt at least has a purpose to his madness (almost always). Critic Michael Jensen contends that "part of the joy in watching this show is that almost everyone is morally compromised, especially the show's two main characters—Walt and Jesse—and yet you end up caring deeply about them";[24] however, Jensen wrote this comment prior to meeting Todd and his white supremacist family. The white supremacists were the necessary bad guys to end Walt's tragic tale, because "what brought . . . Walt down was not the hubris . . . it's the elemental, unpredictable forces of violence and nature that can best even the most calculated, powerful of men. The neo-Nazis are not foes nearly on the level of Walt in terms of cunning and forward thinking, but they prove better than anything else on *Breaking Bad* how inadequate his power truly is."[25] The fact that the bad guys at the end of Season 5 were unlikable, morally repugnant animals provides one reason why so many fans remained Team Walt until the end.

Todd has no redeeming qualities. He is like John Steinbeck's Lenny from *Of Mice and Men*, but worse because he intends to kill. Li describes him as "cold, calm, disturbing Todd, polite to the point of creepy, incapable of reason, fully capable of killing."[26] Todd *is* polite. He tells Walt, "I'm sorry for your loss," as he releases him from his handcuffs after Uncle Jack shoots Hank (Episode 5.14, "Ozymandias"). He calls Skyler "ma'am," as he threatens to murder baby Holly if Skyler says anything about Lydia to the DEA (Episode 5.15, "Granite State"). When he visits Andrea, he is polite as he tells her it is "nice to meet you." He then tells her, "Just so you know, this isn't personal," right before he caps Andrea in the back of the head (Episode 5.15, "Granite State"). And it is not personal—for Todd. The politeness is jarring in juxtaposition with his quick trigger finger and complete lack of remorse for taking another person's life. When the neo-Nazis sit around watching Jesse's taped confession (Episode 5.15, "Granite State"), Todd swells with pride when he is revealed as the killer of Drew Sharp. Unlike Walt, Todd does not have to justify or rationalize his actions. He does what has to be done. In Episode 5.6 ("Buyout") when he explains why he killed Drew, he says, "It's not like I wanted to," but "I saw a threat and I took care of it." The writers smartly give Todd some layers beyond a killing machine. For example, Todd takes the jarred tarantula from Drew's jacket home with him after the cleanup. It could be seen as a trophy from his victim, but the way he gazes at it in his car seems to indicate that he himself is just a boy, fascinated with the same things that intrigued young Drew. And not everybody thinks Lydia is intolerably wound like a top; Todd falls in love with her. His unrequited schoolboy crush makes him seem young. While none of these are examples of endearing qualities, it does set up Todd as more complicated than a remorseless hit man. The terror with Todd is that he seems like a polite young man, and then we find out Buffalo Bill is just below the surface. Todd needs Jesse to cook the quality of meth Lydia requires to sell the product, so into the pit Jesse goes (*it puts the lotion on its skin or else it gets the hose again*).

WALT AND THE BAD ANTAGONISTS: NOT YOUR TYPICAL *HARDY BOYS* TALE

Walt does share some traits with some of the bad guys. Like Tuco, he reacts impulsively on his emotions. He is cruelest to Jesse when he is angry, calling him a junkie, telling him he will never be as good a cook, and insisting his hands are dirty with blood money. In Episode 5.9

("Blood Money"), Walt writes off his angry comments: "It was in the heat of the moment. I was trying to win an argument." This is probably the truest statement Walt has made to Jesse in over a year, but the deeper truth is that in anger, Walt wishes Jesse dead time and again. It is in anger that he calls Jesse and his girlfriend Jane "junkies," refusing to give Jesse his cut of the money from the initial deal with Gus (Episode 2.12, "Phoenix"). It is his anger that sends a terrified Jesse to Mexico with Gus without any help from Walt (Episode 4.9, "Bug"). And it is in anger that he turns Jesse over to Uncle Jack, condemning him as Todd's meth-making slave (Episode 5.14, "Ozymandias"). Like Gus, he can be meticulous; he is a scientist, after all. Walt's pro/con list in Episode 1.2 ("Cat's in the Bag . . .") is an example of this. He constantly asks Jesse to detail the steps in a plan, forcing him to think through the scenarios and plan ahead for contingencies. Like Lydia, he does not want to face the repercussions of his choices, attempting to put the past behind him and not think about it (or take responsibility for all the lives he has ruined). These traits are indicative of corruption and power, as a man becomes a monster, and a tragic figure encounters other people with wayward moral compasses. Pitting the protagonist against the bad guys, even as he became one of them, encourages fans to pick a side; and hey, at least Walt never enslaved anyone.

9

THE ANTI-WALTS OF *BREAKING BAD*

Jesse and Hank

It's a job he was doing before he even met Walt, and yet, in my mind, I sense that Jesse's version of meth dealing was a kinder, gentler version [laughs] that did not involve a high body count—or, in fact, a body count at all. He seemed happier when he was making peanuts. I think pretty much everyone roots for Jesse, more or less. He needs a hug. He's not cut out for this life.—Vince Gilligan[1]

Hank wants to be the guy to fight injustice. . . . And I think Vince does, too. That's part of Vince's character. That there's some sort of, you know, karmic justice in the world.—Dean Norris[2]

Fans of *Breaking Bad* are either rooting for Walt, Jesse, or Hank. They are like Chuck Klosterman's Luke Skywalker, Han Solo, Darth Vader identities:[3] each represents a specific philosophy about life, an ideology to live by. The men's goals are frequently in competition with one another, so making a choice means having an understanding that the other two cannot possibly succeed. In the first chapter of this book, I made an argument that *Breaking Bad* is not a show about an antihero, but instead about a tragic figure whose flaws are his downfall. I cannot conclude without exploring the roles that the two other most prominent male figures in the series have in Walt's tragic journey of despair. If Walt is the tragic figure in this narrative, then Jesse and Hank are the anti-Walts in the story and each fulfills a unique role. For all intents and purposes,

Jesse initially acts as Walt's moral compass in the world of corruption and depravity, a guiding tool Walt frequently ignores as he goes off trail. Jesse then becomes Walt's opposite, two repelling ends of a magnet, and he helps us see Walt's flaws more clearly. Hank is the sheriff to Walt's cowboy (later bandit), wearing the white hat and making us like him in spite of his machismo and underlying racism. As the goals of these characters are rarely compatible, they are pitted against one another in the series, placing the audience in an intense game of tug-of-war.

JESSE PINKMAN: NOT *BAD* ENOUGH

One of the most repeated urban legends of *Breaking Bad* is that Jesse was supposed to die in the first season, and Walt would then avenge his death. Vince Gilligan corrects this rumor, saying that it was one of many possibilities, but as soon as they saw Aaron Paul in action they knew Jesse Pinkman was here to stay.[4] It is hard to imagine the show without him. Gilligan comments, "When you first meet Jesse, in that pilot episode, he's really kind of a prick . . . but I wrote that before I met the actor. And Aaron Paul is so sweet and kind in real life that those qualities rubbed off on the writing and therefore on Jesse. I mean, he'd still say 'Yo, bitch' and smoke a lot of pot and be kind of annoying, but we realized he had heart."[5]

Jesse begins the series as Walt's opposite in the criminal world: he has (some) street smarts, where Walt has book smarts; he has connections and history in the drug world, where Walt is (initially) inept in the seedy underbelly; Walt says the cook is about science, and Jesse tells him it is about art (Episode 1.1, "Pilot"). The men are contrasted in almost every conceivable way, but also connected: "However you viewed Walter White (Bryan Cranston) and Jesse Pinkman (Aaron Paul) . . . the two men will forever be linked as the blackened heart and corroded soul" of the series.[6] With the flip of a coin (Episode 1.2, "Cat's in the Bag . . ."), Jesse also becomes Walt's moral opposite within a criminal world.

Because Walt is the one who lost the coin toss, the murder of Krazy-8 keeps Jesse and Walt on opposite ends of the moral spectrum from the beginning, even as drug partners. Jesse did not help with the murders of either Emilio or Krazy-8. His brilliant plan when Emilio and Krazy-8 bring out their guns at the cook site in the middle of the secluded desert is to yell, "Run, Mr. White! Run!" only to trip on his baggy pants and knock himself out on a rock. He was not even capable of handling the disposal of Emilio's body by himself, when he ignored Walt's list and tried to use his bathtub instead of the necessary plastic container. The depiction of Walt, post-Emilio's murder and pre-Krazy-8's, shows a man grappling with ideas of right and wrong, but he is the one who follows through with the plan, chinking his moral armor forever after (Episode 1.3, ". . . And the Bag's in the River").

Early in their partnership, Jesse smartly tries to convince Walt to take a slower foray into the unpredictable world of drugs. After watching Tuco beat No-Doze with seemingly no provocation, Jesse and Walt are visibly shaken, breathing heavily as they collapse in Jesse's car; however, Jesse is the only one of the pair who starts thinking they need to back out (Episode 2.1, "Seven Thirty-Seven"). Walt begins to do the math, estimating how much money he will need to leave his family, and how much longer that means he will need to work with Tuco. He estimates only eleven more deals "in a public place from now on." Jesse looks incredulous. As far as he is concerned, they need to stop working with Tuco altogether. Later, when an undercover police officer busts Badger in Episode 2.8 ("Better Call Saul"), Saul suggests it would be cheaper to let Badger take a deal with the DEA and get killed in prison. Walt seems to consider it for a moment, but Jesse will not allow his friend to die, and Walt (slightly chagrined by his instinct) agrees. It is expensive having a conscience, as it costs the men $80,000 to hire someone to take the fall as Heisenberg, and keep Badger alive and out of jail.

In Episode 2.11 ("Mandala"), Walt tells Jesse they need to expand the territory, and a rival group kills Combo, one of Jesse's crew members and friends. When a distraught Jesse tells Walt about the murder, Walt asks, "Which one was he?" and Jesse hangs up on him. Walt treats Combo's death as part of the business plan, but Jesse feels the moral responsibility weigh heavily on him. Walt seems more concerned with the resulting lack of distribution (and consequently, money) if everybody is too afraid to sell. Jesse continually tries to keep people alive, telling both Mike and Walt that Lydia should live (Episode 5.4, "Fifty-One" and Episode 5.5, "Dead Freight"). In Episode 5.3 ("Hazard Pay"), when Mike says they owe Gus's former men hazard pay, Jesse is willing to let Mike take it all from his stash, whereas Walt pushes back against Mike. Jesse lives by a moral code in the world of crime, and Walt lives by a business model.

Although the two men are contrasted in a number of ways, there are three key characteristics that highlight their differences throughout the series. One, Jesse is not dumb, but he says and does dumb things . . . until he doesn't. Our first vision of Jesse is watching him fall half-naked out the window of a bedroom next to the drug raid, where he was busy having sex with the neighbor (Episode 1.1, "Pilot"). Later in the same episode, when checking out the cook site, Jesse informs Walt that the coast is clear because all he can see in the distance is a "cow house." When Walt questions his use of the phrase "cow house," Jesse responds, "Yeah. Where they live. The cows." He is not being ironic. The contrast between the buttoned-up intellectual Walt (who knows the term "barn") and the stoner Jesse is not just entertaining but also a necessary emphasis for Walt's tragic flaw of ego.

In Episode 2.9 ("4 Days Out"), Walt convinces Jesse they need to use up "expiring" methylamine because Walt fears he is going to die sooner rather than later. Their cook starts with a bickering Walt and Jesse, where first Walt will not let Jesse use his cell phone, then he complains about having too little water, and he finally lectures Jesse about finding a safe place for the keys, since it is their only set and they are "a million miles away from anyone." Jesse puts the keys in the ignition for safekeeping, which unwittingly causes him to drain the battery. Jesse is endearing but such a disaster in this episode that it is hard not to see him as a major screwup and sympathize with Walt's anger. Walt siphons out the gas for the backup generator, and then Jesse spills the gas, which lights the generator on fire. Walt runs to get the fire extinguisher, and Jesse, who thinks fast on his feet, uses the rest of their limited water supply to put it out instead. His lack of ability to think ahead spotlights Walt's resourcefulness by contrast.

Eventually, Jesse stops saying and doing the dumb things of a young stoner and becomes a capable man. In one of my favorite Jesse scenes, when he has to show the cartel how to cook in Mexico (Episode 4.10, "Salud"), the writers make us realize how far Jesse has come from that first cook in the desert. When Gus, Mike, and Jesse show up at the lab, the cartel's head chemist points to Jesse and asks if this is a joke. When the chemist says they will make their own phenylacetic acid, Jesse leans into Gus and says, "Look I get my phenylacetic acid from the barrel with the 'B' on it. That's how I know." The head chemist is appalled to be trained by someone like Jesse, who does not know enough chemistry to make phenylacetic acid. It does not help that Jesse is covered in cuts and bruises from his fistfight with Walt the night before (Episode 4.9, "Bug"). Jesse invokes the spirit of Mr. White when he turns and critiques the shoddy lab setup, saying, "Don't you have standards? This place is disgusting." Jesse uses Walt's words: "If he wants to learn how to make my product, he will have to do it my way. The right way." Reminiscent of Walt's command during the fly episode (Episode 3.10, "Fly"), Jesse announces to the heavily armed cartel, "We are going to clean up any possible source of contamination, and only then will we cook." Gus looks amused, and Jesse's 96 percent pure cook only further accentuates his growth from Season 1.

When Walt becomes a monster in Season 5, Jesse is the one who smartly offers solutions to two major problems. In Episode 5.1 ("Live Free or Die"), Walt realizes he forgot about the recordings from the cameras in the lab, which Mike informs them reside on Gus's laptop, now in police custody. As Mike and Walt engage in a pissing contest about how they will or will not be able to steal the computer, it is Jesse who astutely suggests they use a magnet to erase the information. Although not moral and certainly illegal, it does keep the guard of the evidence room safe from an explosion, which was Walt's solution to the problem. Again in the fifth season (Episode 5.5, "Dead Freight"), in an attempt to avoid killing the train engineers, Jesse cleverly suggests they rob the train without anybody knowing what they are doing. The decision by the writers to make it Jesse's idea serves the purpose of showing how far he has come from exclamations like "Yeah, science" in the first episode, to being able to mastermind a brilliant train heist.

The second key characteristic that distinguishes Walt's tragic downfall from Jesse's opportunity for redemption is that kids are Jesse's kryptonite. Episode 2.6 ("Peekaboo") makes me sob like a baby at the end, every single time I see it. The little boy living in a filthy drug den is a heartbreaking image on its own, but Jesse makes sure to get the kid out so he does not see the bloody remains of his father, and that is what gets me. He plays peekaboo with the little boy and tells him to "have a good rest of your life, kid," but we know that the little boy's future is bleak.

Jesse's downward spiral in part two of Season 5 begins with the murder of Drew Sharp, the little boy who may or may not have witnessed the great train heist of methylamine (Episode 5.5, "Dead Freight"). Jesse is livid with Todd for shooting the kid and wants out of the meth business as a direct result of Drew's death. It is debilitating for Jesse to know that the little boy's parents do not know what happened to their son. He asks Saul to figure out a way to gift over $2 million to the parents (Episode 5.9, "Blood Money"), to try to temper his guilt over the blood money sitting in his home. In Episode 5.11 ("Confessions"), Jesse realizes it was Walt who poisoned Brock after all, and he strikes out on a drug-fueled rampage intent on murder. When Hank stops him at the Whites' home in Episode 5.12 ("Rabid Dog"), Jesse screams, "He poisoned a little kid . . . he can't keep getting away with this!" Although Jesse is not comfortable with any more murders period, it is children getting hurt that Jesse cannot stomach.

Season 5 is not the first time Jesse demonstrates that kids are the line you do not cross with him when he finds out Gus's crew used Andrea's brother Tomás to kill Combo. In Episode 3.12 ("Half Measures"), Jesse is not afraid to stand up to Gus when he finds out he is using kids to sell his drugs, but Walt will not do the same. Jesse wants to kill the two men in Gus's crew for using a kid to kill Combo, but Walt initially stops him by ratting him out to Gus. Jesse's motive for murder is focused on morality and justice. Walt's intention is to keep Gus happy.

When the two men kill Tomás and Jesse decides to kill them anyway, he has to get high first. We will never know if he would have been able to follow through, as Walt interrupts Jesse's plans just as he pulls his gun to begin the shoot-out. Walt instead drives over the two men with his car and tells Jesse to "run!" Walt makes this decision because he knows that Gus will kill Jesse if the two men are shot, and he knows that Gus still needs him to cook. Walt's sole instinct in this situation is to keep Jesse alive, but by being the one to run over the two men with his car, he also keeps Jesse pure. The choice of the writers to then have Jesse commit his first murder in the next episode (Episode 3.13, "Full Measure") by shooting the peace-loving Gale Boetticher in the face is all the more jarring.

Jesse handles the emotional weight of Gale's murder differently than Walt handled the death of any of his victims. Even though Jesse now also has blood on his hands, he still represents a moral contrast to Walt. And this highlights the third major difference between Walt and Jesse. As Walt further amplifies his flaws by the perpetual justification and rationalization of his immoral decisions, we see the raw emotional effects of Jesse's enormous guilt. For example, after the murder of Gale, Jesse sits in shocked silence in the lab as Walt obliviously pontificates about how Victor is going to screw up the batch (Episode 4.1, "Box Cutter"). Walt seemingly has no idea how distraught Jesse is about what he did to Gale. A.V. Club writer Todd VanDerWerff argues, "From the moment Jesse killed Gale Boetticher in the season three finale, he suddenly became aware of the world he occupied, a place where good and bad exist and where he had cast his lot with a very evil man, yet seemed unable to break free of him."[7]

I argue this shift with Jesse's idea of Walt actually happens at the end of Season 4, when he originally suspects Walt of poisoning Brock (Episode 4.12, "End Times"). He knows exactly how it happened (he suspects Huell and Saul immediately), but he cannot bring himself to kill Walt, so he has to convince himself that Walt is telling him the truth. But VanDerWerff highlights an important shift for Jesse, because the way he deals with Gale's murder is revealing. Jesse surrounds himself with people, noise, and debauchery loud enough to let him stop reliving the moment. Episode 4.7 ("Problem Dog") is when we finally hear Jesse articulate what he has been dodging emotionally through drugs and noise, as he describes killing Gale. He calls Gale a "problem dog" because he is telling this story to a drug-support group. Jesse says, "This whole thing is about self-acceptance. . . . So, I should stop judging and accept what I do. . . . No matter how many dogs I kill, I just what, do an inventory and accept?" Jesse differs from Walt here because he refuses to rationalize his actions, or even call what he did a mistake or necessity. He is the "bad guy," but we want to see him allow himself to move on, and that is only because he cannot let himself.

Over time, Jesse becomes the character through which we see Walt more clearly. After getting clean at the Serenity rehab facility where Walt took Jesse after Jane died, Jesse comes home clean and gets closer to finding self-actualization. Walt, feeling guilty because he let Jane die, tells Jesse this situation "could be looked at as a wake-up call for both of us . . . get our lives back together . . . back on the straight and narrow" (Episode 3.1, "No Más"). Walt tells Jesse he is not responsible for everything that happened (meaning Jane's death and the plane crash), but he rationalizes his own involvement at the same time. Walt uses the phrase there are "many factors at play" multiple times in this episode, first with Skyler when she guesses he is a drug dealer (he says "angles"), and then here with Jesse. Walt continues, "I blame the government." Jesse looks at him and says, "You either run from things or you face them. . . . I accept who I am . . . the bad guy." Walt is not accepting responsibility, instead resorting to rationalization and justification for terrible decisions where people end up dead.

After the conclusion of the series, there was a panel at the Tribeca Film Festival devoted to understanding television's love of the psychopath. Bryan Cranston was on the panel as well as Terence Winter, creator of HBO's *Boardwalk Empire*. The other panel member was Dr. James H. Fallon, and he argued that Walter White possessed the checklist of psychopathic tendencies with his narcissism, ego, and deep rationalization and justification for his decisions, which equated to a lack of empathy.[8]

As Walt gets crueler in Season 5, Jesse's character reminds us how out of touch with humanity Walt has become. Particularly, we start to see Walt's lack of morality when it comes to taking responsibility for his actions. Gilligan argues that Jesse "doesn't belong in this business," and this is in part because Jesse acknowledges the effect their actions have taken on the lives of those around them.[9] Jesse refuses to accept killing people as collateral damage, something that Skyler astutely calls Walt out on as he tries to justify her actions with Ted (Episode 5.4, "Fifty-One"). Walt tells her, "Skyler, you can't beat yourself up . . . you did what you had to do to protect your family. It doesn't make you a bad person. It makes you a human being." Skyler tells Walt he is justifying his actions. She explains that justification does not make the outcome of hurting people any less horrifying.

Jesse is a more acceptable moral counterbalance to Walt than Skyler because he finds morality within the same world in which Walt exists. Jesse is a satisfying anti-Walt because he is also flawed, but he grows emotionally and intellectually as the series progresses. As Walt retreats deeper into the psychopathic world of justifications and rationalizations for his behavior, Jesse eventually finds more appropriate ways to handle his guilt and grief. At the end of the series some fans wanted to see Walt live; however, Jesse's ending is more satisfying because we can see a better life for him in the future. Cranston comments, "I like how it ends, because it's not like, 'Oh, he's got the money.' No. He's just got his life, so he has a chance—just a chance."[10] In a tale centered on a tragic figure, Jesse does not come out unscathed (he was kept as a slave and brutalized for months, after all); but he does get to live.

HANK SCHRADER: THE WHITE HAT

Compared to Jesse, Hank offers a more traditional foil for Walt, because he represents an antagonist on the opposite side with the law. It sets up a dynamic between Hank and Walt that is akin to a sheriff and an outlaw, except the outlaw is pretending to be the local general store owner. Vince Gilligan and his writers willingly draw connections between *Breaking Bad* and the western genre. He notes, "We take a lot of inspiration from the 'spaghetti westerns' of Sergio Leone." He continues, "*Once upon a Time in the West* is a particular favorite, and the first fifteen minutes of that movie is something that I have potential directors of the show watch before they start directing for us."[11] The final eight episodes of the series all occur after Hank realizes Heisenberg has been barbecuing in his own backyard this whole time. Dean Norris comments, "Because once that secret is out, it just [explodes] . . . really it's a Hank-Walt showdown now, because it's opened up. It's like boom, and that's what it starts with."[12] The scene after Walt warns Hank to "tread lightly," as Walt walks away from the garage and stands at his car, visually looks like a Wild West showdown (Episode 5.10, "Buried"). Walt and Hank stand facing each other, staring directly into each other's eyes. As soon as Hank hits the button to close the garage door, Walt races into his car to call Skyler and warn her that Hank knows. Hank shoots first, beating Walt to the punch, and convinces Skyler to meet with him before Walt can stop her. It sets up the Hank and Walt relationship after the big reveal as a classic western quarrel.

When I picture ASAC Hank Schrader as the sheriff of a town overrun with cowboys and outlaws smack in the middle of the Wild West, I put a very large white hat on his head. Not to symbolize how good he is, but rather, to accommodate his enormous ego. Early in the series his misogynist and racist comments are bitter pills to swallow, like when Hank uses a derogatory term like "beaner" with his Latino subordinate Steve Gomez. Midseries, when Hank is laid up in bed, miserably pining for his lost career (and the ability to move his legs), his treatment of Marie borders on emotional abuse. In Episode 5.12 ("Rabid Dog"), Hank's callous disregard for Jesse's life when Gomez suggests he might be in danger is infuriating. Yes, it is sometimes hard to like Hank, but the wonderful acting of Dean Norris, and his characterization as the crude sheriff in the

ASAC Hank Schrader: Episode 5.14, "Ozymandias." *AMC/Photofest © AMC*

Wild West of meth lets us oscillate in our feelings for him. According to Vince Gilligan:

> Hank was never going to be that important a character. . . . But as the shooting progressed and I got to know Dean Norris, I realized that this is a very interesting guy with a lot of emotional layers to him . . . so a lot of his substance rubbed off on Hank and changed the way I perceived the character. And therefore Hank is a much more rich and rounded character than he otherwise might have been.[13]

Hank can be obnoxious, but his sweetness with Marie, his relationship with Walt Jr., and his faithfulness to remaining honest to the law make him endearing overall. It is these positive qualities that also create a sharper contrast to Walt, making Hank an anti-Walt figure in the series.

In the premiere episode (Episode 1.1, "Pilot"), Hank's bravado commands the room at Walt's surprise birthday party, a setting where Walt himself tends to blend into his surroundings. Hank loves his job and is very good at it, whereas Walt loves chemistry but does not seem to connect with his students or enjoy being in the classroom. Jesse did not like his class, and we see evidence of that when Jesse finds an old test where Walt offered him the helpful advice "Apply Yourself!" (Episode 1.4, "Cancer Man"). Walt offers another failing student the same advice in Episode 2.7 ("Negro y Azul"). It is the vague catchphrase of a frustrated teacher. In contrast, Hank is depicted as loving his job and being particularly skilled at what he does. This gives him a confidence that Walt does not possess until he also finds a job he loves.

Walt claims that his choices are made entirely for his family (up until the final episode, "All for the family" is his mantra), but Hank's actions are much more clearly family focused. When Walt Jr. gets in trouble for trying to get an off-duty police officer to buy beer for him and his buddies (it is not fair—he can't run!), Hank reprimands him for calling him instead of Walt (Episode 1.5, "Gray Matter"). Hank asks him how he thinks his dad is going to feel about that decision. In a previous episode (Episode 1.3, ". . . And the Bag's in the River"), Marie convinces Hank to scare Walt Jr. straight when she thinks he is smoking pot. Hank reluctantly agrees, citing as his hesitation that Walt should be the one to talk to his son. In contrast, Walt uses Junior as a pawn in his terrible game of chess with those around him. This first happens when he gives Junior multiple shots of tequila in response to Hank telling him he should stop, which culminates with his son puking into their pool as Walt continues to drink, glaring at Hank (Episode 2.10, "Over"). The next morning, when a more sober Walt apologizes, Walt Jr. is pleased with himself for keeping up with Walt and Hank in number of drinks. His comment, so telling of an immature underage drinker, reinforces the realization that Walt has used his son to send a message to Hank, and the moment is heartbreaking.

Later, Walt encourages his son's anger with Skyler, when the teenager blames his mom for kicking Walt out of the house for "no reason" (Episode 3.3, "I.F.T."). Walt knows that Skyler does not want Walt Jr. to know about his father, so she just sits there and takes the abuse. One of the worst moments comes in Season 5 when Walt lies to Junior, telling him the cancer is back (Episodes 5.11, "Confessions"). His only goal here is to keep Walt Jr. from going over to Hank and Marie's house. Walt Jr.'s face in this scene, as he experiences the fear he has clearly held in since his dad went into remission, is debilitating for the viewer. We know Walt is only telling his son about the cancer to manipulate him into staying home, and he lets Walt Jr. feel that pain.

When it comes to family first, the strongest comparison between Hank and Walt is how they react when they get emergency phone calls. In Episode 2.11 ("Mandala"), Gustavo Fring agrees to buy Walt and Jesse's remaining thirty-eight pounds of meth. A frantic Walt only has one hour to get the product to a truck stop and he cannot get ahold of Jesse. While Jesse rides a heroin high with Jane, Walt leaves him furious messages: "I need the product. I need the product now!" Walt breaks through the back door to find an unresponsive Jesse. Walt gets him to mumble that the drugs are under his sink. Walt furiously bags up the meth and gets a "Baby Coming" message. At that point, he makes a choice. He keeps bagging the product and misses the birth of his daughter, ignoring numerous phone calls from Skyler and Marie. In contrast, when Hank gets a call that Marie has been in a car accident (Walter, you sunk to a new low here!), he does not even stop to call in backup to the junkyard where he has Jesse (and Walt) held hostage in the RV (Episode 3.6, "Sunset"). He immediately peels out and races to the hospital, terrified that Marie is hurt.

Finally, Hank's adherence to his moral code within a legal realm makes him an anti-Walt throughout the series. In Episode 3.7 ("One Minute"), after giving his side of the story as to why he beat Jesse close to death following the realization that the call about Marie was a ploy, we see him clean out his desk. Hank sobs on Marie's shoulder on the way down in the elevator. When he has to attend a formal hearing for his actions, Marie suggests he lie, but he refuses. Hank will not go down that road. The fact that he will not even consider lying about what happened sits in sharp contrast with Walt at this point in the series, who cannot help himself from lying when it does not even matter. For example, in the hospital after Hank is attacked, Walt gets a phone call and attempts to lie to Skyler about who it was, but Skyler just walks away because she does not care to hear his lies or even need to know what the call was about (Episode 3.8, "I See You"). They are separated and she did not ask him any questions. Lying is like a habit to Walt now. Walt's justification that his choices are for his family are foiled with Hank, who has a clear line between right and wrong and refuses to invoke his family as an excuse for his bad behavior.

Hank functions as a contrast to early Walt, but he is also the comparison for the monster Walt becomes. He is not perfect, but he is out for the side of justice, and this is perhaps the reason the comparison to westerns frequently comes up with *Breaking Bad*. Vince Gilligan comments, "I absolutely see *Breaking Bad* as a modern Western."[14] Above all, Hank wears the white hat, although sometimes a little askew, and *New York Times* writer Ross Douthat suggests that "having a good man on Walt's tail has actually made *Breaking Bad* more *realistic* than shows that deliberately write virtue and heroism out of their storylines entirely."[15] In the creative revolution of this third golden age of television, the obsession with the bad boy helps us understand why Hank had to die. Episode 5.14 ("Ozymandias") is a tearjerker. The catch in his voice as he explains to Walt, "You are the smartest guy I ever met. And you are too stupid to see. He made up his mind ten minutes ago." Not only does Hank die at the hands of a terrible man like Jack Welker, the result of a situation Walt could not talk his way out of, but he also gets buried in the desert. Ah, and Marie! This will kill her.

With the death of Hank, Walter White's mantra of "family" is pelted back in his face like an icy-cold snowball. Walt's family will suffer because of his choices, and that fact is never clearer than when Hank dies. Hank's death was unequivocally the worst moment in a series filled with "oh my God" moments, but it was absolutely necessary for the moral/ ethical/legal superior to our tragic figure to die: "Hank isn't the hero. There are no heroes. There is only Walter White and what he hath wrought."[16] Hank's death causes Walt to hand Jesse over to Todd's group. Jesse's enslavement is what causes Walt's early demise, when he takes a bullet to the gut. Only one can succeed out of this trio of men, and although Jesse walks away with his life, it is Walt who gets the end he deserves.

CONCLUSION

A Perfect Ending

Have you ever been sitting at your desk and you crumple up a piece of paper and, without even looking, you just toss it over your shoulder and it goes straight into the wastebasket? You didn't think about it. You didn't stress about it. You just did it. And now that you're thinking about it, you could never do it again in a million years, no matter how hard you tried. That's what this was like.—Vince Gilligan[1]

I have learned a lot from watching *Breaking Bad*, not the least of which is how to get rid of a body with acid. Although, I should note that I have not confirmed the validity of the show's execution of this, as I do not want to have a search on my computer for "getting rid of a body in acid melting porcelain?"—just in case somebody in my life goes missing and I become the prime suspect. As a writer, scholar, and educator, the biggest take-away for me is in the brilliant advice from Gilligan and his team of writers: never paint yourself into a corner, and tie up the loose ends.

In an interview with *Entertainment Weekly*, when asked about the final episode, Gilligan responded, "It finally dawned on us one wonderful day that the key to satisfying an audience doesn't necessarily reside within surprising them. . . . Walt's the engine of his own destruction, but in a way that's hopefully satisfying."[2] The finale *was* deeply satisfying, praised as near perfection by critics across the board. Contributing writer for *Forbes* Allen St. John contends:

Making meth has always been a thinly veiled metaphor for the making of *Breaking Bad.* The alchemy of putting smart people together, each giving everything they have to give, and unaccountably, the total of their talent and hard work produces something remarkable, something enduring, something far greater than the sum of its parts.[3]

Luckily, unlike meth production, writing for television is still legal, and Gilligan and his fellow writers fared better in the end than did Walter White.

Before the second half of the fifth season aired, Vince Gilligan commented, "There are things in these last eight episodes that are going to surprise people. There are also things where people will say, 'I kind of saw that coming.' But maybe the obvious choice is the right one sometimes."[4] In a television culture that desperately tries to shock its viewers with a twist conclusion that "no one saw coming!" it is not surprising that some viewers and critics refused to take the final story at face value. After the finale aired, there were a few people who insisted that the end was not what we thought it was. Although Gilligan refers to it as "definitive," both Emily Nussbaum of the *New Yorker* and comedian Norm MacDonald, in addition to a segment of viewers, argue that Walt actually died in the snow-covered car in New Hampshire, and everything after that is a dying fantasy.[5] Gilligan specifically contends he would never use a dream ending, as that is the "antithesis to a satisfying" conclusion.[6] However, he also acknowledges that once the story is out of the writers' room, it is open to interpretation. About the finale, he argues, "I mean, yes, it's mine. But it's also everyone else's, at this point. Up until these episodes aired, they were simply mine and the writers' and the crew's and the actors'. Now they sort of belong to everybody. Like, it's up to the viewer to decide what happened to Jesse."[7] Although Gilligan and the writers have a specific intention in mind when they write, and they can confirm or deny whether various viewer interpretations fit the original goal, it does not mean that audience members are wrong about alternative theories. Gilligan notes, "I hear interpretations of the show . . . that are marvelous. Just way better than anything I could come up with."[8]

The finale was entertaining, funny, and tragic, all in keeping with what we have come to expect from this wonderful series. The use of Badger and Skinny Pete as the "hit men" who compel Gretchen and Elliott Schwartz to do Walt's bidding was a delightful way to let fans say goodbye to these endearing characters. Allowing Jesse to violently strangle

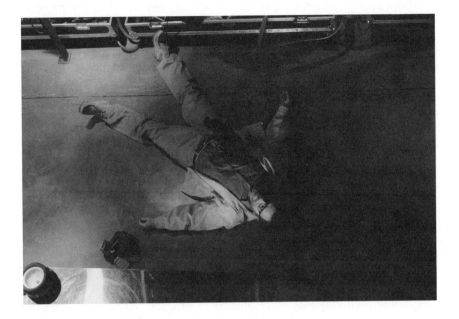

A satisfying end for Walter White. *AMC/Photofest © AMC*

Todd with the same chains used to keep him in servitude was the ultimate catharsis. There was additional closure in knowing that Skyler would have a bargaining chip, and Marie would have Hank's body to bury. And, as I have argued throughout this book, Walt's death was necessary and also perfect as he dies on the floor of a meth lab: the place where he felt most alive.

There were a number of unanswered questions with five episodes left, and the writers tied everything up. Who is the gun for? Who will get the ricin? Did something happen to Walt's family? Why does a fence surround the Whites' house? What happened to Walt's money? Did Jesse turn him in? Does Walt ever tell Jesse the truth about Jane's death? Gilligan and his crew answered every single one of these questions with no hokey gimmicks. The finale was an example of clever writing and solid acting that made every second captivating. At the end, viewers need to see Walter White acknowledge his role in the mess he left behind, and we have to see Jesse get out of the pit. *Rolling Stone* writer Scott Neumyer asserts, "*Breaking Bad*'s finale pulled in nearly every net the show had cast during its five-season run."[9] The writers of *Breaking Bad* sewed up the loose ends and gave us, the loyal viewing audience, our own sense of retribution. As Vince Gilligan and his writers moved on to the popular and critically acclaimed spin-off *Better Call Saul*, they left us with a litany of cultural themes to endlessly debate and a new take on the "bad guy."

Due to a variety of ways the audience can watch television in our contemporary media-saturated landscape, multiple interpretations are inevitable. Critic James Poniewozik argues, "More than ever, even those of us who watch the same TV show—in an age of smaller and smaller audiences—don't really see the same thing."[10] The experience of binge-watching a television series—through streaming, downloading, and on demand—might allow marathon viewers to notice rich details and connections, whereas the weekly watchers may get the benefit of ruminating on the show's themes between episodes and also being the first to know the spoilers. Not only has this changed the landscape for marketers, as I detailed in chapter 6, but this also changes the writing. Like any piece of written work, understanding the audience is the first step, but with television today, that audience is composed of different consumers. As with any popular product on the market, the beauty of *Breaking Bad* is that it can appeal to people from all walks of life.

Above all, the value of creative television resides in the communicative function it holds for our cultural conversations. The audience is supposed to debate, interpret, and analyze smartly written television. Gilligan states, "We do strive very hard to not answer every question in every episode, so that people can indeed argue over certain moments."[11] He notes the intelligence of the audience, and the value in assuming they are smarter than the writers. Case in point, in the second season of *Better Call Saul*, the writers hid a message for astute fans, announcing "Fring's Back" by concealing the phrase in the first letter of the episode titles. Fans figured it out immediately, and Gilligan notes that he should have known he and the writers would have to try harder to surprise this devoted of an audience. Audience members spend their time continuing the conversation, researching clues, and generally engaging with the series outside of the boundaries of the specific viewing space. In other words, the value of a series has to be measured not just by the ratings of the shows, but also by the engagement of the fans on a variety of media.

The success of *Breaking Bad*, which set a Guinness World Record for the highest-rated TV series with a MetaCritic.com rating of 99/100,[12] is not the only indication of its cultural value. The significance of this series is in the conversations that it still inspires as fans meet other fans, or rewatch the series, and even as new viewers start watching for the first time. *Breaking Bad* is why it is important to have quality television that challenges our interpretations of life and requires us to think about the way our world works outside of the fictional universe of Walter White.

Watching *Breaking Bad* is like taking the best aspects from every course you can imagine, and then immediately using that knowledge in the real world. As viewers, we are then a combination of the student and the astronomer of Walt Whitman's "When I Heard the Learn'd Astronomer," a famous poem now forever tied to Gale Boetticher and *Breaking Bad*. He tells Walt the lab is magic because it is experiential learning, rather than academic. However, the academic learning as a foundation is what makes magic possible in the lab. Similarly, analyzing the media we consume has to be built on a foundation of knowledge, whether that research occurs on discussion boards or in off-line conversations with friends, family, and colleagues. Neil Landau, a screenwriter and professor, interviewed Vince Gilligan. The interview highlights the theme of learning versus teaching. Gilligan comments:

> Walt is an excellent student. He drinks in this criminal world around him very quickly. Yet, he is arrogant enough that he has trouble thinking of himself as a student. He prefers to think of himself as the master. That is what chafed so much in the season where Walt was under Gus Fring's thumb. I think what chafed him the most was not that Gus wanted him dead but that Gus was the master and Walt was the indentured servant. [13]

Gilligan argues that he has "nothing but respect for" teachers,[14] and in many ways Gilligan became one as he offered lessons about human nature against a background of cultural issues and anxieties.

The series functions as a case study for media literacy, when themes of family, morality, drugs, and consequences all permeate discussion, but not as a hit-you-over-the-head cautionary tale. Vince Gilligan and his writers' desire to create an organic story allowed them to acknowledge that their original intention—for the fans to turn on Walter White when he becomes a monster—was not experienced by all the viewers. Instead of making him so evil that there would be no way to enjoy the rest of the series, Gilligan et al. joined the conversation by "fomenting arguments" about why Walter White should win.[15] It says something about our culture that a man like Walt can be read as a sympathetic character, whether he gets the label of antihero, villain, or tragic figure. While some say it explains a political shift in our cultural landscape,[16] others claim it is a sign of being an adult.[17] Gilligan suggests it is part of human nature to love stories about the bad guys. He observes, "It's that much harder to build a really compelling drama around an essentially good guy. I don't know why that is. It's just some basic truth about human nature."[18] No matter the explanation, Walter White is part of the cultural conversation, and it is important to think about all the possibilities for what that says about the mind-set of America.

Writing for *GQ*, Brett Martin contends, "If there was one person this year who gave us a National Cultural Moment—the kind of shared group experience that isn't supposed to happen anymore, at least not without the word *Bowl* appended to its title—it was Vince Gilligan."[19] I love this sentiment, partially because my pop-culture-loving and sports-annoyed self rejoices in the idea that television can be as unifying as America's favorite pastime. The thought of experiencing creative television as a cultural moment harkens back to the goals of this book, which are to explore how media is both a mirror and creator of reality. I have hopefully demonstrated that *Breaking Bad* provides ample opportunity for rich analysis regarding culture, drugs, economics, power, and human nature, both via the characters and through conversations about the series. To Vince Gilligan, the writers, the cast and crew, and the marketers of *Breaking Bad*: thank you for reminding us what good television looks like, and for giving the fans five seasons worth of gripping and thought-provoking entertainment. Well done, yo.

THE EPISODES

An Opinionated Compendium

Episode 1.1: "Pilot" (January 20, 2008)

We meet Walter White, an Albuquerque chemistry teacher who receives a death sentence in the first twenty minutes of the show. This
episode spans three weeks—from Walt's diagnosis of terminal lung cancer to his failed suicide attempt—and reveals White's rapid transformation from a bland and beaten-down never-was to a drug manufacturer
who, in the words of his partner and former student Jesse Pinkman,
understands the *art* of cooking meth. Even in the pilot, we can detect
hints of Heisenberg in Walt's brilliance and bravado. This episode introduces the characters of Walt's family, as well as the complexity of the
drug world that Jesse, Walt's former student turned drug partner, is involved in. Jesse and Walt establish their drug-making base in a run-down
RV in the middle of the desert. The quality of the drugs, and suspicions
about the bust of Jesse's former partner, Emilio, trigger the unwelcome
interest of drug dealer Krazy-8. The episode concludes with Walt igniting
a chemical explosion to kill both Emilio and Krazy-8, in order to save
himself and Jesse.

Episode 1.2: "Cat's in the Bag . . ." (January 27, 2008)

The conclusion of this episode is where many viewers gave up on the
series, becoming too squeamish with the blood and gore. Understandably:

the sight of the pinkish-red muck formerly known as Emilio falling through the ceiling is horrifying. However, this second episode offers a glimmer of the depth of what is to come later in the series. This episode starts Walt and Jesse down a path much more sinister than making and selling drugs. Jesse and Walt both struggle with the magnitude of what has happened, and what still has to be done, with Walt spending the entire episode keeping Krazy-8 alive rather than killing him. Walt takes a major stand against Skyler's nagging (also known as a wife wanting to know why her husband is disappearing and keeping secrets), telling her to "climb down out of my ass." The construction of Skyler's character is cemented as the ultimate prude when she visits Jesse to warn him away from selling marijuana to Walt.

Episode 1.3: ". . . And the Bag's in the River" (February 10, 2008)

Walt and Jesse start the episode by getting into a comical fight, when Walt walks in on Jesse using some of their inventory. Walt attempts to flush the drugs, and Jesse saves the bag of meth by throwing it out the window onto the lawn below. The two men rush out of the house after it, slapping and kicking at each other, as they roll down the stairs. This is a particularly delightful scene to watch in hindsight, as the level of acceptable violence against one another escalates throughout the series and becomes far less humorous. There is a discussion of chemistry and the soul, when Walt talks with former girlfriend Gretchen in a flashback. This conversation occurs as Walt tries to build up to killing Krazy-8. Is Walt losing his soul? Is it Krazy-8's soul that keeps Walt from being able to kill him? Walt makes a pros/cons list about whether to kill, with the only pro the desire to save his family. Krazy-8 smartly tries to convince Walt that he just wants to live and will not attempt to retaliate against him. He is unsuccessful when Walt realizes he has kept a shard of broken plate and now has a weapon. Prior to his demise Krazy-8 pointed out to Walt that if he wanted to kill him, he could have just poisoned the food. Tellingly, Walt's chosen method of execution is death by strangulation; it's personal and emotional, repeatedly saying "sorry" as he pulls the bike lock as tight as he can and snuffs out Krazy-8's life. Each violent act moves him closer to becoming Heisenberg. Walt gets out of trouble with

Skyler by finally telling her he has cancer, implying that his diagnosis is the cause of his strange behavior (a partial truth).

Episode 1.4: "Cancer Man" (February 17, 2008)

Jesse and Walt cut ties with one another, as the cleanup of both bodies is complete. Both men go home in this episode. Walt is forced into revealing his cancer diagnosis to his extended family when Skyler begins crying at the dinner table. Walt's animosity toward Hank's machismo is emphasized in this episode when he refuses Skyler's suggestion that they ask Hank and Marie for money to pay for treatment. Additionally, Hank reassures Walt that he will take care of his family if anything happens, which does not sit well with Walt. Jesse goes to his parents' home after fleeing his own house during a paranoid drug delusion. It is revealed that his addiction has taken a toll on his family, but, in the end, he attempts to keep his little brother off the same path. Perhaps the biggest fulcrum of the episode is Ken, a loudmouth, egotistical, parking-spot-stealing douche bag. Walt stands by silently when he first encounters Ken at the bank but, by the end of the episode, stumbles upon him again and lights his precious sports car on fire, blowing it up. The scenes with Ken emphasize a theme of siding with the underdog, which is peppered throughout the series.

Episode 1.5: "Gray Matter" (February 24, 2008)

Walt's hubris is emphasized throughout this episode, as he gives up an opportunity to make a lot of money for his family and receive medical insurance and treatment for free. Walt turns down Elliott's offer to hire him on at Gray Matter, the company Walt and Elliott started before he bought Walt out many years before achieving financial success. Walt is initially excited about the opportunity to prove himself as a chemist again, but refuses the help when he realizes Skyler revealed his cancer diagnosis to Elliott, who is framing the offer as charity. Walt tells Skyler he does not want treatment and she organizes a family intervention to try to convince him otherwise. Hank and Marie surprise Skyler by siding with Walt and saying the choice of treatment should be up to him. Walt makes a speech about choice and survival but, the next day, agrees to attempt treatment. Meanwhile, Jesse tries to get a job in sales, only to be told that the job he's interviewing for is a sign holder. He enlists the help of a druggie friend to get him Sudafed so that he can make meth on his own. We see Jesse in comparison to his friend, as someone who won't settle for simply good enough with the meth production. He's learned something from Walt, thus reinforcing the teacher-student relationship that defines their dynamic throughout the series. At the end of the episode, Gretchen calls Walt to try to convince him to take the money that "belongs" to him, but he can't or won't, and asks Jesse, "Wanna cook?"

Episode 1.6: "Crazy Handful of Nothin'" (March 2, 2008)

Jesse realizes why Walt has turned to making meth, and Walt demands that they find a way to make more money and move more product. Jesse gets a contact to Tuco Salamanca, a major drug distributor in the area, but is hesitant to reach out. Walt tells him to "grow some fucking balls!" Jesse sets a meeting and gets brutally beat up by the insane Tuco (played by the fantastic Raymond Cruz), landing him in the hospital. Walt visits Jesse in the hospital, sees the damage, and visits Tuco himself. Initially, Walt's visit to Tuco appears to be about revenge when he sets off a chemical explosion blasting out the windows of the building. However, Walt ends up making a deal with Tuco for more money and product, thus sealing his (and Jesse's) fate with insanity. A little side note here: instead of using the Wilhelm stock audio, the scream produced right after the explosion is from the 2004 presidential candidate Howard Dean's "Dean Scream."

Episode 1.7: "A No-Rough-Stuff-Type Deal" (March 9, 2008)

After Walt wins the respect and business of Tuco, he informs Jesse that he has made a deal to deliver more meth than they can make. Jesse says the problem is procuring enough Sudafed, and Walt finds a bypass that requires them to steal methylamine. Jesse does not want to work with the "insane ass-clown, dead-eyed killer" Tuco, but Walt knows that the only way to make the money he needs for his family is to expand the operation to the level that a partnership with Tuco offers. The scene where Jesse and Walt steal the barrel of methylamine is like watching a hilariously hyped-up version of *The Odd Couple*. This is much-needed comic relief, but is followed up with a scene that reveals the danger of working with

Tuco. At the end of this episode (and Season 1), Tuco brutally beats No-Doze, one of his associates who had tried to remind Walt and Jesse that Tuco was in charge.

Episode 2.1: "Seven Thirty-Seven" (March 8, 2009)

The writers do not simply ease us into Season 2, which begins with the (recurring) image of a plastic eyeball floating in a pool, but rather fling us in with a catapult. The episode repeats the last scene from the final episode of Season 1, with Tuco beating up No-Doze. It continues as Walt and Jesse get into the car to leave the lot, and Jesse looks as though he is about to throw up. Walt looks equally disturbed but then shifts his focus to figuring out how many more deals they will have to get through with Tuco to save enough money to provide for his family. He estimates he will need $737,000, also the title of the episode, and a type of plane, foreshadowing a major plot point at the end of the season. Tuco comes back and demands that Walt/Heisenberg save the now dying No-Doze. He can't and Tuco orders his other associate, Gonzo, to get rid of the body, which Gonzo does rather unwillingly, as he does not want to leave his friend's body in the junkyard. Walt returns home, dazed, and apparently sexually excited, as he attempts to have rough sex with a very unwilling Skyler. Walt and Jesse fear that Tuco will come after them as witnesses to the murder, and Jesse purchases a gun. Walt comes up with a different weapon: ricin, a poison that becomes a recurring plot driver throughout the remainder of the series. Their fears are solidified when Gonzo shows up dead. The episode ends with Walt about to tell the frustrated Skyler all his woes, but he stops short when he has to leave the house to yell at Jesse who has shown up unexpectedly. When he gets to Jesse's car, Tuco is in the backseat with a gun, and he kidnaps Walt.

Episode 2.2: "Grilled" (March 15, 2009)

Hank is now in charge of the official manhunt for Tuco Salamanca and the unofficial manhunt for the disappeared Walt. Walt's family fears he has gone off to take his own life, but in reality, Tuco has kidnapped Jesse and Walt and taken them out to the desert to his disabled Tio Hector's house. Jesse and Walt soon realize that Tuco does not know that Gonzo is dead, instead furiously (and mistakenly) condemning him as a police informant. Tuco has big plans for Walt, to join him in Mexico and make the blue meth "24/7." Walt saves Jesse's life, insisting to Tuco that he needs him. Walt and Jesse plot to poison Tuco with the ricin, but Tio Hector is more alert than he appears and painstakingly (via the use of a single bell) warns Tuco not to trust the two men. The already paranoid and meth-high Tuco is easily pushed to the extreme, taking Jesse out to the yard to murder him. As Walt distracts Tuco, Jesse strikes him with a rock and the two men attempt a blundering escape. Hank shows up, having tracked the LoJack on Jesse's car, and after a spectacular shoot-out hits Tuco between the eyes with a bullet. Walt and Jesse run out into the desert and avoid being seen by Hank.

Episode 2.3: "Bit by a Dead Bee" (March 22, 2009)

An elaborate alibi plan is set into motion with Walt walking naked into the Hi-Lo grocery store, and Jesse paying Wendy to place him in her room all weekend. Walt fakes a fugue state, comes clean (partially) to a hospital psychiatrist, and eventually gets released from the hospital, with his family all thinking he is weaker than they ever have before. Hank targets Jesse as a possible link to Tuco when his car shows up at the crime scene. He brings him in for questioning and takes the bag of getaway money that Jesse left in the car. Hank thinks he has a way to implicate Jesse when he brings in Tio Hector, who refuses to turn Jesse in (he hates the police more than he hates his nephew's killer). Hector poos on the floor to add insult to injury. The episode ends with Skyler asking Walt about his second cell phone, Walt lying and telling her he doesn't have one, and Skyler dodging his kiss as she rolls over to go to sleep.

Episode 2.4: "Down" (March 29, 2009)

We get one more piece to the foreshadowing puzzle as a man in a hazmat suit pulls the pink bear out of the pool and lines it up with other evidence bags along the side of the pool. Something big is coming. Walt and Jesse are both dealing with deteriorating home lives, and both men are attempting to gain control by manipulating and lying to their families to get what they want. Walt makes breakfast for the family, but his efforts to fix things are thwarted when he refuses to come clean about the cell phone, causing Skyler to repeatedly leave the house without telling Walt where she is going. Jesse's parents kick him out of his aunt's former house when they find out he has been using it as a meth lab. He tells Walt that he deserves half of the money he has left, since he lost his in the situation with Tuco; Walt disagrees. A series of unfortunate events then plague Jesse as he loses his crash pad, his crotch rocket, and what was left of his belongings. Jesse falls into a latrine as he breaks into the tow yard where the RV is stored. It is an absolutely hilarious scene, only tempered by Jesse's crying with ultimate despair as he falls asleep on the RV floor, wearing a gas mask due to the latrine stench. Jesse and Walt later get into a brutal fight, where Jesse stops himself from strangling and then beating Walt. Walt relents gives him half of his stash, and then offers to make him breakfast. This final scene emphasizes the growing dependency of the Walt-Jesse dynamic: they only have each other in this moment.

Episode 2.5: "Breakage" (April 5, 2009)

I like to call this episode "Jesse Has Potential." He needs an apartment, storage for the RV, and a distribution plan to sell. By the end of the episode, he has accomplished all of these goals. He is the one who sees that they need to cut out the middleman and become their own distributors. He refers to Walt by his first name in this episode and firmly sets up the terms of the partnership where he is in charge of selling the drugs, while Walt is in charge of cooking. This comes back to bite him later when junkies Spooge and Spooge's Woman (yes, that is how she is credited), steal Skinny Pete's stash and Walt insists Jesse handle it like Tuco. However, his distribution chain is working out, for the most part, and both men are making money. Meanwhile, the pressure is mounting when Hank receives a promotion and has a panic attack, both associated with his killing Tuco. The end of the episode shows him throwing Tuco's plastic-encased grill into the river, attempting to rid himself of the emotional baggage associated with taking someone's life and almost losing his own.

Episode 2.6: "Peekaboo" (April 12, 2009)

If you want people to think you are made of stone, do not watch this episode. "Peekaboo" emphasizes Jesse's soft spot for kids and highlights a general decency regarding innocent people that Walt lacks. Jesse attempts to recover the money for the stolen drugs, but finds a neglected child at the junkies' house. His soft spot earns him a lump on the head, but ultimately he gets the money back without having to be the one to kill. Walt shows a much darker side when he meets with Gretchen, who finds out from Skyler that Walt has been lying about whom the money for his treatment is coming from. Lesson learned from this episode? Don't call Spooge's Woman a "skank."

Episode 2.7: "Negro y Azul" (April 19, 2009)

This episode introduces the crossover of what is to come in the next few seasons with the drug cartel in Mexico. "The Ballad of Heisenberg" joins the two worlds, as Walt and Jesse's business grows. Jesse becomes a blowfish with his new reputation as a killer and Walt convinces him to expand their territory. Hank has been reassigned to go after the cartel, but his new group doesn't find him as delightful as Gomez does, when he can't speak Spanish, doesn't take the time to get to know the way things work, and breaks out a racist Hispanic accent that would have gone over well in his Albuquerque office. Shit gets real for Hank when he sees a cartel snitch's head mounted on a tortoise (Tortuga on a Tortuga), and he turns to throw up or have another panic attack. The guys on his team make fun of him for reacting that way, but then they all explode as the bomb in the Tortuga's head goes off and various limbs and people are scattered. Hank stumbles around trying to help—it's a very Tarantino-esque moment. Meanwhile, Skyler gets a job at her old company and rekindles a friendship with the owner, Ted Beneke, who previously tried to kiss her at a company party. Jane holds hands with Jesse.

Episode 2.8: "Better Call Saul" (April 26, 2009)

Jesse sleeps with Jane and finds out she is eighteen months sober. Badger gets arrested and thus creates the impetus for the introduction of Saul Goodman, a character who became so popular that it launched a spin-off series, *Better Call Saul*. Saul helps them figure a way out of the DEA deal Badger gets offered in exchange for turning in Heisenberg because, as Jesse says, "When the going gets tough, you don't want a criminal law-yer. You want a *criminal* lawyer." Some people prefer prison to real life and Saul finds a fake Heisenberg who is willing to take the heat for

$80,000. The hijinks associated with the scene where Badger picks the wrong guy, and Walt distracts Hank by acting like a befuddled ninety-year old man, while Jesse points to the right guy is hilarious, but also reveals where some of Walt's anger comes from in later episodes. He is seen as a fool by Hank, somebody who would stumble into a stakeout and "Mr. Magoo" his way through the world, when in actuality, he is the puppet master. Unfortunately for Hank, Walt is not content staying behind the curtain.

Episode 2.9: "4 Days Out" (May 3, 2009)

The beginning of this episode has Walt anticipating bad news about his cancer, which makes him panic with a need to make as much meth as possible. He convinces a reluctant Jesse that the methylamine is going bad and they need to cook; four days out in the middle of nowhere. Jesse accidentally drains the battery on the RV and the cook becomes a catastrophe. The backup generator catches fire, Jesse pours out the remainder of their water, and Skinny Pete can't follow directions (go figure). Walt coughs up blood, and Jesse realizes he lied about the methylamine. Eventually, Walt "MacGyvers" his way out and he and Jesse share a touching moment where he trusts Jesse to take care of his family and get them his share of the money. In the end, Walt's tumor has shrunk by 80 percent, and he beats up a towel dispenser as he deals with his emotions.

Episode 2.10: "Over" (May 10, 2009)

Another flash-forward at the beginning of this episode shows the ominous stuffed pink bear as well as a crime scene of two dead bodies on Walt's driveway. His car windshield is smashed and we anticipate major trouble ahead for Walt and his family. In the present time during this episode, Walt begins repairs at home, both literally and metaphorically, after he encourages Walt Jr. to drink shots of tequila. Walt Jr. throws up into the pool at the culmination of an incredibly tense scene between Walt and Hank. Walt works tirelessly to make home repairs but misses a major crack in the foundation as a romance buds between a very pregnant Skyler and Ted Beneke. In another relationship, Jesse introduces himself to Jane's father, and she pretends to barely know him and later hurts his feelings when she acts as though their relationship doesn't matter to her.

The episode ends with Walt threatening two meth makers out of his territory, foreshadowing a return to cooking in the near future.

Episode 2.11: "Mandala" (May 17, 2009)

After a child on a bike shoots Combo point-blank, Walt and Jesse discuss other options for selling meth. Saul puts them in contact with Gustavo Fring, owner of Los Pollos Hermanos (a local fast-food chain) and a brilliant drug kingpin. Skyler and Walt pick a birthday for Holly, and back at the office, Skyler sings "Happy Birthday, Mr. President" to Ted Beneke in a Marilyn Monroe voice. Everybody in the office claps and laughs, instead of cringing from the awkwardness of the very pregnant Skyler and clearly smitten Ted flirting at a workplace function. Shortly after that, Skyler finds out Ted is cooking the books, and she has to decide if she will help him or leave the company. She stays, because she likes flirting with him. On the meth front, Gus decides to give Walt and Jesse a chance and agrees to buy their remaining thirty-eight pounds of meth for $1.2 million. Jesse, unable to deal with his role in Combo's death, has turned to heroin with the help of Jane, who is off the wagon again. Unable to rouse Jesse, Walt breaks into his house and takes the meth, getting to the required pickup location with barely enough time. He misses the birth of his daughter to make the deal.

Episode 2.12: "Phoenix" (May 24, 2009)

Money is an issue in the White house. Everybody except Walt thinks the family is desperate for money, and Walt is desperate to tell somebody about the money he made. Walt Jr. sets up a donation website for his dad, and Walt shows his disdain for charity, first to Skyler and then to Saul. When Jesse realizes what happened to the drugs, he wants his cut of the money, but Walt won't give it to him until he gets clean. When Walt calls Jane Jesse's "junkie girlfriend," Jesse shatters a beaker over the head of a very surprised Walt. Jane's dad finds out she's been using again and, after roughing up Jesse, he gives her one more day before rehab. Jane finds out about the money Walt owes Jesse and convinces him to let her blackmail Walt into getting what he's owed. After they get the money, Jesse and Jane agree to get clean together, but only after one more night. After a discussion with Jane's dad (unbeknownst to Walt), Walt visits Jesse and inadvertently turns Jane onto her back. She begins to throw up, and Walt rushes over to save her, but he changes his mind and lets Jane choke to death on her own vomit.

Episode 2.13: "ABQ" (May 31, 2009)

Jesse, Jane's dad, and Walt all deal with the repercussions of Jane's death. This episode opens with Jesse futilely trying to revive a long-dead Jane. When Walt gets the call from Jesse, he promises to help him, and we meet Mike for the first time when he shows up to clean the scene. He removes the drug paraphernalia and tells Jesse what to say to the police, temporary pulling him out of his shock with a hard slap across the face. Jesse can't deal with his complicity in Jane's death and blames himself, and Walt gets him set up at a rehab facility. Walt goes in for surgery, gets some relaxation drugs, and accidentally confirms to Skyler that he does have a second cell phone. After waiting out his recovery, Skyler packs her bags and tells Walt that she is giving him time to move out. She knows he has been lying about everything. Jane's dad picks out a dress for Jane for the funeral and eventually returns to work as an air traffic controller, where he loses focus. The second-season finale ends with a plane crash and a pink bear floating in the pool, finally revealing the ominous event that has foreshadowed the entire season.

Episode 3.1: "No Más" (March 21, 2010)

In the third-season opener, the twin Cousins crawl onto the scene. Our first shot of them is of one of their silver skull-tipped snakeskin boots as they visit a shrine to Santa Muerte, a saint said to give protection against violent death. The Cousins light a candle and pin a sketch of Heisenberg to the wall of the shrine. Over the border, the plane crash that killed 167 people is the focus of the town and media, and Walt is trying to deal with the role he played in the situation. Skyler pursues a divorce but will not tell anybody why she is leaving Walt, except Walt when she guesses he is a drug dealer. She thinks it is marijuana and Walt tells her it is methamphetamine. A horrified Skyler says she will not tell Hank or the kids what he has done, but only if he signs the divorce papers and stays out of their lives. Gus offers Walt $3 million for three months of this time. Walt declines, thinking this will keep his family together. The Cousins end the episode by brutally gunning down a truckload of immigrants and the coyote driver, and then blowing up the scene of the crime.

Episode 3.2: "Caballo Sin Nombre" (March 28, 2010)

Walt is going downhill after receiving divorce papers from Skyler. He gets pepper-sprayed by a police officer when he becomes unhinged after getting pulled over for a cracked windshield. Hank bails him out and then tries to help him again by asking Skyler what happened to cause her to keep Walt from the kids. Skyler tells him to mind his own business. Walt Jr. is mad at his mom and tries to move in with his dad. Walt sees an opportunity for reconciliation with Skyler when he returns his son back home. He also picks up dinner. Skyler does not let him through the door, and the pizza ends up on the roof. Jesse, forty-five days sober, buys his aunt's house from his parents, after he has Saul negotiate the deal of a lifetime. When Mike visits Walt's house to install listening devices, he secretly observes Walt moving (breaking) back in, against Skyler's wishes. The Whites' house is a revolving door that day, when the Cousins visit briefly before getting a call to back down.

Episode 3.3: "I.F.T." (April 4, 2010)

When Skyler gets home to find Walt has moved back in, she calls the Albuquerque police, who show up but tell her there is nothing they can do unless she has some information they can use against him. Walt manipulates everybody in the room, playing the perfect father with grilled cheese making and one-handed bottle-feeding. Skyler refuses to tell the police about his illegal activities, but she locks herself into the bedroom with Holly that night. We find out Gus is a big deal in the Mexican cartel, and his territory boundaries require that he bless the killing of Walt, which the twins want as revenge for their cousin Tuco's death. He asks the Cousins to hold off for now, but this request is not guaranteed. Jesse is struggling with Jane's death. He calls her cell phone repeatedly, just to hear her voice-mail message. One day, the phone number is disconnected and Jesse starts cooking again. Hank is losing it. He starts a fight in a dive bar and Gomez has to cover for him. Walt shows Skyler the money he made, tells her it was all for the family, and asks that she accept it. She goes to work, kisses Ted, and has sex with him. She comes home that night and tells Walt what she did.

Episode 3.4: "Green Light" (April 11, 2010)

Walt tries to fight Ted Beneke but only manages to embarrass Skyler at work. Mike shows up in time to keep Walt from sneaking into the building through the air vents. Walt fires Saul and forces Mike to remove the listening devices. Mike sees a sign that the Cousins are still watching Walt, but luckily Gus has Mike watching Walt, too. Hank gets a lead on the blue meth and skips his flight back to El Paso. Jesse proudly shows a recently fired Walt the result of his solo cook, and Walt takes the opportunity to berate him. Gus, the ultimate puppet master, makes a deal to buy Jesse's meth, hoping to make Walt angry.

Episode 3.5: "Más" (April 18, 2010)

A flashback starts this episode and we find out that back in the beginning, Jesse spent the majority of Walt's life savings on strippers and alcohol for his friends instead of the RV. It turns out the RV they have been using as a meth lab was stolen from Combo's mom. Oh, Jesse. Flash forward and we see Skyler appreciating the finer things in life with Ted Beneke's heated tile bathroom floors. Marie confides in Skyler about Gomez getting Hank's job in El Paso and makes her think about how people change after traumatic events. Walt visits Gus to tell him that he knows the money was a ploy to get him to cook, but he is not that prideful. Gus calls his bluff, shows him the lab, and Walt is impressed. Walt still tells him no, because he does not want to harm his family. Gus reminds him that children are always your family. Walt considers this. Skyler finds the money in Holly's room and opens the bag to admire it. She visits her lawyer to talk through the situation, and the lawyer advises her to tell Walt Jr. and the authorities about Walt. Skyler says she did not marry a criminal, and the lawyer tells her that she is married to one now. A conflicted Skyler comes home to find that Walt has signed the divorce papers, and left them in Holly's crib (unpack that metaphor!). Walt then visits Jesse at Saul's office and lets him know how he cut him out of the deal with Gus: "I'm in. You're out." An enraged Jesse throws a cinder block through Walt's windshield. Hank finds his white whale.

Episode 3.6: "Sunset" (April 25, 2010)

This episode should be called "Hank's Bad Day." Hank knows Jesse owns the RV, but he does not know where Jesse is keeping it. He sits on Jesse's house, watching as Badger and Skinny Pete come and go. Jesse is trying to start his own business and get his dealers back in line. He tells them things will be different, smarter than before. Walt starts his first day at the lab, meets Gale Boetticher, and finally has a lab assistant worthy of Walt's praise. They make meth, talk philosophy and politics, and drink some damn fine coffee. Marie suggests Hank ask Walt about Jesse, considering Walt used to buy marijuana from him (ha!). Walt realizes Hank will find the RV and his prints, and gets Badger's cousin to tow the RV to a junkyard. Badger calls Jesse to tell him what is happening and a furious Jesse screams into the junkyard to confront Walt. Walt realizes Hank followed him, and an incredibly intense scene takes place as Hank tries to break into the RV, only to be stopped by the owner of the junkyard, who expertly outsmarts Hank with legalese. Hank, knowing he cannot break and enter, tries to convince Jesse to come out. With Walt playing Cyrano, Jesse tells Hank, "This is my own private domicile and I will not be harassed. Bitch." Jesse brilliantly adds the last word. Hank says he will wait for the search warrant. Walt, seeing no way out of the RV without Hank spotting him, reluctantly calls Saul and has him pretend Marie was in a terrible car accident to get Hank to leave the junkyard, which he does immediately. Jesse and Walt then watch as the RV is crushed into a small rectangle of metal. Hank gets to the hospital, frantically looking for Marie, who calls right then and asks if he plans to be home for dinner. Relief and then rage cross Hank's face. Gus has run out of time to hold off the Cousins from killing Walter White. He gives his blessing to go after Hank instead, even though their boss says DEA agents are off limits.

Episode 3.7: "One Minute" (May 2, 2010)

A furious Hank beats the crap out of Jesse, who does not see it coming. The police (whom Hank presumably called) question him as Jesse gets wheeled out of the house on a stretcher into a waiting ambulance. Walt visits Jesse in the hospital, and Saul tells him, "You are now officially the cute one of the group" as Walt takes in the massive bruises and swelling that Hank inflicted on Jesse's face and body. Jesse is furious. He threatens to ruin Hank's life and Walt's life, saying if he gets caught making drugs, he will just turn Walt into the police. Saul suggests that Jesse needs to be taken care of, but Walt thinks he can fix it. Walt negotiates with Gus for Jesse to be his lab assistant instead of Gale. Jesse eventually agrees after emotionally painful conversations with Walt, including an admission that Jesse's "meth is good. As good as mine." Hank writes out a true statement about what happened with Jesse, refusing to lie to save face, and turns in his badge and gun. Jesse drops the charges against Hank, and Hank stops by the store to get Marie something to celebrate the good news. Back in his car, he receives a warning call telling him he has one minute before men are coming to kill him. He does not have a gun when the Cousins attack. During the shoot-out, one of the twins is pinned behind his car, and the other brother comes in for the kill. He wounds Hank and then goes for his ax because shooting him is "too easy." Hank sees one bullet that fell out of the brother's pocket, struggles to load it into the leftover gun, hands shaking and slick with his own blood, and shoots the back of the twin's head off. The ax falls to the pavement.

Episode 3.8: "I See You" (May 9, 2010)

Jesse gets out of the hospital. His eye is still swollen shut, his battered body screams in protest as he attempts to get dressed, and he is angry. As he waits for Skinny Pete to pick him up after discharge, an ambulance blares into the emergency room drive-up and Jesse sees Hank rushed into the hospital. Incredulous, he gets into the car with Skinny Pete and smiles a wicked grin, happy with the turn of fate. He shows up for his first day on the job, issuing orgasmic-like shouts of happiness as he surveys the new digs, just as Walt is letting a baffled Gale go. Gus's man reminds Walt he owes them two hundred pounds of meth a week, which Walt wants to start on immediately. Jesse realizes Walt does not have cell service, and thus does not know about Hank. Walt rushes to the hospital. Marie is a mess, waiting for information on Hank's condition. The entire police force has shown up in solidarity. Marie finds out Hank didn't have his gun and she yells at his boss and Gomez, telling them it is their fault. When Walt can't get away to cook, he lies to Gus, telling him that Gale really screwed up their progress. Walt does not know that Gus knows he is Hank's brother-in-law. Gomez offers to show Walt the guy who tried to kill Hank. The twin opens his eyes, sees Walt, and furiously crawls with his bloody bandaged stump legs across the floor, smearing a trail of blood as he tries to get to Walt. Walt begins to worry for his own safety. Gus supplies food for the entire force at the hospital and offers a $10,000 reward for any information about the attack. Marie is grateful, and Walt is worried; he's been caught in a lie with his new boss. Gus tells him not to worry about the Cousins, and shortly afterward, we see Mike dispose of a syringe as the last brother dies. Hank's condition is stable. Marie insists the entire family get to see him, including Walt. The audience sees the family stare at Hank in his hospital bed, and Marie grabs his hand.

Episode 3.9: "Kafkaesque" (May 16, 2010)

The beginning of this episode visually depicts the extent of Gus's operation, as we watch the various pieces of the drug business at work. Jesse also begins to understand the extent of Gus's empire, estimating that he makes $96 million, while Jesse and Walt make $1.5 million each. In a bit of a switch from previous episodes, it is Jesse who gets greedy about money. He starts taking the overage from the bins to sell on the side. He thinks he knows the perfect location: his group therapy meetings. Money is also on Marie's and Skyler's minds as Marie finds out how much therapy their insurance will not cover. She refuses to limit Hank's recovery, saying they will find a way to pay for the extra appointments. Gomez visits Hank, tells him they have a lead on the blue meth. Skyler puts two and two together and asks Walt if they are safe. Walt visits Gus to praise his cunning removal of competition in the Mexican cartel and to find out what happens after the three months of contracted work are up. Gus offers Walter $15 million for another year, and Walt agrees. On the way home, he closes his eyes while driving, swerves over the line, and almost gets hit by a semi. Back at the hospital, Skyler decides Walter will help pay for Hank's treatments, and concocts a story about Walt's gambling addiction. Walt humble-brags that he is very good at gambling and that he has a stash in the "7 figure" range. Walt mistakenly thinks Skyler's story means she is on his side, and he is thrilled with her quick lie, but she quickly brings him back down to earth when she tells him that he owes Hank this money because she is pretty sure that Walt helped put him in the hospital bed.

Episode 3.10: "Fly" (May 23, 2010)

The love-it-or-hate-it episode of the series, "Fly" primarily takes place in the chemistry lab below Gus's laundry facility. In the opening of the episode, we see Walt staring at the blinking red light of the smoke detector above his bed. He has not slept all night. Off to work, Jesse and Walt scrub the entire lab clean, and then Walt crunches the numbers, realizing they are missing a quarter to half a pound from each batch. Jesse tries to offer some explanations, hoping to divert attention away from the fact that he is stealing the overage. Jesse leaves for the day and Walt becomes distracted by a fly. The next day, Jesse shows up for work and can barely get the door open. An agitated Walt runs to the door and yells about the room being pressurized. Jesse realizes Walt never went home and has spent the entire evening trying to kill the fly. Walt insists the fly is going to contaminate the product and refuses to allow any cooking until it is caught. Jesse tries to appease the crazy Walt and help him but eventually gives up, and a classic Walt-Jesse scuffle ensues as they try to best each other with hijinks to get control over the lab. Eventually Jesse drugs Walt's coffee with sleeping pills, and a groggy Walt begins revealing his internal conflicts. Walt brings up Jane, tells Jesse he is sorry, that he ran into Jane's dad the night before her death, and is nail-bitingly close to revealing his culpability in her death, but stops before Jesse understands what he means. Eventually Walt falls asleep and Jesse finishes the batch on his own. The episode ends with Walt warning Jesse that if he is stealing the overage, he can't protect him. An angry Jesse asks, "Who's asking you to?"

Episode 3.11: "Abiquiu" (May 30, 2010)

Jesse misses Jane. He flashes back to a conversation they had about the meaning of art and life at the Georgia O'Keeffe Museum they went to before Jane died. At work, Walt won't let Jesse weigh the product, and indicates the cameras are watching. Skyler gets involved in the cover story, primarily because she now needs to protect Hank and Marie if anything goes awry. She suggests Walt buy his former car wash, and she will be the person who helps him launder the money. Walt starts to trust Skyler more than Saul. Jesse tells his crew that they will not have more meth for a while, but finds out Badger and Skinny Pete are having a hard time selling to the people in the meetings. They don't think it is morally right to do so. Jesse attempts to show them how it is done, and meets Andrea and her son, Brock. His soft spot for kids starts to bring out a bit of the old Jesse again, and he also can't follow through on selling the blue meth to Andrea. When she asks for it, Jesse yells at her and questions her ability to be a mother. Andrea yells back and swears she will not let her son get involved with gangs like her brother, Tomás. Jesse finds out that Tomás was the one who killed Combo. Gus invites Walt over to dinner, where he advises Walt to never make the same mistake twice.

Episode 3.12: "Half Measures" (June 6, 2010)

Jesse wants to kill the guys who use Tomás to sell drugs. He tells Walt his plan: he is going to use ricin and have Wendy deliver it with the burgers she brings them when she picks up her meth for the week. Walt tries to dissuade Jesse to no avail. He then tries to get Saul to get Jesse locked up for thirty days to cool off. When Saul rejects that idea, he then turns to Mike for help, and realizes they have the same boss. Mike tells Walt never to take half measures when a full measure is needed. Walt tells Gus what Jesse is planning, and Gus tells Jesse it will not happen. Gus tells Jesse to shake hands with the two men and that there will be peace. All three men agree, reluctantly, and, at Jesse's insistence, Gus says they are not to use children to sell drugs anymore. Tomás is almost immediately shot to death. A furious Jesse prepares to kill the two men. He gets high and walks across the road with his gun ready, as the two men who work for Gus get out of their car with their guns ready. Just as they are all about to open fire, Walt's car crashes into the two men. Walt jumps out, shoots one of the men struggling on the ground, and tells an incredulous Jesse to "run!"

Episode 3.13: "Full Measure" (June 13, 2010)

Another very Tarantino-esque episode with Mike and the balloons: Mike hands one to his precious granddaughter and uses the rest as a distraction to kill a bunch of people. The cartel is nosing around, testing their boundaries. And this isn't Gus's only problem. Walt hides Jesse from Gus and Mike and, in refusing to give him up, challenges Gus's authority. Gus turns to Gale, asking him to make sure he knows Walt's procedure for making the blue meth. Walt knows what he has planned and he asks Jesse to kill Gale. Jesse refuses and tries to get Walt to go to the police instead, but Walt says he will do it. Victor and Mike move quicker than he thought. Walt tries to plead with Mike to save his life and offers him Jesse. Mike lets Walt call Jesse, and Walt tells Jesse he has to kill Gale. A smug Walt tells Mike he will need to hold off, as Victor runs to try to head off Jesse. Gale opens the door and Jesse pulls out the gun, with tears in his eyes. Gale realizes what is happening and tells him he doesn't have to do this, but he does have to do this. Jesse pulls the trigger.

Episode 4.1: "Box Cutter" (July 17, 2011)

Gus is a bad dude. Jesse killed Gale and Victor shows up too late. He hauls Jesse into the chemistry lab, and a smug Walt believes he now has an advantage. Walt declares that nobody else can do the cook. Victor decides to show him he is wrong about that and begins a flawless cook, much to Walt's concern. Jesse appears to be in shock. Gus comes to the lab, walks right up to Walt to stare at him, and then slowly and methodically undresses to put on a protection suit. Walt vacillates between challenging Gus and pleading for his life (and Jesse's). Gus walks back to Walt with a box cutter and slices Victor straight across the throat. He dumps the body in front of Walt and Jesse, who, along with Mike, look horrified by this turn of events and tells them to "get back to work." After cleaning up the mess, in homage to *Pulp Fiction*, Walt and Jesse debrief over breakfast. Jesse tells Walt they are safe, but the message from Gus is "if I can't kill you, you'll sure as shit wish you were dead."

Episode 4.2: "Thirty-Eight Snub" (July 24, 2011)

Everybody is on the "verge" in this episode. Jesse, Walt, Saul, Mike, Marie, Hank, and Skyler are all trying to deal with the stress in their lives. Jesse surrounds himself with noise to block out having to deal with the fact that he killed Gale. Walt buys a gun and decides he needs to kill Gus. Saul hires security. Mike watched Gus kill one of his men, and now he has to deal with Walt, who feels cornered and desperate. Marie has to deal with Hank's nastiness in the wake of his depression and frustration with the slow progress of his recovery. Hank begins to hoard minerals (not rocks, Marie!). And, dealing with her own frustration with Walt's lack of action, Skyler tries to buy the car wash from Walt's old boss Bogdan and finds out Walt did not leave on good terms. Lesson learned in this episode? Don't try to get Mike to turn on Gus.

Episode 4.3: "Open House" (July 31, 2011)

Hank (finally) starts to turn a corner by the end of this episode. Marie slips over the edge, stealing from open houses as a way to escape the problems of her life. She gets caught and Hank has to call his friend Tim from Homicide to bail her out of jail. Tim visits Hank and asks for his help with Gale's case. He knows it is connected to drugs, but if he hands it over to Gomez, the DEA will take it. Hank hedges and tries to refuse, but Tim leaves Gale's notebook to see if Hank can find any leads. Meanwhile, Skyler rejects any other business idea but the car wash, and when she tells Walt what Bogdan said about him when she first made the offer, Walt also refuses to consider any other business. Skyler gets creative with some water and chemical testing, and convinces Bogdan to sell her the car wash for less than she originally offered. Walt celebrates the good news with a $320 bottle of champagne, and Skyler questions his showy spending. The episode ends with Hank, up in the middle of the night, as he opens up the notebook Tim left him.

Episode 4.4: "Bullet Points" (August 7, 2011)

This episode starts with Mike bundled up in the back of a freezer truck lined with Los Pollos Hermanos product buckets. The truck gets stopped and shot up—a message from the cartel to Gus. Mike survives, kills the two men who ambushed the truck, and disgustingly tries to reposition the tip of his bloody ear. Skyler writes a story to explain Walt's gambling addiction, as they head to dinner at Hank and Marie's house. Walt grumbles about some of her creative choices but ultimately is humbled when he is shown crime scene photos of Gale's death and convincingly shows remorse for his actions. Hank is shocked but seems to buy the gambling story. Hank asks for Walt's help to decipher the initials in a clue from Gale's lab notes: "To my W.W. My star, my perfect silence." Hank muses it could stand for Walter White, to which Walt jokingly confesses and then points Hank toward the Walt Whitman poem that the quote references. A spiraling Jesse, who has shaved his head, challenges Mike's authority and ends up on a ride-along to who knows where.

Episode 4.5: "Shotgun" (August 14, 2011)

Walt is convinced Mike is taking Jesse to his death, as he races through the streets, leaving instructions for Saul and a good-bye message for Skyler. He shows up at Los Pollos Hermanos and waits for Gus with a gun in his pocket. Mike calls and tells Walt he will have to do the cook alone that day because Jesse is with him. A frustrated Walt struggles to do everything alone, and Gus sends a heavy lifter, but no Jesse. Walt and Skyler sign the paperwork for the car wash, Skyler hears the message Walt left for her proclaiming his undying love, and they have sex. Skyler says Walt should move back into the house. Once Jesse realizes that Mike is not going to kill him, he gets bored with the day of driving around picking up money. As Mike makes the last stop, Jesse thwarts a robbery, and Mike softens a little (tiny) bit toward him. Walt has too much to drink at Hank and Marie's house and suggests that Gale was not the mastermind genius behind the meth. The next day, Hank questions the connection between Gale and Los Pollos Hermanos.

Episode 4.6: "Cornered" (August 21, 2011)

Two excellent and often quoted lines of the series come from this episode. After Walt's drunken evening at Marie and Hank's house, Skyler worries about the family's safety. Walt tries to reassure her that the family will be fine, but she insults his ego by saying he must be scared. Walt turns on Skyler and asks her whom she thinks she is speaking to. He warns her that he is "the danger" because "I am the one who knocks." A scared Skyler leaves the house. Jesse continues to work with Mike, and Walt starts to get suspicious about Gus's motives. He tries to get Saul to help him hire a hit man to kill Gus. After Walt's declaration, Skyler disappears with Holly to Four Corners State Park, and plays a game of coin toss to determine her next steps. Unhappy with the signs of fate, she returns home where Walt has bought Walt Jr. a brand-new sports car. She tells Walt that he has to return it, as it is not sticking to the story they put together. Skyler tells Walt, "Someone has to protect this family from the man who protects this family."

Episode 4.7: "Problem Dog" (August 28, 2011)

Walt agrees to take Walt Jr.'s car back but then takes it for a $52,000 joyride. He gets it stuck and decides to blow it up instead. Saul refuses to help Walt find a hit man for Gus, so Walt visits Jesse instead. Jesse agrees to kill Gus, and Walt cooks up a final batch of ricin for the occasion. Gus has bigger problems, as the cartel wants a piece of his business. Jesse decides not to shoot Gus in the back when he has the chance. He then visits the drug-support group and describes the "problem dog" that he had to put down recently. He conveys his emotional struggle as he talks about Gale (the dog as far as the group knows). Hank suspects Gus as the drug kingpin, and lifts his prints from a Los Pollos Hermanos cup to get some proof. When he presents his findings to his former boss and Gomez, Hank wants to know why Gus's prints were at Gale's apartment.

Episode 4.8: "Hermanos" (September 4, 2011)

Gus visits Hector Salamanca and tells him he killed Hector's nephews (the Cousins) as revenge. The DEA brings Gus into the station and asks about his fingerprints being at Gale's apartment, to which he tells them he had dinner with Gale. Everybody but Hank seems satisfied with this response. Skyler has more money than she can launder through the car wash, so she hides stacks of bills in between her clothes and vacuum seals the bags. These end up in the crawl space of the house. Hank tells Walt his suspicions about the owner of Los Pollos Hermanos and asks Walt to put a GPS tracker on Gus's car. Walt swears to Gus that he will keep Hank off his trail, but he visits Jesse to tell him to move quicker with the ricin poisoning. Jesse says he has not had a chance yet, but Walt sees a text on his phone that makes him think Jesse may be lying. We find out why Gus hates Hector; he killed his partner, Max, decades prior, when the cartel was uninterested in the "poor man's cocaine," a.k.a. meth.

Episode 4.9: "Bug" (September 11, 2011)

Hank is doggedly in pursuit of the suspect, and Walt is his somewhat unwilling chauffeur for the hunt. Hank finds nothing in the GPS data but wants to check out Gus's warehouse. Walt manages to hold him off and warn Mike. We see Jesse and more of Mike's guys removing the concealed meth from the buckets. The cartel sends Gus a message when a sniper shoots one of Mike's guys right in front of Jesse. Jesse narrowly avoids getting shot himself, as Mike pushes him out of the way. Gus walks defiantly toward the shooter, bullets pinging off the ground in front of him; he makes a call and tells the cartel the answer is yes. Gus has Jesse over for dinner, and Jesse considers whether this is his opportunity to use the ricin. Gus asks if Jesse can cook alone, and he tells Gus he won't do it if it means Walt is dead. Ted Beneke shows up at the car wash and tells Skyler he owes the IRS more than $620,000 in taxes and fines for the books Skyler cooked for him. Skyler worries this will bring a spotlight on her family, and she dresses up like a dumb mob girlfriend to convince the auditor that it was ignorance instead of criminal intent. She is not out of the woods yet, as Ted tells her he cannot pay his bills. Walt visits a terrified Jesse, who tells him that Gus wants Jesse to go to Mexico to show the cartel chemists how to cook their formula. He wants help and an angry Walt refuses, telling him he will fail and end up in a barrel. Jesse finds out Walt bugged his car and the two men break into a bloody fight. It ends badly, with Jesse telling Walt to "never come back."

Episode 4.10: "Salud" (September 18, 2011)

It is Walt Jr.'s birthday and Skyler bought him a car; it is a reliable PT Cruiser and Jr. is underwhelmed, to say the least. Gus, Jesse, and Mike travel to Mexico where Jesse commands the lab, showing up the snobby scientists, and Walt, by producing a successful batch of 96.2 percent pure meth. After celebrating his success, his bubble bursts when he finds out he will be the cartel's unwilling new cook. Walt has a touching moment with Walt Jr. as he takes care of his dad during an emotional breakdown over Jesse, fueled by painkillers and beer. Skyler finds out Ted is spending the money she "willed" him on a Mercedes and payroll, instead of paying his bills. Gus risks death in order to settle an old debt. He poisons all of the cartel members as retribution for trying to take his business, and for the death of his beloved partner decades prior. Don Eladio falls into the same pool that Max bled out into. Gus manages to vomit up most of the poison, but Mike gets shot. Jesse murders for the second time, when he kills the man shooting at them during their getaway.

Episode 4.11: "Crawl Space" (September 25, 2011)

Bryan Cranston submitted this episode to secure his 2012 Emmy nomination win, and many people (Cranston included) cite the ending as Walt's turn into Heisenberg. It opens with Jesse furiously driving the car with a dying Gus and Mike to a medical tent set up about six miles from the Texas border. The doctor refuses to touch Mike until Gus is taken care of first, and Jesse finds out Gus had provisions for all three of the men. With Mike in stable condition, Gus takes Jesse to visit Tio Hector, where he informs the old man that Jesse murdered his nephew, the elderly Salamanca's only remaining family. Walt chauffeurs Hank first to the warehouse, and then toward the laundry, before turning directly into oncoming traffic in order to avoid getting Hank too close to the lab. Ted tries to return the money, but Skyler thinks he is just blackmailing her to get even more. She calls Saul, and his men show up to make Ted see reason. Ted attempts to escape, trips on his rug, and lands headfirst into a wall. Walt tries to talk to Jesse, who thinks Walt brought Hank to the laundry on purpose, but Jesse tells him to get lost. Tyrus tases Walt and brings him out to the desert, tied up with a bag over his head. Gus says he has put a hit out on Hank and threatens Walt's entire immediate family if he interferes. A terrified Walt convinces Saul to call in a threat on Hank's life to the DEA, and help him disappear with his family. Saul tells him it will cost about $500,000 for all four. Walt races home to gather the money from the crawl space, only to find out Skyler gave it to Ted. In what feels like a scene from a horror film, a terrified Skyler stares at Walt as he laughs maniacally from the crawl space.

Episode 4.12: "End Times" (October 2, 2011)

The DEA agents show up to take Skyler and Holly over to Hank and Marie's house. Walt refuses to come, saying nobody will be safe if he is there. He tells Hank he has too much to take care of at the car wash and he will come as soon as he can get away. Marie and Walt Jr. are furious with both Skyler and Hank for not forcing Walt to join the family. Hank, thinking the death threat is a result of his investigation of Gus, convinces Gomez to check out the laundry facility for him. Saul is getting ready to skip town and he calls Jesse to come pick up the rest of his money. Later that day, Jesse gets a call from Andrea saying that Brock is in the hospital with flu-like symptoms. Jesse immediately realizes the cigarette hiding the ricin is missing from his pack. He tells Andrea to warn the doctors and then shows up at Walt's house and accuses him of having Saul's bodyguard Huell pickpocket the cigarette from Jesse at Saul's office. He threatens to kill him, but Walt convinces him that he did not take the cigarette or poison Brock, and Jesse does not/cannot pull the trigger. Walt persuades him that Gus would be willing to poison a child, and both men agree he needs to die. Jesse refuses to leave the hospital, and Gus visits him there, ultimately telling him to take his time. While the two men talk, Walt has planted a bomb on Gus's car, but, as if he has supernatural abilities, Gus suspects something is amiss and leaves without his car.

Episode 4.13: "Face Off" (October 9, 2011)

By the end of Season 4, the writers did not know if they would have a Season 5, so the final episode had to stand in as both the season and a possible series finale. In this incredible episode, Walt wins against Gus. He finds out that Gus and Hector are enemies, and his enemy's enemy is now his friend. Detectives, who want to know why he suspected ricin poisoning, pick up Jesse at the hospital and take him in for questioning. As he leaves the station, Jesse gets tased and dragged to the lab to complete a cook under gunpoint. Gus, thinking Hector has ratted him out to the DEA, lectures the old man about the code of the cartel. Hector finally looks Gus in the face for the first time as he furiously rings his bell, triggering the bomb explosion that Walt hooked up to his wheelchair. As the scene ends, Gustavo Fring walks out of Hector's room, straightening his tie as the camera pans around to view him full on, and we realize he only has half a face. Walt shows up and kills the two men keeping Jesse hostage. Walt and Jesse get to work torching the lab, using the dead bodies as chemist decoys. Walt waits as Jesse finds out that Brock will pull through after having been poisoned by lily of the valley berries. Walt looks relieved. Skyler wants to know if he had anything to do with Gus's death, and Walt tells her it is over and they are safe. The closing shot of the season is a pan into the Whites' backyard, focusing on a large pot of lily of the valley.

Episode 5.1: "Live Free or Die" (July 15, 2012)

The first episode of the final season opens in a flash-forward, where we see a haggard Walt eating his birthday breakfast at a diner. He breaks up his bacon to make a "52" on the plate like Skyler did in the premiere episode of the series. He purchases a machine gun and a car, and we are left to figure out what gets him to this point. Who has he killed? Who wants to kill him? And, who will the machine gun be used on? Back to the present, Walt runs around cleaning up the remaining evidence of his plot against Gus and finds out Skyler is afraid of him. Mike is furious when he finds out Gus is dead, and he races home, not quite fully recovered yet. Jesse and Walt inform him that the police have Gus's laptop, and the rest of the episode is focused on getting rid of the recordings from the lab cameras. Jesse brilliantly suggests a magnet to erase everything on the laptop ("Yeah, bitch! Magnets!"), and they visit their old friend at the junkyard to buy a supermagnet to do the job. It works, even though Walt tips their truck with his overzealous charge, and the computer is destroyed. Saul tries to end his relationship with Walt, but Walt won't let him. Skyler is forgiven.

Episode 5.2: "Madrigal" (July 22, 2012)

The corporate entity fronting Gus's operation gets a face, albeit temporarily, with the hungry Mr. Schuler. He kills himself rather than face the police by jump-starting his already beating heart. Jesse drives himself crazy trying to find the ricin cigarette; he is worried that a little kid will pick it up, or somebody will accidentally smoke it. Walt plants a fake ricin cigarette (the real vial of ricin is hidden behind an outlet in the Whites' bedroom) and a relieved Jesse breaks down. Walt says he wants to get back to cooking, and they try to convince Mike to join them. Mike, the Greek chorus of the show at this point, tells Jesse to run from Walt. He then finds out the DEA has the bank account numbers for all the men on Gus's payroll, and Mike's granddaughter's money is gone. This is the episode where we meet Lydia, a nervous Nellie who wants to murder all those who can link her from Madrigal to Gus. Mike refuses to kill the men on her list, and she puts a hit out on him. Mike decides not to kill Lydia, because she can help him get methylamine; he's in with Jesse and Walt. Skyler is terrified of Walt.

Episode 5.3: "Hazard Pay" (July 29, 2012)

Walt moves back into the family house, much to Skyler's dismay. Saul shows Walt, Jesse, and Mike some options for the cook site and nothing works out until they find an exterminator. They will use the homes that are tented for extermination to cook a batch, and then pack up and turn on the poison as they leave; it's brilliant! Andrea and Brock come over as Walt and Jesse are finalizing details, and Jesse invites Walt to stay for a beer. Walt sits down next to Brock and eyes him like a predator. Prior to the first cook, we meet Todd who tells Walt that he disabled a nanny cam in the living room. During the cook, Walt talks to Jesse about his future with Andrea. Tells him he trusts him to make the right decision about how much to tell her. Jesse consequently breaks up with Andrea, maybe fearing for her life with Walt around? Skyler breaks down, and a worried Marie waits to talk to Walt. Walt blames Skyler's mood on Ted Beneke's condition and reveals she had an affair. When Skyler wakes up to gunshots, she leaves the bedroom to find Walt, Walt Jr., and Holly watching *Scarface* in the living room. Skyler is horrified with the picture. After the first cook, Mike divvies up the money and says they need to cover the hazard pay for Gus's men. Walt disagrees, but Jesse offers to let Mike take it all from his portion. Walt relents, but warns Jesse that Mike is overstepping his bounds.

Episode 5.4: "Fifty-One" (August 5, 2012)

Walter White made it another year. He turns fifty-one at the beginning of the episode and buys himself a birthday present: a brand-new Chrysler 300 SRT8. He also buys Walt Jr. another Dodge Challenger SRT8, which sends a clear message to Skyler: Walt is in charge. Worried about Walt's reckless spending, when Skyler finds out Walt is back in business she tries to convince him to send the kids away. Walt laughs her off and then forces Skyler to throw him a birthday dinner. Walt says he wants something small, but he secretly hopes for a party. If wishes were horses, then beggars would ride, and Walt finds out Skyler planned exactly what he asked for, no more, no less. Jesse goes to pick up a barrel of methylamine and Lydia finds a tracker on the bottom of the barrel. Mike thinks she was the one to plant it. When Hank and Marie come over for the dinner, at her wit's end and worried for her children, Skyler walks into the deep end of the swimming pool and fakes a suicide attempt. Walt agrees to let Holly and Walt Jr. stay with Hank and Marie for a while so that Skyler and Walt can "work on their relationship," but Walt is furious with Skyler for orchestrating these events. She tells him she hates him and is just waiting for him to die from the cancer. Jesse buys Walt a birthday gift, and Walt tells Skyler that she will change her mind about him.

Episode 5.5: "Dead Freight" (August 12, 2012)

Using a giant magnet to clear a computer was just the tip of the iceberg. In this episode, Mike, Jesse, and Walt (with the help of Todd) rob a train, stockpiling a thousand gallons of methylamine. The heist is Lydia's idea, when she attempts to save her life by offering them another solution to get methylamine. Mike, thinking she planted the tracker on the barrel, wants to kill Lydia; Jesse does not; and Walt as the deciding vote keeps her alive. On the home front, Walt Jr. is furious that he has been sent away; he attempts to come home, but Walt will not let him stay. Skyler says she will never change her mind about him. The heist nail-bitingly goes off just as planned, until the end when they realize a little boy on a dirt bike is watching. He waves at the trio, and Todd waves back. Then he pulls a gun and shoots, as Jesse screams, "No, NO!"

Episode 5.6: "Buyout" (August 19, 2012)

Jesse takes the death of Drew Sharp (the boy on the dirt bike) hard, punching out Todd after he makes a flip comment about the murder. Todd defends his decision to shoot the boy and Walt decides to keep him on the payroll. During their next cook, Jesse sees a news report for Drew and breaks down in grief for his parents; he leaves the cook early and listens to Walt happily whistle immediately following a proclamation that he was sick about Drew's death. Walt finds out Mike and Jesse want out of the business. Mike finds a buyer for the methylamine, but Walt does not want to sell his share. Jesse visits the Whites' home to try to convince Walt to sell and gets invited to the most awkward dinner of his life. Aaron Paul's facial expressions during this episode are laugh-out-loud funny every single time. It is like being at dinner with George and Martha. When Skyler excuses herself with the bottle of wine, Walt informs Jesse the cook is all he has left. The next day, Mike ties Walt up at gunpoint in order to ensure the deal goes through. Walt MacGyvers his way out of the room and hides the methylamine. He's worked out a plan where "everybody wins."

Episode 5.7: "Say My Name" (August 26, 2012)

In what is arguably the saddest episode of the series until "Ozymandias," Walt hides the methylamine at Skyler's car wash to keep Jesse and Mike's deal from moving forward. He strikes a new deal with Declan that gets Mike his $5 million. Walt makes it known that Heisenberg was the one to kill Gus, demanding Declan say his name. Walt witnesses a touching moment between Mike and Jesse and gets jealous. Walt does not want to let Jesse go, and he tries to verbally manipulate him into continuing to cook with him, offering him his own lab. Jesse walks away without his money, refusing to cook, and more importantly refusing to be part of more bloodshed. Walt brings in Todd as his new protégé. Mike makes sure his nine guys get their hazard pay out of his cut. Hank's boss reprimands him for spending too much time and money on the Fring case, especially for his obsession with Mike. Hank instead turns to the lawyer helping Mike with the money. Walt finds out the lawyer plans to flip, and warns Mike, who, to escape, has to leave his granddaughter alone at the park. He calls Saul to help him get his "go bag," and Walt offers to take care of it for him. Walt meets up with Mike in a remote location and demands the nine names of the men in prison. Mike refuses and, after a heated exchange, yells, "You. And, your pride and your ego . . . if you had done your job and known your place, we'd all be fine right now." A furious Walter gets his gun and shoots Mike through the car window. A wounded Mike attempts to drive off but quickly diverts into a rock. Shocked, Walter follows Mike's bloody trail to the riverbed, where he apologizes. He sadly realizes he could have gotten the names from Lydia all along. Mike dies.

Episode 5.8: "Gliding over All" (September 2, 2012)

Walt watches a fly (and hears a collective groan from half the viewing audience). In the part-one Season 5 finale, Walt and Todd get rid of Mike's body. Walt reaches out to Lydia for the list of ten names (including the lawyer planning to flip). Lydia convinces Walt he can go global with his empire, and he decides to let her live. Walt retapes the ricin vial he had planned to use on her behind the outlet at home. With the help of Todd's uncle Jack, Walt orchestrates a carefully timed mass murder of all ten prisoners. Walt's empire grows, and a montage of cooking, distributing, and laundering ensues to the song we've all been waiting for: "Crystal Blue Persuasion." Walt is tired. Skyler takes him to the storage unit where she has been stashing the cash, and he looks at the block of money he has amassed. She wants this to be enough. Walt visits Jesse; they reminisce and Walt leaves Jesse duffle bags filled with his $5 million cut. After Walt leaves, Jesse sinks to the floor relieved, and pulls out the gun he stuffed in the back of his pants when he saw Walt at the door. Walt tells Skyler he is done cooking. Flash forward a month, and Hank and Marie come to dinner. While using the bathroom, Hank finds the Walt Whitman book from Gale with the inscription to W.W.

Episode 5.9: "Blood Money" (August 11, 2013)

The part-two season opener (directed by Bryan Cranston) starts with another flash-forward as a bearded Walt shows up at the condemned White house. He uses a crowbar to open his front door, revealing the house in shambles; "Heisenberg" is scrawled in graffiti on the wall. Walt retrieves the ricin vial from behind the outlet. Who is he going to use that on? What happened to the house? Where is his family? That is all the information we get for now. Back to the present, Hank is reeling from his discovery of the W.W. note in the front of Walt's book. He takes the book, hightails it out of the party, and immediately crashes the car as he has a panic/rage attack. He compares the inscription to his notes from Gale's file, and the handwriting matches. Walt is Heisenberg. Lydia shows up at the car wash to try to convince Walt to come back to work for just a week to get the quality back up on the product. Walt declines and Skyler tells Lydia to go and never come back. Jesse tries to give away his money, first to Drew Sharp's parents and then to Mike's granddaughter. Saul tells Walt, who brings the money back to Jesse. Jesse tells him it is blood money and then he tells Walt that he thinks Walt killed Mike. Walt swears he did not kill Mike. Jesse drives around stoned and gives a homeless man a stack of bills. He realizes he wants to give it away to others and starts to throw the money from his car; it rains down like early morning newspapers. Walt cannot find the *Leaves of Grass* book from

Gale and starts to question Hank's strange behavior at dinner the other night. His suspicions are confirmed when he finds a tracking device on his car. Walt visits Hank, who closes the garage door. Walt tells Hank the cancer is back; Hank says he will do everything he can to make sure Walt rots in jail.

Episode 5.10: "Buried" (August 18, 2013)

Jesse is quickly sliding downhill after throwing millions of dollars into the street and pulling into a park to ride the merry-go-round. Hank and Walt have a standoff in the driveway, and Hank gets ahold of Skyler before Walt does. Skyler meets Hank at a restaurant and he asks her to turn on Walt. After realizing Hank does not have her best interest at heart, or any evidence against Walt, Skyler refuses and leaves loudly and emotionally. Walt worries that his money is not safe and takes it out to the desert to bury. Marie shows up to talk to Skyler. She realizes that Skyler knew about Walt before Hank got shot, and that Walt's connection to that world is to blame for all their misery. She slaps Skyler hard and then tries to take Holly away with her. Skyler refuses to let her leave with the baby and Hank has to intervene. He makes Marie leave Holly with Skyler. An exhausted Walt returns home and passes out in the bathroom as Skyler is trying to assess the risk. When he wakes up, Skyler suggests their best move is to "keep quiet." Lydia needs a higher-quality product, so she offs Declan and his men to replace them with Todd. Hank finds out Jesse is in the interrogation room.

Episode 5.11: "Confessions" (August 23, 2013)

Hank tries to get Jesse to flip, but he will not bite. Walt and Skyler meet with Hank and Marie at a Mexican restaurant, and when they cannot come to a resolution, Walt slides a DVD across the table. It holds a taped confession from Walt that implicates Hank as the mastermind kingpin behind everything. Hank finds out Marie took money from Walt and Skyler to pay for his treatment. Saul drives Jesse out to a remote location where Walt attempts to manipulate Jesse into leaving town. Jesse calls out Walt for the manipulation and tells him to be honest. Walt walks over and hugs Jesse, who resists but eventually breaks down sobbing on his shoulder. Saul makes the call and Jesse gets ready for a new life. Waiting for the guy to show up, he reaches for his bag of pot and realizes Huell lifted it in Saul's office. Jesse stares at his cigarette packet and puts two and two together. At gunpoint, Saul admits to Jesse that Walt asked him to lift the ricin cigarette. Jesse races to the Whites' house and violently throws gasoline around the front room to end the episode.

Episode 5.12: "Rabid Dog" (September 1, 2013)

Walt comes home to find Saul's car parked catawampus on his front drive. He sneaks in through the backyard and sees the gasoline can sitting in his family room, but cannot find Jesse. He rushes to get everything cleaned up before Skyler gets home, and regales his family with a ridiculous story about a gasoline pump gone wrong. Skyler smells a lie (in addition to the gasoline), but agrees to stay at a hotel. Walt meets with Saul, who recommends Jesse get taken out "Old Yeller" style. Walt refuses. Skyler gets more of the story from Walt, and also suggests that Jesse needs to be dealt with permanently. Walt tries to convince Jesse to meet with him so that he can explain why he poisoned Brock. We find out Hank walked in before Jesse could light the match and burn down the Whites' house. He convinces Jesse to turn on Walt, tapes his confession, and then sets him up with a wire. Jesse thinks it is a trap and he backs out on the meeting, telling a furious Hank he knows how to really hurt him. Walt calls Todd.

Episode 5.13: "To'hajiilee" (September 8, 2013)

Lydia needs a higher-quality product from Todd, and one that is blue. Todd has fallen in love with Lydia and aims to please her. Walt asks Todd and Uncle Jack to kill Jesse. Hank and Gomez find out that the biggest piece of evidence they can get against Walt is something he would never destroy: his money. Saul is concerned because Huell is missing, but Hank convinced him he is next on Walt's list. Huell reveals enough information about the whereabouts of the money that they are able to trick Walt into leading them right to it. A cornered Walt calls Jack and gives him the coordinates. He then realizes Jesse is with Hank and tells Uncle Jack and his men to stand down. Walt comes out from his hiding place behind a rock, hands up in surrender, and Hank slaps the cuffs on him. Hank calls Marie to tell her the good news. Jack and his

gang pull up, as Walt screams for them to leave. The neo-Nazis open fire and the episode concludes with the start of a shoot-out.

Episode 5.14: "Ozymandias" (September 15, 2013)

Three 2014 Emmys were awarded for this episode in the Writing, Lead Actor, and Lead Actress categories. Hailed by critics as the best episode of the series, and for some the best episode on television ever, "Ozymandias" packs one emotional punch after another. We open to the standoff between Hank and Gomez versus the neo-Nazis. After a blaze of gunfire, Gomez lies dead and Hank wounded. Walt pleads for Hank's life in vain as Uncle Jack shoots him midsentence. It is a punch to the gut, and Walt demonstrates the audience's reaction when he drops to his knees sobbing in grief. The neo-Nazis find Walt's barrels of money, and due to Todd's respect for "Mr. White," Uncle Jack leaves him one barrel and the car. Walt gives up Jesse's hiding place, finally telling him that he watched Jane die. A frantic Walt heads home to gather supplies and his family, but Walt Jr. and Skyler refuse to leave when they find out Hank is dead. Skyler grabs a knife and she and Walt scuffle, with Walt Jr. eventually jumping in to protect his mom. Junior calls the police and Walt takes off with Holly. A horrified Skyler races down the street after them, but Walt disappears. Jesse appears beaten, cuffed, and locked in a caged pit. Todd collects a terrified Jesse and brings him to the lab, chaining Jesse on a lead like a dog. A picture of Andrea and Brock is held to a post as a warning; Jesse will cook for Todd. Walt calls Skyler as the police listen in and provides a cover story that makes Skyler the unwilling victim in Walt's grand scheme, hoping to buy her some leeway with the police. Skyler cries, Marie cries, and the viewing audience cries. Walt delivers Holly to a fire station and waits for the vacuum repairman.

Episode 5.15: "Granite State" (September 22, 2013)

Saul also needs a vacuum repaired. Ed, the repairman, tells Saul he has to share a basement with Walt as they both wait to disappear. Walt plots his revenge, and Saul counsels Walt to turn himself in and face the music. Saul tells Walt that he is leaving Skyler and the kids "high and dry," but Walt refuses to listen and continues with his plan to kill the neo-Nazis. Saul refuses to help and tells Walt, "It's over." Skyler's house is being watched, but the neo-Nazis slip in and warn her to keep her mouth shut. Lydia wants to end the business deal, but Todd tells her he has Pinkman, a 92 percent purity, and the blue is back. Walt arrives at his New Hampshire residence. He complains about the DVD selection and the lack of Internet, and insists he needs to conduct some business (kill the neo-Nazis). Ed tries to explain the gravity of Walt's situation. Jesse picks his locks and attempts to escape. Todd kills Andrea and threatens Brock next if he ever tries to run away again. Many months later, a bearded Walt with a full head of hair opens the gate for Ed's monthly delivery. Ed brings supplies, news, and his chemo treatment. Skyler is a pariah and can only afford a young public defender. A lonely Walt pays Ed $10,000 for one extra hour of company. Later that night, Walt's wedding ring slips from his finger and we know he does not have much time left. He breaks Ed's rule and ventures into town, where he tries to contact Walt Jr. to send him some money. A distraught Jr. tells Walt to keep his money and die. Walt calls the DEA to turn himself in. While he waits with a drink at the bar, he sees Gretchen and Elliott Schwartz on *Charlie Rose* discounting his initial contribution to Gray Matter. As the episode concludes, the police descend, and Walt is no longer sitting at the bar.

Episode 5.16: "Felina" (September 29, 2013)

The conclusion to Walter White's saga is magnificent. Walt finds a car and makes a plan. His first stop is Gretchen and Elliott's place, where he sits quietly in the shadows for them to come home and then walks right in the front door. He tells them they will use his money, and only his money, to set up a trust in Walt Jr.'s name for $9,720,000. Sensing Gretchen's unspoken refusal and Elliott's too willing agreement to anything Walt says, he tells them if they do not follow through on his plan, he has hired two hit men to kill them. Skinny Pete and Badger (playing the hit men with laser pointers instead of guns) inform Walt that his blue meth is on the streets and "better than ever." Walt thinks Jack has partnered with Jesse. We see a sequence of Jesse making a box in woodworking shop, lovingly carving and oiling it down to perfection. Reality hits when Jesse's lead gets stuck and we realize he is imagining the shop in order to escape the horrors of his enslavement as a meth cook. Walt sits down with a horrified Lydia and surprised Todd to tell them he has a new way to cook meth that will not require the hard-to-come-by methylamine.

Lydia tells Todd to kill Walt. We see Walt building a robot in the desert, as his wedding ring, still secure to the string around his neck, slips from his shirt. Marie calls Skyler to warn her Walt has been sighted around Albuquerque, and the camera pans out to show him standing in Skyler's kitchen. She gives him "five minutes." He says he wants a proper good-bye and hands her the lottery ticket with coordinates. He tells her to trade that for a deal with the prosecutor. Walt admits to Skyler that he did everything for himself, because it made him feel good and "alive." She lets him see Holly one last time. Walt shows up at Uncle Jack's and pulls a final Mr. Magoo move to park directly in front of the clubhouse. Jack tells his men to kill Walt, but Walt insists Jack owes him for not killing Jesse. Todd brings Jesse into the clubhouse to show Walt that he is not a willing participant, let alone a partner in their meth business. Walt realizes what he has done to Jesse as he looks at the beaten-down mess of a man before him, and he tackles him, saving Jesse from the machine-gun massacre that takes out almost everybody else in the room. Todd is saved from the gun, and he inches to the window to find out the source of the gunfire. Seeing his chance, Jesse pulls his chains around Todd's neck, violently strangling his captor. A severely wounded Jack offers Walt the whereabouts of his money, but Walt shoots him. It is finally not about the money. Walt tells Jesse to kill him, and Jesse refuses to do anything Walt wants ever again. Jesse takes a car, peeling out around Walt's silent figure, and busts through the gates to freedom. A dying Walt wanders into the lab, fondly tapping gauges as he leaves one last bloody handprint on a shiny vat. As Badfinger's "Baby Blue" plays, Walter White falls to the ground and dies.

NOTES

INTRODUCTION

1. Hillary Busis, "*Saturday Night Live* Taps *Breaking Bad* for Trump's Next Cabinet Pick," *Vanity Fair*, December 10, 2016, http://www.vanityfair.com/hollywood/2016/12/saturday-night-live-breaking-bad-donald-trump-walter-white.

2. Tom Schnauz and Peter Gould, "*Breaking Bad* Writers: 'This Is It; There Is No More,'" interview by Terry Gross, *Fresh Air*, NPR, October 3, 2013.

3. Allen St. John, "Why *Breaking Bad* Is the Best Show Ever and Why That Matters," *Forbes*, September 16, 2013, http://www.forbes.com/sites/allenstjohn/2013/09/16/why-breaking-bad-is-the-best-show-ever-and-why-that-matters/.

4. James Poniewozik, "Breaking Point," *Time* 182, no. 7 (August 12, 2013).

5. Ann Larabee, "Editorial: The New Television Antihero," *Journal of Popular Culture* 46, no. 6 (2013): 1131.

6. Steven Johnson, *Everything Bad Is Good for You: How Today's Popular Culture Is Actually Making Us Smarter* (New York: Riverhead Books, 2006).

7. Greg Smith, "'It's Just a Movie': A Teaching Essay for Introductory Media Classes," *Cinema Journal* 41, no. 1 (2001): 127–34.

8. Andrew Leonard, "The Downward Spiral," *Rolling Stone*, no. 11133 (June 23, 2011).

9. Megan McCluskey, "See All the Ways *Breaking Bad* Was Inspired by *Pulp Fiction*," *Time*, October 21, 2015, http://time.com/4081446/breaking-bad-inspired-by-pulp-fiction/.

10. Dan Snierson, "*Breaking Bad*: Creator Vince Gilligan Explains the Series Finale," *Entertainment Weekly*, September 30, 2013, http://ew.com/article/2013/09/30/breaking-bad-finale-vince-gilligan/.

11. Smith, "'It's Just a Movie,'" 133.

12. M. Keith Booker and Bob Batchelor, Mad Men: A Cultural History (Lanham, MD: Rowman & Littlefield, 2016): ix.

I. ANTIHERO OR VILLAIN

1. Kevin Clarke, "Broken, Bad, Redeemed?" America Magazine, October 7, 2013.

2. Tad Friend, "The One Who Knocks," New Yorker 89, no. 28 (September 16, 2013).

3. Jaime J. Weinman, "What Makes Breaking Bad So Good." Maclean's 123, no. 20 (May 31, 2010).

4. Dan Snierson, "Bad Boys, Bad Boys . . . Whatcha Gonna Do?" Entertainment Weekly, July 20, 2012.

5. Emily Nussbaum, "Child's Play," New Yorker 88, no. 25 (August 27, 2012), http://www.newyorker.com/magazine/2012/08/27/childs-play-5.

6. Clarke, "Broken, Bad, Redeemed?"

7. Chuck Klosterman, I Wear the Black Hat (New York: Scribner, 2013), 48.

8. "Bryan Cranston and Breaking Bad Get Ready for the End," Minneapolis Star Tribune, August 10, 2013, http://www.startribune.com/bryan-cranston-and-breaking-bad-get-ready-for-the-end/218927041/.

9. Bryan Cranston, "Psychos We Love," Tribeca Film Festival, interviewed by Juju Chang, April 23, 2014, https://tribecafilm.com/stories/recap-psychos-bryan-cranston-terence-winter-james-fallon-panel.

10. Cranston, "Psychos We Love."

11. Friend, "One Who Knocks."

12. Cranston, "Psychos We Love."

13. James Poniewozik, "Elements of Style," Time, July 17, 2011, http://content.time.com/time/Arts/article/0,8599,2082963,00.html.

14. Jean MacKenzie, "The Rise of the American Antihero," PRI: Public Radio International, June 11, 2013, http://www.pri.org/stories/2013-06-11/rise-american-antihero.

15. Thomas Batten, "Mad Men: How Don Draper and Walter White Prepared Us for Donald Trump," Guardian, August 10, 2015, https://www.theguardian.com/tv-and-radio/tvandradioblog/2015/aug/10/donald-trump-antihero-mad-men-breaking-bad.

16. Ashley M. Donnelly, Renegade Hero or Faux Rogue (Jefferson, NC: McFarland, 2014), 13.

17. Chuck Klosterman, "Chuck Klosterman on Batman, Bad Guys and Wearing 'The Black Hat,'" interview by Audie Cornish, All Things Considered, NPR,

July 9, 2013, http://www.npr.org/2013/07/09/200141185/chuck-klosterman-on-batman-bad-guys-and-wearing-the-black-hat.

18. Klosterman, *I Wear the Black Hat.*

19. M. Keith Booker and Bob Batchelor, Mad Men: *A Cultural History* (Lanham, MD: Rowman & Littlefield, 2016).

20. "Bryan Cranston and *Breaking Bad* Get Ready for the End," *Minneapolis Star Tribune*, August 10, 2013, http://www.startribune.com/bryan-cranston-and-breaking-bad-get-ready-for-the-end/218927041/.

21. "Bryan Cranston and *Breaking Bad.*"

22. Batten, "Mad Men."

23. Donna Bowman, "What's the Right Way to Watch *Breaking Bad?*" A.V. Club, August 5, 2013, http://www.avclub.com/article/whats-the-right-way-to-watch-ibreaking-badi-101143.

24. Todd VanDerWerff, "How *Breaking Bad* Broke Free from the Clockwork-Universe Problem," A.V. Club, August 7, 2013, http://www.avclub.com/article/how-ibreaking-badi-broke-free-of-the-clockwork-uni-101278.

25. Rich Bellis, "Which Great Literary Work Explains *Breaking Bad* Best?" *Atlantic*, October 2, 2013, http://www.theatlantic.com/entertainment/archive/2013/10/which-great-literary-work-explains-em-breaking-bad-em-best/280149/.

26. Tom Schnauz and Peter Gould, "*Breaking Bad* Writers: 'This Is It; There Is No More,'" interview by Terry Gross, *Fresh Air*, NPR, October 3, 2013.

27. Alan Sepinwall, "*Breaking Bad* Star Bryan Cranston Looks Back at Walter White's Greatest Hits, Part 2," UPROXX, July 13, 2012, http://uproxx.com/sepinwall/breaking-bad-star-bryan-cranston-looks-back-at-walter-whites-greatest-hits-part-2/.

28. Sepinwall, "*Breaking Bad* Star Bryan Cranston."

29. Bill Bradley, "Vince Gilligan Finally Reveals Why Walter White Left Gray Matter," *Huffington Post*, March 17, 2016, http://www.huffingtonpost.com/entry/vince-gilligan-walter-white-gray-matter_us_56e85f27e4b0b25c91838d57.

30. Jessica Hecht, "Q&A—Jessica Hecht (Gretchen)," AMC.com, May 2009, http://www.amc.com/shows/breaking-bad/talk/2009/05/jessica-hecht-interview.

31. Klosterman, *I Wear the Black Hat.* (See for a discussion of why it is ironic that this is such a powerful image of villainy.)

2. THE EVOLUTION OF HEISENBERG

1. Tad Friend, "The One Who Knocks," *New Yorker* 89, no. 28 (September 16, 2013).

2. Bryan Cranston, "Actor Bryan Cranston, 'Breaking' with Type," interview by David Bianculli, *Fresh Air*, NPR, March 19, 2010.

3. Alan Sepinwall, "*Breaking Bad*: Bryan Cranston/Vince Gilligan Q&A," *Newark (NJ) Star-Ledger*, March 6, 2009, http://www.nj.com/entertainment/tv/index.ssf/2009/03/breaking_bad_bryan_cranstonvin.html.

4. "*Breaking Bad*: Two Surprising Actors Who Could Have Taken Bryan Cranston's Role," *Hollywood Reporter*, July 16, 2012.

5. "*Breaking Bad*: Two Surprising Actors."

6. Friend, "One Who Knocks."

7. Sepinwall, "Bryan Cranston/Vince Gilligan Q&A."

8. Friend, "One Who Knocks."

9. Bryan Cranston, "Psychos We Love," Tribeca Film Festival, interview by Juju Chang, April 23, 2014, https://tribecafilm.com/stories/recap-psychos-bryan-cranston-terence-winter-james-fallon-panel.

10. Vince Gilligan, "*Breaking Bad*: The Network & GEITF Joint Session Masterclass," Edinburgh International Television Festival, interview by Charlie Brooker, published online September 11, 2013, accessed November 6, 2016, https://www.youtube.com/watch?v=lXVJ8eRIRrc.

11. Krysten Ritter, "Krysten Ritter on *Breaking Bad*: Team Walter White until the Bitter End," Vulture.com, September 24, 2013, http://www.vulture.com/2013/09/krysten-ritter-breaking-bad-essay.html.

12. Emily Nussbaum, "Child's Play," *New Yorker* 88, no. 25 (August 27, 2012), http://www.newyorker.com/magazine/2012/08/27/childs-play-5.

13. Chuck Klosterman, *I Wear the Black Hat* (New York: Scribner, 2013), 49.

14. Gilligan, "Network & GEITF Joint Session."

15. Alan Sepinwall, "*Breaking Bad* Star Bryan Cranston Looks Back at Walter White's Greatest Hits, Part 2," UPROXX, July 13, 2012, http://uproxx.com/sepinwall/breaking-bad-star-bryan-cranston-looks-back-at-walter-whites-greatest-hits-part-2/.

16. Friend, "One Who Knocks."

17. Donna Bowman, "What's the Right Way to Watch *Breaking Bad*?" A.V. Club, August 5, 2013, http://www.avclub.com/article/whats-the-right-way-to-watch-ibreaking-badi-101143.

18. Friend, "One Who Knocks."

19. Cranston, "Psychos We Love."

3. DOES WALT WANT TO DIE?

1. Jarre Fees, "He's Not 'Bad,' Just Written That Way," *Television Week* 27, no. 17 (June 2, 2008).

2. Fees, "He's Not 'Bad.'"

4. MORALITY, LEGALITY, AND EVERYTHING IN BETWEEN

1. Vince Gilligan, "*Breaking Bad*: Vince Gilligan on Meth and Morals," interview by Terry Gross, *Fresh Air*, NPR, September 9, 2011.

2. Vince Gilligan, "Vince Gilligan on How *Breaking Bad* Almost Didn't Happen," *Newsweek*, July 16, 2012, http://www.newsweek.com/vince-gilligan-how-breaking-bad-almost-didnt-happen-65529.

3. Scott Meslow, "The Moral Universe of *Breaking Bad*," *Atlantic*, July 16, 2012, http://www.theatlantic.com/entertainment/archive/2012/07/the-moral-universe-of-breaking-bad/259860/.

4. Maureen Ryan, "*Breaking Bad* Does *Scarface*: Is Al Pacino a Fan of Walter White?" *Huffington Post*, July 30, 2012, http://www.huffingtonpost.com/2012/07/29/breaking-bad-scarface_n_1716848.html.

5. *Breaking Bad: The Complete Series*. Directed by Bryan Cranston, Adam Bernstein, Bronwen Hughes, Charles Haid, Colin Bucksey. 2009–2013. Culver City, CA: Sony Pictures Home Entertainment. Home Video, 2014. DVD.

6. Lane Brown, "In Conversation: Vince Gilligan on the End of *Breaking Bad*," Vulture.com, May 12, 2013, http://www.vulture.com/2013/05/vince-gilligan-on-breaking-bad.html.

7. Jonathan Merritt, "The Death of Moral Relativism," *Atlantic*, March 25, 2016, http://www.theatlantic.com/politics/archive/2016/03/the-death-of-moral-relativism/475221/.

8. Helen Rittelmeyer, "Moral Relativism, R.I.P." *American Spectator*, September 17, 2012, http://spectator.org/35020_moral-relativism-rip/.

9. Merritt, "Death of Moral Relativism."

10. Meslow, "Moral Universe of *Breaking Bad*."

5. JUST SAY NO?

1. Lane Brown, "In Conversation: Vince Gilligan on the End of *Breaking Bad*," Vulture.com, May 12, 2013, http://www.vulture.com/2013/05/vince-gilligan-on-breaking-bad.html.

2. Chuck Klosterman, *I Wear the Black Hat* (New York: Scribner, 2013).

3. Klosterman, *I Wear the Black Hat*.

4. Patrick Radden Keefe, "The Uncannily Accurate Depiction of the Meth Trade in *Breaking Bad*," *New Yorker*, July 13, 2012, http://www.newyorker.com/culture/culture-desk/the-uncannily-accurate-depiction-of-the-meth-trade-in-breaking-bad.

5. Office of National Drug Control Policy, *Fact Sheet: Methamphetamine Trends in the United States*, July 2010.

6. Brown, "In Conversation."

7. Brown, "In Conversation."

8. Jessica Hecht, "Q&A—Jessica Hecht (Gretchen)," AMC.com, May 2009, http://www.amc.com/shows/breaking-bad/talk/2009/05/jessica-hecht-interview.

9. Alan Sepinwall, *"Breaking Bad* Star Bryan Cranston Looks Back at Walter White's Greatest Hits, Part 2," UPROXX, July 13, 2012, http://uproxx.com/sepinwall/breaking-bad-star-bryan-cranston-looks-back-at-walter-whites-greatest-hits-part-2/.

10. Brown, "In Conversation."

11. Klosterman, *I Wear the Black Hat*, 49.

12. Brown, "In Conversation."

13. Klosterman, *I Wear the Black Hat.*

14. Klosterman, *I Wear the Black Hat*, 49.

15. David Ury and Dale Dickey, "Q&A—David Ury (Spooge) and Dale Dickey (Spooge's Woman)," AMC.com, 2010, http://www.amc.com/shows/breakingbad/talk/2011/01/david-ury-dale-dickey-interview.

16. Dan Snierson, *"Breaking Bad*: Creator Vince Gilligan Explains the Series Finale," *Entertainment Weekly*, September 30, 2013, http://ew.com/article/2013/09/30/breaking-bad-finale-vince-gilligan/.

17. Maia Szalavitz, "'Unbroken Brain' Explains Why 'Tough' Treatment Doesn't Help Drug Addicts," interview by Terry Gross, *Fresh Air*, NPR, July 7, 2016, http://www.npr.org/sections/health-shots/2016/07/07/485087604/unbroken-brain-explains-why-tough-treatment-doesnt-help-drug-addicts.

18. Keefe, "Uncannily Accurate Depiction."

6. MARKETING *BREAKING BAD*

1. Lane Brown, "In Conversation: Vince Gilligan on the End of *Breaking Bad*," Vulture.com, May 12, 2013, http://www.vulture.com/2013/05/vince-gilligan-on-breaking-bad.html.

2. Donna Bowman, "What's the Right Way to Watch *Breaking Bad*?" A.V. Club, August 5, 2013, http://www.avclub.com/article/whats-the-right-way-to-watch-ibreaking-badi-101143.

3. Alessandra Stanley, "When Going Gets Tough, a Not-So-Tough Turns to Meth," *New York Times*, January 18, 2008, http://www.nytimes.com/2008/01/18/arts/television/18brea.html.

4. Tom Shales, "There's a Meth to AMC's Madness in *Breaking Bad*," *Washington Post*, January 19, 2008, http://www.washingtonpost.com/wpdyn/content/article/2008/01/18/AR2008011803342.html.

5. Owen Van Spall, "*Breaking Bad*: The Finest Thing You Haven't Seen," *Guardian*, August 21, 2009, https://www.theguardian.com/culture/tvandradioblog/2009/aug/21/breaking-bad.

6. Gary Levin, "Nielsens: 'Runway' Finale Rules on Cable," *USA Today*, March 11, 2008, http://usatoday30.usatoday.com/life/television/news/2008-03-11-nielsens-analysis_N.htm.

7. Eliana Dockterman, "A Record-Breaking 10.3 Million People Watched the *Breaking Bad* Finale," *Time*, September 30, 2013, http://entertainment.time.com/2013/09/30/a-record-breaking-10-3-million-people-watched-the-breaking-bad-finale/.

8. Greg Gillman, "TheGrill: Ted Sarandos—Vince Gilligan Thanked Netflix for Saving *Breaking Bad*," TheWrap.com, September 24, 2013, http://www.thewrap.com/thegrill-netflixs-ted-sarandos-on-arrested-development-its-only-a-matter-of-when-and-what-form-it-takes/.

9. Dorothy Pomerantz, "Netflix, *Breaking Bad* and the Business Triumph of Quality Television," *Forbes*, September 27, 2013, http://www.forbes.com/sites/dorothypomerantz/2013/09/27/breaking-bad-and-the-triumph-of-quality-television/.

10. Dan Snierson, "Bad Boys, Bad Boys . . . Whatcha Gonna Do?" *Entertainment Weekly*, July 20, 2012.

11. James Poniewozik, "Go Ahead, Binge-Watch That TV Show," *Time*, July 10, 2012, http://entertainment.time.com/2012/07/10/go-ahead-binge-watch-that-tv-show/.

12. John Jurgensen, "Binge Viewing: TV's Lost Weekends," *Wall Street Journal*, July 13, 2012, http://www.wsj.com/articles/SB10001424052702303740704577521300806686174.

13. Jurgensen, "Binge Viewing."

14. Poniewozik, "Go Ahead."

15. Jurgensen, "Binge Viewing."

16. Jurgensen, "Binge Viewing."

17. Joshua Brustein, "Why Did AMC Split *Breaking Bad*'s Final Season into Two?" *Bloomberg Businessweek*, September 9, 2013, https://www.bloomberg.com/news/articles/2013-09-09/why-did-amc-split-breaking-bads-final-season-into-two.

18. Jeff Jensen, "*Breaking Bad* and *Mad Men*: Why Splitting Final Seasons Isn't a Good Idea," *Entertainment Weekly*, September 18, 2013, http://ew.com/article/2013/09/18/breaking-bad-mad-men-split-season/.

19. Gillman, "Vince Gilligan Thanked Netflix."

20. Bowman, "Right Way to Watch *Breaking Bad?*"

21. Vince Gilligan, "I Am Vince Gilligan, AMA," Reddit.com, 2015, https://www.reddit.com/r/IAmA/comments/34g1us/i_am_vince_gilligan_ama/.

22. John Foley, "*Breaking Bad* Meets Modern Marketing: 5 Rules for High-Impact Content," *Forbes*, November 1, 2013, http://www.forbes.com/sites/oracle/2013/11/01/breaking-bad-meets-modern-marketing-5-tips-for-high-impact-content/#44db0d285b9d.

23. "AMC Announces Chris Hardwick as Host of *Talking Bad*, Premiering August 11," AMC.com, July 2013, http://www.amc.com/shows/talking-bad/talk/2013/07/amc-announces-chris-hardwick-as-host-of-talking-bad-premiering-august-11.

24. "Sunday Cable Ratings: *Breaking Bad* Wins Night, *True Blood*, *Low Winter Sun*, *Devious Maids*, *Dexter*, *The Newsroom* & More," TV by the Numbers, August 13, 2013, http://tvbythenumbers.zap2it.com/sdsdskdh279882992z1/sunday-cable-ratings-breaking-bad-wins-night-true-blood-low-winter-sun-devious-maids-dexter-the-newsroom-more/197129/.

25. "Sunday Cable Ratings: *Breaking Bad* Wins Big, *Talking Bad*, *Homeland*, *Boardwalk Empire*, *Masters of Sex* & More," TV by the Numbers, October 1, 2013, http://tvbythenumbers.zap2it.com/sdsdskdh279882992z1/sunday-cable-ratingsbreaking-bad-wins-big-talking-bad-homeland-boardwalk-empiremasters-of-sex-more/205986/.

26. Megan McCluskey, "Here's the *Breaking Bad* Easter Egg Even Vince Gilligan Missed," *Time*, April 13, 2016, http://time.com/4292409/breaking-bad-easter-egg-vince-gilligan-missed/.

27. Bowman, "Right Way to Watch *Breaking Bad?*"

28. Laura Bennett, "The Hidden Secrets of TV Posters," *New Republic*, July 18, 2013, https://newrepublic.com/article/113874/breaking-bad-mad-men-newsroom-posters-their-hidden-secrets.

29. Rob Tannenbaum, "Vince Gilligan: 'Walt Is Not Darth Vader,'" *Rolling Stone*, September 25, 2013, http://www.rollingstone.com/tv/news/vince-gilligan-walt-is-not-darth-vader-20130925.

30. glass_daggers, "All Hail the King Season 5 Promo Image," Reddit.com, 2013, https://www.reddit.com/r/breakingbad/comments/uk8n5/all_hail_the_king_season_5_promo_image/.

31. Bennett, "Hidden Secrets of TV Posters."

32. Bowman, "Right Way to Watch *Breaking Bad?*"

33. Gilligan, "I Am Vince Gilligan."

34. Tim Nudd, "'Remember My Name,' Says Walter White on *Breaking Bad*'s Imposing Final Poster," *AdWeek*, June 24, 2013, http://www.adweek.com/adfreak/remember-my-name-says-walter-white-breaking-bads-imposing-final-poster-150684.

35. *"Breaking Bad* Poster Features Walter White and 'Remember My Name' Slogan," *Huffington Post*, June 25, 2013, http://www.huffingtonpost.com/2013/06/25/breaking-bad-poster-walter-white_n_3497339.html.

36. Judy Berman, "Does the New *Breaking Bad* Poster Foreshadow Walter White's Death?" *Flavorwire*, June 25, 2013, http://flavorwire.com/400411/does-the-new-breaking-bad-poster-foreshadow-walter-whites-death.

37. Richard Lawson, "Is Walter White Going to Die?" *Atlantic*, June 25, 2013, http://www.theatlantic.com/entertainment/archive/2013/06/walter-white-going-die/313914/.

38. Bennett, "Hidden Secrets of TV Posters."

39. Joanna Robinson, *"Better Call Saul* Creators Didn't Expect You to Solve Their Gus Fring Puzzle," *Vanity Fair*, April 19, 2016, http://www.vanityfair.com/hollywood/2016/04/better-call-saul-gus-frings-back-title-anagram-finale.

40. Foley, *"Breaking Bad* Meets Modern Marketing."

7. BAD ASS MAMA

1. Anna Gunn, "I Have a Character Issue," *New York Times*, August 23, 2013, http://www.nytimes.com/2013/08/24/opinion/i-have-a-character-issue.html?_r=0.

2. Ethan Richardson, "Why *Does* Everyone Hate Skyler White?" Mockingbird.com, September 4, 2013, http://www.mbird.com/2013/09/why-does-everyone-hate-skyler-white/.

3. Gunn, "I Have a Character Issue."

4. Lane Brown, "In Conversation: Vince Gilligan on the End of *Breaking Bad*," Vulture.com, May 12, 2013, http://www.vulture.com/2013/05/vince-gilligan-on-breaking-bad.html.

5. Paul MacInnes, *"Breaking Bad* Creator Vince Gilligan: The Man Who Turned Walter White from Mr. Chips into Scarface," *Guardian*, May 19, 2012, https://www.theguardian.com/tv-and-radio/2012/may/19/vince-gilligan-breaking-bad.

6. Brown, "In Conversation."

7. Louis C.K., director, *Louis C.K.: Chewed Up*, Art & Industry, 2008.

8. Richardson, "Why *Does* Everyone Hate Skyler White?"

8. BREAKING DOWN THE BAD GUYS

1. Greg Braxton, "Sympathy for Gus: Giancarlo Esposito Talks *Breaking Bad*," *LA Times Blogs*, October 10, 2011, http://latimesblogs.latimes.com/showtracker/2011/10/sympathy-for-gus-giancarlo-esposito-talks-breaking-bad.html.

2. Shirley Li, "Forget Gus: Todd Is the Most Dangerous Villain on *Breaking Bad*," *Entertainment Weekly*, September 7, 2013, http://ew.com/article/2013/09/17/breaking-bad-dangerous-villain-todd/.

3. John Hanlon, "*Breaking Bad*: How Walter White Became Each of His Enemies," *The Week*, September 30, 2013, http://theweek.com/articles/459468/breaking-bad-how-walter-white-became-each-enemies.

4. Rob Tannenbaum, "Vince Gilligan: 'Walt Is Not Darth Vader,'" *Rolling Stone*, September 25, 2013, http://www.rollingstone.com/tv/news/vince-gilligan-walt-is-not-darth-vader-20130925.

5. Hanlon, "*Breaking Bad*."

6. Rachel Simon, "*Breaking Bad* Characters Ranked from Least to Most Evil: Where Does Walt Finish?," *Bustle.com*, September 25, 2013, https://www.bustle.com/articles/5697-breaking-bad-characters-ranked-from-least-to-most-evil-where-does-walt-finish.

7. Tom Schnauz and Peter Gould, "*Breaking Bad* Writers: 'This Is It; There Is No More,'" interview by Terry Gross, *Fresh Air*, NPR, October 3, 2013.

8. Hanlon, "*Breaking Bad*."

9. Luis Moncada, "Q&A—Daniel and Luis Moncada (the Cousins)," AMC.com, May 2010, http://www.amc.com/shows/breaking-bad/talk/2010/05/the-cousins-interview.

10. Stacey Wilson Hunt, "Emmys 2012: Mark Margolis, the Year's Only Silent Nominee, Reflects on *Breaking Bad*, *Scarface*," *Hollywood Reporter*, August 23, 2012, http://www.hollywoodreporter.com/news/emmys-2012-breaking-bad-mark-margolis-364842.

11. Dan Snierson, "Bad Boys, Bad Boys . . . Whatcha Gonna Do?" *Entertainment Weekly*, July 20, 2012.

12. Perri Nemiroff, "*Breaking Bad*: Giancarlo Esposito on Taking Gus from One-Episode Character to Iconic Villain," Collider.com, July 17, 2015, http://collider.com/breaking-bad-giancarlo-esposito-on-taking-gus-from-one-episode-character-to-iconic-villain/.

13. Patrick Radden Keefe, "The Uncannily Accurate Depiction of the Meth Trade in *Breaking Bad*," *New Yorker*, July 13, 2012, http://www.newyorker.com/culture/culture-desk/the-uncannily-accurate-depiction-of-the-meth-trade-in-breaking-bad.

14. Braxton, "Sympathy for Gus."

15. Braxton, "Sympathy for Gus."

16. Braxton, "Sympathy for Gus."

17. Vince Gilligan, "*Breaking Bad* Insider Podcast 408," Breaking Bad *Insider Podcast*, September 6, 2011, AMC, https://itunes.apple.com/us/podcast/breaking-bad-insider-podcast/id311058181?mt=2.

18. Braxton, "Sympathy for Gus."

19. Giancarlo Esposito, "Q&A—Giancarlo Esposito (Gus Fring)," AMC.com, September 2011, http://www.amc.com/shows/breaking-bad/talk/2011/09/giancarlo-esposito-interview.

20. Rob Tannenbaum, "*Breaking Bad*'s Lydia: She's a Clean-Cut, Bonkers Sociopath,'" *Rolling Stone*, September 28, 2013, http://www.rollingstone.com/tv/news/breaking-bads-lydia-shes-a-clean-cut-bonkers-sociopath-20130926.

21. Tannenbaum, "*Breaking Bad*'s Lydia."

22. Katy Rich, "Why *Breaking Bad*'s Neo-Nazis Are the Perfect Villains for the End of the Series," CinemaBlend, 2013, http://www.cinemablend.com/television/Why-Breaking-Bad-Neo-Nazis-Perfect-Villains-End-Series-59132.html.

23. Li, "Forget Gus."

24. Michael Jensen, "Interpreting 'Partner' on This Week's *Breaking Bad*," *Logo* (blog), September 7, 2011, http://www.newnownext.com/interpreting-partner-on-this-weeks-breaking-bad/09/2011/.

25. Rich, "*Breaking Bad*'s Neo-Nazis."

26. Li, "Forget Gus."

9. THE ANTI-WALTS OF *BREAKING BAD*

1. Rob Tannenbaum, "Vince Gilligan: 'Walt Is Not Darth Vader,'" *Rolling Stone*, September 25, 2013, http://www.rollingstone.com/tv/news/vince-gilligan-walt-is-not-darth-vader-20130925.

2. Andrew Romano, "'To'hajiilee' Is the Finest Episode of *Breaking Bad* Yet," *Daily Beast*, September 8, 2013, http://www.thedailybeast.com/articles/2013/09/08/to-hajiilee-is-the-finest-episode-of-breaking-bad-yet.html.

3. Chuck Klosterman, *I Wear the Black Hat* (New York: Scribner, 2013).

4. Vince Gilligan, "*Breaking Bad* Series Creator Vince Gilligan Answers Viewer Questions, Part I," AMC.com, 2011, http://www.amc.com/shows/breaking-bad/talk/2011/10/vince-gilligan-interview.

5. Vince Gilligan, "Vince Gilligan: Kingpin of the Year 2013," interview by Brett Martin, *GQ.com*, November 26, 2013, http://www.gq.com/story/vince-gilligan-men-of-the-year-kingpin.

6. Dan Snierson, "Bryan Cranston and Aaron Paul Discuss Ending of *Breaking Bad* Finale," *Entertainment Weekly*, September 30, 2013, http://ew.com/article/2013/09/30/breaking-bad-finale-bryan-cranston-aaron-paul/.

7. Todd VanDerWerff, "*Breaking Bad* Ended the Anti-hero Genre by Introducing Good and Evil," A.V. Club, September 30, 2013, http://www.avclub.com/article/ibreaking-badi-ended-the-anti-hero-genre-by-introd-103483.

8. Bryan Cranston, "Psychos We Love," Tribeca Film Festival, interview by Juju Chang, April 23, 2014, https://tribecafilm.com/stories/recap-psychos-bryan-cranston-terence-winter-james-fallon-panel.

9. Gilligan, "Kingpin of the Year."

10. Snierson, "Bryan Cranston and Aaron Paul."

11. Gilligan, "Viewer Questions, Part I."

12. Laura Prudom, "'Under The Dome': Dean Norris on Big Jim's Duplicitous Nature and the *Breaking Bad* Finale," *Huffington Post*, July 8, 2013, http://www.huffingtonpost.com/2013/06/18/under-the-dome-dean-norris-big-jim_n_3458143.html.

13. Gilligan, "Viewer Questions, Part I."

14. Andrew Romano, "*Breaking Bad* Finale: Lost Interviews with Bryan Cranston & Vince Gilligan," *Daily Beast*, September 29, 2013, http://www.thedailybeast.com/articles/2013/09/29/breaking-bad-finale-lost-interviews-with-bryan-cranston-vince-gilligan.html.

15. Ross Douthat, "The Hero of Breaking Bad," *New York Times*, September 18, 2013, http://douthat.blogs.nytimes.com/2013/09/18/the-hero-of-breaking-bad/.

16. Andrew Romano, "'To'hajiilee.'"

CONCLUSION

1. Vince Gilligan, "Vince Gilligan: Kingpin of the Year 2013," interview by Brett Martin, *GQ.com*, November 26, 2013, http://www.gq.com/story/vince-gilligan-men-of-the-year-kingpin.

2. Dan Snierson, "Vince Gilligan's Very Good *Breaking Bad* Year," *Entertainment Weekly*, December 31, 2013, http://ew.com/article/2013/12/31/breaking-bad-vince-gilligan-better-call-saul-community/.

3. Allen St. John, "In a Perfect Finale, *Breaking Bad* Proves It's a Love Story," *Forbes*, September 30, 2013. http://www.forbes.com/sites/allenstjohn/2013/09/30/in-a-perfect-finale-breaking-bad-proves-its-a-love-story/3/#4c66d9a663fc.

4. Lane Brown, "In Conversation: Vince Gilligan on the End of *Breaking Bad*," Vulture.com, May 12, 2013, http://www.vulture.com/2013/05/vince-gilligan-on-breaking-bad.html.

5. Emily Nussbaum, "The Closure-Happy *Breaking Bad* Finale." *New Yorker*, September 30, 2013, http://www.newyorker.com/culture/culture-desk/the-closure-happy-breaking-bad-finale.

6. Snierson, "Gilligan's Very Good *Breaking Bad* Year."

7. Gilligan, "Kingpin of the Year."

8. Maureen Ryan, "*Breaking Bad* Does *Scarface*: Is Al Pacino a Fan of Walter White?" *Huffington Post*, July 30, 2012, http://www.huffingtonpost.com/2012/07/29/breaking-bad-scarface_n_1716848.html.

9. Scott Neumyer, "Five Revelations from the Near-Perfect *Breaking Bad* Finale," *Rolling Stone*, September 30, 2013, http://www.rollingstone.com/tv/news/lessons-of-the-breaking-bad-series-finale-20130930.

10. James Poniewozik, "Go Ahead, Binge-Watch That TV Show," *Time*, July 10, 2012, http://entertainment.time.com/2012/07/10/go-ahead-binge-watch-that-tv-show/.

11. Ryan, "*Breaking Bad* Does *Scarface*."

12. Mike Janela, "Breaking Bad Cooks Up Record-Breaking Formula for Guinness World Records 2014 Edition," GuinnessWorldRecords.com, September 4, 2013, http://www.guinnessworldrecords.com/news/2013/9/breaking-bad-cooks-up-record-breaking-formula-for-guinness-world-records-2014-edition-51000.

13. Neil Landau, *The TV Showrunner's Handbook: 21 Navigational Tips for Screenwriters to Create and Sustain a Hit TV Series* (Burlington, MA: Focal, 2013).

14. Rob Tannenbaum, "Vince Gilligan: 'Walt Is Not Darth Vader,'" *Rolling Stone*, September 25, 2013, http://www.rollingstone.com/tv/news/vince-gilligan-walt-is-not-darth-vader-20130925.

15. Ryan, "*Breaking Bad* Does *Scarface*."

16. Thomas Batten, "Mad Men: How Don Draper and Walter White Prepared Us for Donald Trump," *Guardian*, August 10, 2015, https://www.theguardian.com/tv-and-radio/tvandradioblog/2015/aug/10/donald-trump-antihero-mad-men-breaking-bad.

17. Chuck Klosterman, *I Wear the Black Hat* (New York: Scribner, 2013).

18. Tannenbaum, "'Walt Is Not Darth Vader.'"

19. Gilligan, "Kingpin of the Year."

BIBLIOGRAPHY

"AMC Announces Chris Hardwick as Host of *Talking Bad*, Premiering August 11." AMC.com. July 2013. http://www.amc.com/shows/talking-bad/talk/2013/07/amc-announces-chris-hardwick-as-host-of-talking-bad-premiering-august-11.

Batten, Thomas. "Mad Men: How Don Draper and Walter White Prepared Us for Donald Trump." *Guardian*, August 10, 2015. https://www.theguardian.com/tv-and-radio/tvandradioblog/2015/aug/10/donald-trump-antihero-mad-men-breaking-bad.

Bellis, Rich. "Which Great Literary Work Explains *Breaking Bad* Best?" *Atlantic*, October 2, 2013. http://www.theatlantic.com/entertainment/archive/2013/10/which-great-literary-work-explains-em-breaking-bad-em-best/280149/.

Bennett, Laura. "The Hidden Secrets of TV Posters." *New Republic*, July 18, 2013. https://newrepublic.com/article/113874/breaking-bad-mad-men-newsroom-posters-their-hidden-secrets.

Berman, Judy. "Does the New *Breaking Bad* Poster Foreshadow Walter White's Death?" *Flavorwire*, June 25, 2013. http://flavorwire.com/400411/does-the-new-breaking-bad-poster-foreshadow-walter-whites-death.

Booker, M. Keith, and Bob Batchelor. Mad Men: *A Cultural History*. Lanham, MD: Rowman & Littlefield, 2016.

Bowman, Donna. "What's the Right Way to Watch *Breaking Bad*?" A.V. Club. August 5, 2013. http://www.avclub.com/article/whats-the-right-way-to-watch-ibreaking-badi-101143.

Bradley, Bill. "Vince Gilligan Finally Reveals Why Walter White Left Gray Matter." *Huffington Post*, March 17, 2016. http://www.huffingtonpost.com/entry/vince-gilligan-walter-white-gray-matter_us_56e85f27e4b0b25c91838d57.

Braxton, Greg. "Sympathy for Gus: Giancarlo Esposito Talks *Breaking Bad*." *LA Times Blogs*. October 10, 2011. http://latimesblogs.latimes.com/showtracker/2011/10/sympathy-for-gus-giancarlo-esposito-talks-breaking-bad.html.

Breaking Bad: The Complete Series. Directed by Bryan Cranston, Adam Bernstein, Bronwen Hughes, Charles Haid, Colin Bucksey. 2009–2013. Culver City, CA: Sony Pictures Home Entertainment. Home Video, 2014. DVD.

"*Breaking Bad*: Two Surprising Actors Who Could Have Taken Bryan Cranston's Role." *Hollywood Reporter*, July 16, 2012.

"Breaking Bad Finale Scores Record 10.3 Million Viewers, 6.7 Million Adults 18–49." TV by the Numbers. October 1, 2013. http://tvbythenumbers.zap2it.com/1/breaking-bad-finale-scores-record-10-3-million-viewers-6-7-million-adults-18-49/205634/.

"*Breaking Bad* Poster Features Walter White and 'Remember My Name' Slogan." *Huffington Post*, June 25, 2013. http://www.huffingtonpost.com/2013/06/25/breaking-bad-poster-walter-white_n_3497339.html.

Brown, Lane. "In Conversation: Vince Gilligan on the End of *Breaking Bad*." Vulture.com. May 12, 2013. http://www.vulture.com/2013/05/vince-gilligan-on-breaking-bad.html.

Brustein, Joshua. "Why Did AMC Split *Breaking Bad*'s Final Season into Two?" *Bloomberg Businessweek*, September 9, 2013. https://www.bloomberg.com/news/articles/2013-09-09/why-did-amc-split-breaking-bads-final-season-into-two.

"Bryan Cranston and *Breaking Bad* Get Ready for the End." *Minneapolis Star Tribune*, August 10, 2013. http://www.startribune.com/bryan-cranston-and-breaking-bad-get-ready-for-the-end/218927041/.

Busis, Hillary. "*Saturday Night Live* Taps *Breaking Bad* for Trump's Next Cabinet Pick." *Vanity Fair*, December 10, 2016. http://www.vanityfair.com/hollywood/2016/12/saturday-night-live-breaking-bad-donald-trump-walter-white.

C.K., Louis, director. *Louis CK: Chewed Up*. Art & Industry, 2008.

Clarke, Kevin. "Broken, Bad, Redeemed?" *America Magazine*, October 7, 2013.

Cranston, Bryan. "Actor Bryan Cranston, Breaking' with Type." Interview by David Bianculli. *Fresh Air*. NPR. March 19, 2010.

———. "Psychos We Love." Tribeca Film Festival. Interview by Juju Chang. April 23, 2014. https://tribecafilm.com/stories/recap-psychos-bryan-cranston-terence-winter-james-fallon-panel.

Dockterman, Eliana. "A Record-Breaking 10.3 Million People Watched the *Breaking Bad* Finale." *Time*, September 30, 2013. http://entertainment.time.com/2013/09/30/a-record-breaking-10-3-million-people-watched-the-breaking-bad-finale/.

Donnelly, Ashley M. *Renegade Hero or Faux Rogue*. Jefferson, NC: McFarland, 2014.

Douthat, Ross. "The Hero of Breaking Bad." *New York Times*, September 18, 2013. http://douthat.blogs.nytimes.com/2013/09/18/the-hero-of-breaking-bad/.

Esposito, Giancarlo. "Q&A—Giancarlo Esposito (Gus Fring)." AMC.com. September 2011. http://www.amc.com/shows/breaking-bad/talk/2011/09/giancarlo-esposito-interview.

Fees, Jarre. "He's Not 'Bad,' Just Written That Way." *Television Week* 27, no. 17 (June 2, 2008).

Foley, John. "*Breaking Bad* Meets Modern Marketing: 5 Rules for High-Impact Content." *Forbes*. November 1, 2013. http://www.forbes.com/sites/oracle/2013/11/01/breaking-bad-meets-modern-marketing-5-tips-for-high-impact-content/#44db0d285b9d.

Friend, Tad. "The One Who Knocks." *New Yorker* 89, no. 28 (September 16, 2013).

Gilligan, Vince. "Breaking Bad: The Network & GEITF Joint Session Masterclass." Edinburgh International Television Festival. Interview by Charlie Brooker. Published online September 11, 2013. Accessed November 6, 2016. https://www.youtube.com/watch?v=lXVJ8eRIRrc.

———. "*Breaking Bad*: Vince Gilligan on Meth and Morals." Interview by Terry Gross. *Fresh Air*. NPR. September 9, 2011.

———. "*Breaking Bad* Insider Podcast 408." Breaking Bad *Insider Podcast*. September 6, 2011. AMC. https://itunes.apple.com/us/podcast/breaking-bad-insider-podcast/id311058181?mt=2.

———. "*Breaking Bad* Series Creator Vince Gilligan Answers Viewer Questions, Part I." AMC.com. 2011. http://www.amc.com/shows/breaking-bad/talk/2011/10/vince-gilligan-interview.

———. "*Breaking Bad* Series Creator Vince Gilligan Answers Viewer Questions, Part III." AMC.com. 2011. http://www.amc.com/shows/breaking-bad/talk/2011/10/vince-gilligan-interview-part-iii.

———. "I Am Vince Gilligan, AMA." Reddit.com. 2015. https://www.reddit.com/r/IAmA/comments/34g1us/i_am_vince_gilligan_ama/.

———. "Vince Gilligan: Kingpin of the Year 2013." Interview by Brett Martin. *GQ.com*, November 26, 2013. http://www.gq.com/story/vince-gilligan-men-of-the-year-kingpin.

———. "Vince Gilligan on How *Breaking Bad* Almost Didn't Happen." *Newsweek*, July 16, 2012. http://www.newsweek.com/vince-gilligan-how-breaking-bad-almost-didnt-happen-65529.

Gillman, Greg. "TheGrill: Ted Sarandos—Vince Gilligan Thanked Netflix for Saving *Breaking Bad*." TheWrap.com. September 24, 2013. http://www.thewrap.com/thegrill-netflixs-ted-sarandos-on-arrested-development-its-only-a-matter-of-when-and-what-form-it-takes/.

glass_daggers. "All Hail the King Season 5 Promo Image." Reddit.com. 2013. https://www. reddit.com/r/breakingbad/comments/uk8n5/all_hail_the_king_season_5_promo_image/.

Gunn, Anna. "I Have a Character Issue." *New York Times*, August 23, 2013. http://www. nytimes.com/2013/08/24/opinion/i-have-a-character-issue.html?_r=0.

Hanlon, John. "*Breaking Bad*: How Walter White Became Each of His Enemies." *The Week*, September 30, 2013. http://theweek.com/articles/459468/breaking-bad-how-walter-white-became-each-enemies.

Hecht, Jessica. "Q&A—Jessica Hecht (Gretchen)." AMC.com. May 2009. http://www.amc. com/shows/breaking-bad/talk/2009/05/jessica-hecht-interview.

Hunt, Stacey Wilson. "Emmys 2012: Mark Margolis, the Year's Only Silent Nominee, Reflects on *Breaking Bad*, *Scarface*." *Hollywood Reporter*, August 23, 2012. http://www. hollywoodreporter.com/news/emmys-2012-breaking-bad-mark-margolis-364842.

Janela, Mike. "Breaking Bad Cooks Up Record-Breaking Formula for Guinness World Records 2014 Edition." GuinnessWorldRecords.com. September 4, 2013. http://www. guinnessworldrecords.com/news/2013/9/breaking-bad-cooks-up-record-breaking-formula-for-guinness-world-records-2014-edition-51000.

Jensen, Jeff. "*Breaking Bad* and *Mad Men*: Why Splitting Final Seasons Isn't a Good Idea." *Entertainment Weekly*. September 18, 2013. http://ew.com/article/2013/09/18/breaking-bad-mad-men-split-season/.

Jensen, Michael. "Interpreting 'Partner' on This Week's *Breaking Bad*." *Logo* (blog). September 7, 2011. http://www.newnownext.com/interpreting-partner-on-this-weeks-breaking-bad/09/2011/.

Johnson, Steven. *Everything Bad Is Good for You: How Today's Popular Culture Is Actually Making Us Smarter*. New York: Riverhead Books, 2006.

Jurgensen, John. "Binge Viewing: TV's Lost Weekends." *Wall Street Journal*, July 13, 2012. http://www.wsj.com/articles/SB10001424052702303740704577521300806686174.

Keefe, Patrick Radden. "The Uncannily Accurate Depiction of the Meth Trade in *Breaking Bad*." *New Yorker*, July 13, 2012. http://www.newyorker.com/culture/culture-desk/the-uncannily-accurate-depiction-of-the-meth-trade-in-breaking-bad.

Klosterman, Chuck. "Chuck Klosterman on Batman, Bad Guys and Wearing 'The Black Hat.'" Interview by Audie Cornish. *All Things Considered*. NPR. July 9, 2013. http://www.npr.org/2013/07/09/200141185/chuck-klosterman-on-batman-bad-guys-and-wearing-the-black-hat.

———. *I Wear the Black Hat*. New York: Scribner, 2013.

Landau, Neil. *The TV Showrunner's Handbook: 21 Navigational Tips for Screenwriters to Create and Sustain a Hit TV Series*. Burlington, MA: Focal, 2013.

Larabee, Ann. "Editorial: The New Television Antihero." *Journal of Popular Culture* 46, no. 6 (2013): 1131–32.

Lawson, Richard. "Is Walter White Going to Die?" *Atlantic*, June 25, 2013. http://www. theatlantic.com/entertainment/archive/2013/06/walter-white-going-die/313914/.

Leonard, Andrew. "The Downward Spiral." *Rolling Stone*, no. 11133 (June 23, 2011).

Levin, Gary. "Nielsens: 'Runway' Finale Rules on Cable." *USA Today*, March 11, 2008. http:// usatoday30.usatoday.com/life/television/news/2008-03-11-nielsens-analysis_N.htm.

Li, Shirley. "Forget Gus: Todd Is the Most Dangerous Villain on *Breaking Bad*." *Entertainment Weekly*, September 7, 2013. http://ew.com/article/2013/09/17/breaking-bad-dangerous-villain-todd/.

MacInnes, Paul. "*Breaking Bad* Creator Vince Gilligan: The Man Who Turned Walter White from Mr. Chips into Scarface." *Guardian*, May 19, 2012. https://www.theguardian.com/tv-and-radio/2012/may/19/vince-gilligan-breaking-bad.

MacKenzie, Jean. "The Rise of the American Antihero." PRI: Public Radio International. June 11, 2013. http://www.pri.org/stories/2013-06-11/rise-american-antihero.

McCluskey, Megan. "Here's the *Breaking Bad* Easter Egg Even Vince Gilligan Missed." *Time*, April 13, 2016. http://time.com/4292409/breaking-bad-easter-egg-vince-gilligan-missed/.

———. "See All the Ways *Breaking Bad* Was Inspired by *Pulp Fiction*." *Time*, October 21, 2015. http://time.com/4081446/breaking-bad-inspired-by-pulp-fiction/.

Merritt, Jonathan. "The Death of Moral Relativism." *Atlantic*, March 25, 2016. http://www. theatlantic.com/politics/archive/2016/03/the-death-of-moral-relativism/475221/.

Meslow, Scott. "The Moral Universe of *Breaking Bad*." *Atlantic*, July 16, 2012. http://www.theatlantic.com/entertainment/archive/2012/07/the-moral-universe-of-breaking-bad/259860/.

Moncada, Luis. "Q&A—Daniel and Luis Moncada (the Cousins)." AMC.com. May 2010. http://www.amc.com/shows/breaking-bad/talk/2010/05/the-cousins-interview.

Nemiroff, Perri. "*Breaking Bad*: Giancarlo Esposito on Taking Gus from One-Episode Character to Iconic Villain." Collider.com. July 17, 2015. http://collider.com/breaking-bad-giancarlo-esposito-on-taking-gus-from-one-episode-character-to-iconic-villain/.

Neumyer, Scott. "Five Revelations from the Near-Perfect *Breaking Bad* Finale." *Rolling Stone*, September 30, 2013. http://www.rollingstone.com/tv/news/lessons-of-the-breaking-bad-series-finale-20130930.

Nudd, Tim. "'Remember My Name,' Says Walter White on *Breaking Bad*'s Imposing Final Poster." *AdWeek*, June 24, 2013. http://www.adweek.com/adfreak/remember-my-name-says-walter-white-breaking-bads-imposing-final-poster-150684.

Nussbaum, Emily. "Child's Play." *New Yorker* 88, no. 25 (August 27, 2012). http://www.newyorker.com/magazine/2012/08/27/childs-play-5.

———. "The Closure-Happy *Breaking Bad* Finale." *New Yorker*, September 30, 2013. http://www.newyorker.com/culture/culture-desk/the-closure-happy-breaking-bad-finale.

Office of National Drug Control Policy. *Fact Sheet: Methamphetamine Trends in the United States*. July 2010.

Pomerantz, Dorothy. "Netflix, *Breaking Bad* and the Business Triumph of Quality Television." *Forbes*, September 27, 2013. http://www.forbes.com/sites/dorothypomerantz/2013/09/27/breaking-bad-and-the-triumph-of-quality-television/.

Poniewozik, James. "Breaking Point." *Time* 182, no. 7 (August 12, 2013).

———. "Elements of Style." *Time*, July 17, 2011. http://content.time.com/time/arts/article/0,8599,2082963,00.html.

———. "Go Ahead, Binge-Watch That TV Show." *Time*, July 10, 2012. http://entertainment.time.com/2012/07/10/go-ahead-binge-watch-that-tv-show/.

Prudom, Laura. "Under the Dome': Dean Norris on Big Jim's Duplicitous Nature and the *Breaking Bad* Finale." *Huffington Post*, July 8, 2013. http://www.huffingtonpost.com/2013/06/18/under-the-dome-dean-norris-big-jim_n_3458143.html.

Rich, Katy. "Why *Breaking Bad*'s Neo-Nazis Are the Perfect Villains for the End of the Series." CinemaBlend. 2013. http://www.cinemablend.com/television/Why-Breaking-Bad-Neo-Nazis-Perfect-Villains-End-Series-59132.html.

Richardson, Ethan. "Why *Does* Everyone Hate Skyler White?" Mockingbird.com. September 4, 2013. http://www.mbird.com/2013/09/why-does-everyone-hate-skyler-white/.

Rittelmeyer, Helen. "Moral Relativism, R.I.P." *American Spectator*, September 17, 2012. http://spectator.org/35020_moral-relativism-rip/.

Ritter, Krysten. "Krysten Ritter on *Breaking Bad*: Team Walter White until the Bitter End." Vulture.com. September 24, 2013. http://www.vulture.com/2013/09/krysten-ritter-breaking-bad-essay.html.

Robinson, Joanna. "*Better Call Saul* Creators Didn't Expect You to Solve Their Gus Fring Puzzle." *Vanity Fair*, April 19, 2016. http://www.vanityfair.com/hollywood/2016/04/better-call-saul-gus-frings-back-title-anagram-finale.

Romano, Andrew. "*Breaking Bad* Finale: Lost Interviews with Bryan Cranston & Vince Gilligan." *Daily Beast*, September 29, 2013. http://www.thedailybeast.com/articles/2013/09/29/breaking-bad-finale-lost-interviews-with-bryan-cranston-vince-gilligan.html.

———. "'To'hajiilee' Is the Finest Episode of *Breaking Bad* Yet." *Daily Beast*, September 8, 2013. http://www.thedailybeast.com/articles/2013/09/08/to-hajiilee-is-the-finest-episode-of-breaking-bad-yet.html.

Ryan, Maureen. "*Breaking Bad* Does *Scarface*: Is Al Pacino a Fan of Walter White?" *Huffington Post*, July 30, 2012. http://www.huffingtonpost.com/2012/07/29/breaking-bad-scarface_n_1716848.html.

Schnauz, Tom, and Peter Gould. "*Breaking Bad* Writers: 'This Is It; There Is No More.'" Interview by Terry Gross. *Fresh Air*. NPR. October 3, 2013.

Sepinwall, Alan. "*Breaking Bad*: Bryan Cranston/Vince Gilligan Q&A." *Newark (NJ) Star-Ledger*, March 6, 2009. http://www.nj.com/entertainment/tv/index.ssf/2009/03/breaking_bad_bryan_cranstonvin.html.

———. "*Breaking Bad* Star Bryan Cranston Looks Back at Walter White's Greatest Hits, Part 2." UPROXX. July 13, 2012. http://uproxx.com/sepinwall/breaking-bad-star-bryan-cranston-looks-back-at-walter-whites-greatest-hits-part-2/.

Shales, Tom. "There's a Meth to AMC's Madness in *Breaking Bad.*" *Washington Post*, January 19, 2008. http://www.washingtonpost.com/wpdyn/content/article/2008/01/18/AR2008011803342.html.

Simon, Rachel. "*Breaking Bad* Characters Ranked from Least to Most Evil: Where Does Walt Finish?" *Bustle.com*, September 25, 2013. https://www.bustle.com/articles/5697-breaking-bad-characters-ranked-from-least-to-most-evil-where-does-walt-finish.

Smith, Greg. "'It's Just a Movie': A Teaching Essay for Introductory Media Classes." *Cinema Journal* 41, no. 1 (2001): 127–34.

Snierson, Dan. "Bad Boys, Bad Boys . . . Whatcha Gonna Do?" *Entertainment Weekly*, July 20, 2012.

———. "*Breaking Bad*: Creator Vince Gilligan Explains the Series Finale." *Entertainment Weekly*, September 30, 2013. http://ew.com/article/2013/09/30/breaking-bad-finale-vince-gilligan/.

———. "Bryan Cranston and Aaron Paul Discuss Ending of *Breaking Bad* Finale." *Entertainment Weekly*, September 30, 2013. http://ew.com/article/2013/09/30/breaking-bad-finale-bryan-cranston-aaron-paul/.

———. "Vince Gilligan's Very Good *Breaking Bad* Year." *Entertainment Weekly*, December 31, 2013. http://ew.com/article/2013/12/31/breaking-bad-vince-gilligan-better-call-saul-community/.

Stanley, Alessandra. "When Going Gets Tough, a Not-So-Tough Turns to Meth." *New York Times*, January 18, 2008. http://www.nytimes.com/2008/01/18/arts/television/18brea.html.

St. John, Allen. "In a Perfect Finale, *Breaking Bad* Proves It's a Love Story." *Forbes*, September 30, 2013. http://www.forbes.com/sites/allenstjohn/2013/09/30/in-a-perfect-finale-breaking-bad-proves-its-a-love-story/3/#4c66d9a663fc.

———. "Why *Breaking Bad* Is the Best Show Ever and Why That Matters." *Forbes*, September 16, 2013. http://www.forbes.com/sites/allenstjohn/2013/09/16/why-breaking-bad-is-the-best-show-ever-and-why-that-matters/.

"Sunday Cable Ratings: *Breaking Bad* Wins Big, *Talking Bad*, *Homeland*, *Boardwalk Empire*, *Masters of Sex* & More." TV by the Numbers. October 1, 2013 http://tvbythenumbers.zap2it.com/sdsdskdh279882992z1/sunday-cable-ratingsbreaking-bad-wins-big-talking-bad-homeland-boardwalk-empiremasters-of-sex-more/205986/.

"Sunday Cable Ratings: *Breaking Bad* Wins Night, *True Blood*, *Low Winter Sun*, *Devious Maids*, *Dexter*, *The Newsroom* & More." TV by the Numbers. August 13, 2013. http://tvbythenumbers.zap2it.com/sdsdskdh279882992z1/sunday-cable-ratings-breaking-bad-wins-night-true-blood-low-winter-sun-devious-maids-dexter-the-newsroom-more/197129/.

Szalavitz, Maia. "'Unbroken Brain' Explains Why 'Tough' Treatment Doesn't Help Drug Addicts." Interview by Terry Gross. *Fresh Air*. NPR. July 7, 2016. http://www.npr.org/sections/health-shots/2016/07/07/485087604/unbroken-brain-explains-why-tough-treatment-doesnt-help-drug-addicts.

Tannenbaum, Rob. "*Breaking Bad*'s Lydia: She's a Clean-Cut, Bonkers Sociopath.'" *Rolling Stone*, September 28, 2013. http://www.rollingstone.com/tv/news/breaking-bads-lydia-shes-a-clean-cut-bonkers-sociopath-20130926.

———. "Vince Gilligan: 'Walt Is Not Darth Vader.'" *Rolling Stone*, September 25, 2013. http://www.rollingstone.com/tv/news/vince-gilligan-walt-is-not-darth-vader-20130925.

Ury, David, and Dale Dickey. "Q&A—David Ury (Spooge) and Dale Dickey (Spooge's Woman)." AMC.com. 2010. http://www.amc.com/shows/breaking-bad/talk/2011/01/david-ury-dale-dickey-interview.

VanDerWerff, Todd. "*Breaking Bad* Ended the Anti-hero Genre by Introducing Good and Evil." A.V. Club. September 30, 2013. http://www.avclub.com/article/ibreaking-badi-ended-the-anti-hero-genre-by-introd-103483.

———. "How *Breaking Bad* Broke Free from the Clockwork-Universe Problem." A.V. Club. August 7, 2013. http://www.avclub.com/article/how-ibreaking-badi-broke-free-of-the-clockwork-uni-101278.

Van Spall, Owen. "*Breaking Bad*: The Finest Thing You Haven't Seen." *Guardian*, August 21, 2009. https://www.theguardian.com/culture/tvandradioblog/2009/aug/21/breaking-bad.

Weinman, Jaime J. "What Makes Breaking Bad So Good." *Maclean's* 123, no. 20 (May 31, 2010).

INDEX

ABOUT THE AUTHOR

Lara C. Stache is an assistant professor in the Division of Communication, Visual, and Performing Arts at Governors State University. She is also an affiliated faculty member in gender and sexuality studies.